*I*rene M. Spry was born in South Africa in 1907 of British parents. She was educated at the London School of Economics, Cambridge University, and Bryn Mawr College. She is professor emeritus of the Department of Economics at the University of Ottawa. In preparing this book she did extensive archival research and field work, including visits to Palliser's descendants in Ireland; a trip to Australia and New Zealand to consult the papers of the expedition's geologist and naturalist, James Hector, and secretary, John Sullivan; and travels in western Canada to retrace the route of the expedition.

Captain John Palliser (left) and Dr. James Hector, in a photograph taken shortly after the expeditions were completed. *Courtesy Provincial Archives of Alberta/P.A.6186*

The Palliser Expedition

The Dramatic Story of
Western Canadian Exploration 1857–1860

IRENE M. SPRY

FIFTH
HOUSE
PUBLISHERS

Front cover painting, *Captain Palliser's Expedition, 1857–1859,* by
C.W. Jefferys, reproduced courtesy Canadian Imperial Bank of Commerce
Frontispiece, "Captain Palliser and Dr. Hector—Explorers," courtesy
Provincial Archives of Alberta/P.A. 6186
Cover and series logo designed by Sandra Hastie/GDL
Map by George Duff

The publisher gratefully acknowledges the support received from
The Canada Council and the Department of Canadian Heritage.

Printed and bound in Canada by Friesens, Altona, MB
06 05 04 03 02 / 7 6 5 4

Canadian Cataloguing in Publication Data

Spry, Irene M.

The Palliser Expedition
2nd ed. —

(Western Canadian classics)
Originally published: Toronto : Macmillan, 1963.
Includes index.
ISBN 1-895618-52-5

1. British North American Exploring Expedition (1857–
1860). 2. Northwest, Canadian - Discovery and
exploration. 3. Canada - Exploring expeditions.
4. Palliser, John, 1817–1887. I. Title. II. Series.

FC3205.1.S68 1995   917.12'04'1   C94-920246-0
F1060.8.S68 1995

FIFTH HOUSE LTD.
#1511, 1800 - 4th Street SW
Calgary AB Canada
T2S 2S5
1-800-387-9776

Contents

Contents

To the memory of my father
Evan E. Biss

ℱOREWORD

𝓘t was just as he had described it. Coming over a hill, with map in hand and a copy of the expedition's report as her guide, Irene Spry was busy retracing the steps of the famous Palliser survey of western Canada. And although much of the land had been turned into farms or ranches over the past century, she was still able to identify a particular feature and pinpoint where the expedition had travelled. Little did anyone realize when Irene had first been asked to look for Palliser material how she would become engrossed with the task—and where it would lead her scholarly career.

Irene Mary Biss was born in 1907 in the Transvaal, South Africa, to parents whose families had helped shape the British Empire both there and in India. At seventeen, she entered the London School of Economics and later attended Cambridge University, where she encountered some of the leading minds in economic theory. She then continued her studies at Bryn Mawr near Philadelphia before being appointed lecturer in the Department of Political Economy at the University of Toronto in 1929. Over the next decade, her academic career flourished, under the inspiration of her mentor and colleague Harold Adams Innis and his emphasis on practical field study. She also became active in the League for Social Reconstruction and its search for answers to the Depression; it was during a League skating party that she met her future husband, Graham Spry, an advocate of public broadcasting and political organizer for the Cooperative Commonwealth Federation.

Graham Spry's 1946 appointment as agent-general for the Province of Saskatchewan in London meant new challenges for Irene. She quickly acquired a reputation as the caring matron of Saskatchewan House, whose doors were always open to a generation of travellers and students. She also handled a number of requests on behalf of her husband, such as when he was asked by the Saskatchewan Archives in 1957 to locate material for a collection commemorating the centennial of Captain John Palliser's famous expedition to the Canadian west.

The Palliser assignment was special for Irene in that it allowed her to draw upon her own experience, in the words of one biographer, as a "child of the British Empire." The forces and motives that had sent Palliser to the western interior of British North America in the mid-nineteenth century were essentially the same forces and motives that had taken her own family to Africa and India. The task also gave her a chance to use the investigative skills she had developed and refined during her first academic career in the 1930s. And she would need them. During the so-called "troubles" in Ireland in 1923, the Palliser home, Comeragh House, had been burned and with it, most of the explorer's papers.

Irene's search efforts took her first to the Commonwealth Office, where she had spotted some old files labelled "Upper Canada" during a previous visit, and then to the Public Record Office and Hudson's Bay Company Archives (later transferred to Winnipeg). She also tracked down several Palliser descendants, as well as pursued a number of local sources in Ireland. She even took advantage of a trip to Australia, as a delegate to the Associated Country Women of the World Conference, to consult the papers of expedition geologist and naturalist James Hector and secretary John Sullivan in New Zealand.

This work was gratifying in itself, but what gave the project added impetus for Irene was a suggestion during a London dinner party from Lovat Dickson, then head of Macmillan Publishers in England and a close friend of Grey Owl. When the Canadian-born Dickson learned what she had been doing, he remarked, "Why not write a book?" The idea appealed to Irene, and she started work on what would eventually result in not one, but two books: a popular account of Palliser's expedition (1963), and an edited collection of his official report and related papers for the Champlain Society (1968). Although both publications were prepared in London, Irene remained faithful to the Innis tradition and made two trips to the Canadian prairies and Rocky Mountains to get a better appreciation of the work of the expedition and the land it traversed.

This combination of archival research and field work, together with Spry's lucid prose, makes *The Palliser Expedition* one of the great works in Canadian exploration literature. She describes what was known about the prairies in the late 1850s and why the British government accepted the Palliser proposal to dispatch a scientific team to examine the area between Lake Superior and the Pacific Coast. She also explains what the expedition learned during its three years in the field (1857–1860), in particular the discovery of new mountain passes, and why it subsequently dismissed the treeless southern grasslands (the so-called "Palliser's Triangle") in favour of the more northern "fertile belt." Above all, she provides an intimate understanding of who the men were, what the region was like, and how the two interacted. In retrospect, it is easy to understand why Irene became absorbed with the expedition and decided to specialize in western Canadian history during her second academic career at the University of Saskatchewan and then Ottawa following her return to Canada in 1967.

In reading *The Palliser Expedition*, it is important to see the party members, as one historian has argued, as original observers of the land; they were assessing the western interior from an entirely new perspective—namely, its potential for agricultural settlement. This critical evaluation of the region, moreover, was being made by outsiders who were unfamiliar with the peculiar prairie environment. Their sweeping generalizations about good and bad land were just that—generalizations—and have been a source of ongoing debate ever since, especially during the Dirty Thirties. Finally, what is often overlooked is that Palliser and his companions travelled peacefully through territory where the Indian was still undisputed master; in fact, without the cooperation of the various tribes, in particular the Blackfoot Confederacy, the expedition could not have completed its work.

The Palliser Expedition is consequently much more than the story of a scientific survey. It provides a revealing snapshot of the last years of the Old Northwest—a time when the western interior was relatively isolated from the outside world; a time when a distinctive way of life existed between the Indian, mixed-blood, fur trader, missionary, and the land; and a time when the idea of the region becoming home to countless thousands of homesteaders probably seemed as unlikely as the sudden disappearance of the great buffalo herds.

BILL WAISER
UNIVERSITY OF SASKATCHEWAN

O ne hundred years ago, when Captain John Palliser got back to London after exploring the country that is now Western Canada, he wanted to write a popular book about his travels. He even went so far as to approach a publisher—John Murray, who had published his earlier best seller about his trip to the Upper Missouri, *Solitary Rambles and Adventures of a Hunter in the Prairies.* The popular book about the prairies and mountains of British North America was never written, as far as we know; certainly it was never published.

What was published was a long and detailed report in the form of a government blue-book. Though even in this official document Palliser's racy style and irrepressible sense of humour break through here and there, it is not easy to read and it is very hard to get hold of. The twenty or thirty copies known to exist are treasured in a few libraries and private collections.

This is a pity, as John Palliser's explorations were full of interest. His own account of his adventures while he was exploring in the country that lies between the head of the lakes and the valley of the Columbia and Kootenay rivers would have made a delightful story. Some of these adventures he thought unsuitable for inclusion in a blue-book; others are barely mentioned. About the long winter of 1858-9, for example, which he spent getting to know the Blackfoot chiefs and hunting with his ill-fated friend Captain Brisco, the Crimean hero, we know almost nothing—only the tantalizing titbits of information you will find in Chapter 15 of this book. There are plenty of other gaps that Palliser would have filled with lively reminiscence; these will be all too evident as you read.

Even so, what we do know about the genial captain and his travels is well worth the telling. Since he did not tell his own story, I have tried to tell it now, with apologies to him for the shortcomings of my version and gratitude to him for the fun he has given me in my efforts to find out something about him and his work as background for the facts that he put into the report. I have used the language of his letters and those of his correspondents and of the report wherever possible. I have kept to established facts where I could; when a guess has been necessary I have tried to make it clear that it is a guess.

I need only add that I could never have come even as near the truth about John Palliser as I may have come, without the generous help of so many people that it would take another book to record them all. I am especially grateful for the help of the Royal Geographical Society, whose part in the exploration will be clear in the story that follows; the Hudson's Bay Company, which helped Palliser and has helped me unstintingly; the Commonwealth Relations Office and Public Record Office in London; the Canadian Archives; the Royal Commonwealth Society, which has most generously allowed me to use its copy of Palliser's Reports for months at a time; the Hocken Library at the University of Otago, New Zealand; the late H.S. Patterson of Calgary and his son, Judge H.S. Patterson, and the late J.N. Wallace of Edmonton, who in 1937 and 1927 respectively collected a most useful fund of material on Palliser and his party; Mr. Ian Fairholme, a descendant of the Fairholme family into which John Palliser's sister married; Major John Gray, who now owns Palliser's old property, Comeragh House, County Waterford in Ireland; and last, but by no means least, the Archives of the Province of Saskatchewan, which started looking for new material about Palliser by way of celebrating the centennial of his explorations, thus initiating my research work, and which have helped me unfailingly throughout my work on this book.

I am also grateful to Mrs. Selwood, Miss Maude, Miss Cook, and Mrs. Jardim for typing and retyping, checking and cross-checking, and doing all sorts of other jobs involved in exploring the life and labours of Captain John Palliser, as well as to the people who, by doing domestic chores, have made it possible for me to work on Palliser.

Without my husband's interest and support this book could never have been written. His help and my family's forbearance in putting up with my preoccupation with Palliser problems are beyond thanks.

I.M.S.

ACKNOWLEDGMENTS

Any Crown copyright material in this book is published by permission of the Controller of Her Majesty's Stationery Office.

Material from the archives of the Hudson's Bay Company is used by permission of the Governor and Committee of the Hudson's Bay Company; from the archives of the Royal Geographical Society, by permission of the Society; from the library of the Royal Botanic Gardens at Kew, by permission of the Director; from the Sir James Hector Papers, by permission of the Librarian of the Hocken Library, University of Otago, New Zealand.

Material in the Palliser Collection of the Saskatchewan Provincial Archives was made available to the author by the Provincial Archivist; in the J.N. Wallace Papers in the Rutherford Collection, by the Librarian of the University of Alberta; in the Public Archives of Canada, by the Dominion Archivist; in the collection of the Glenbow Foundation, by the Archivist.

Mr. Ian Fairholme gave permission to use family papers and His Honour Judge H.S. Patterson gave permission to use the papers of his father, the late H.S. Patterson, Q.C.

The editor of *The Beaver* gave permission to use material from an article the author wrote for that magazine as the basis for the summary in Chapter 12 of what was known about passes through the Rocky Mountains from the headwaters of the two branches of the Saskatchewan River.

I am indebted to Major John Gray, then the occupant of Comeragh House, for his hospitality and local inquiries for sources of information.

To all those who have granted permission for the use of material, and for all the help I have received, I am deeply grateful.

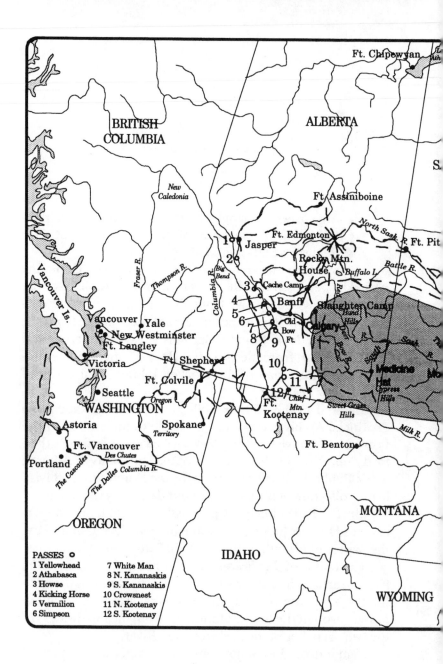

The routes taken by the expedition and its various members have been marked on the map as accurately as possible. Most of them can be followed with reasonable certainty from the journals, itineraries, and maps of the expedition, but in some sections, notably from Fort Ellice to

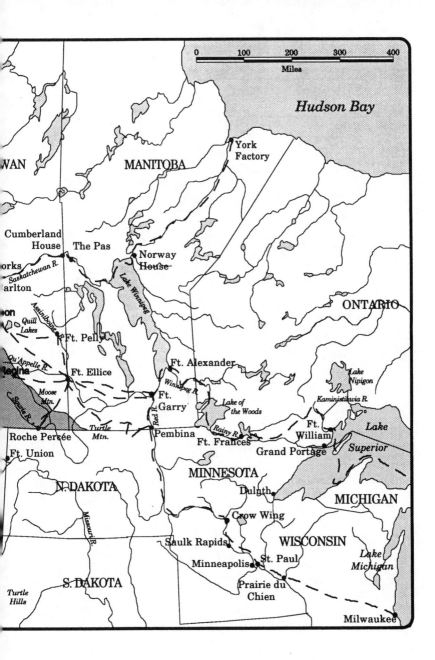

the elbow of the South Saskatchewan, there is some doubt as to the exact line of travel. City names in bold face are contemporary designations and are noted for location only. The darker area in the centre of the map is Palliser's Triangle.

Chapter One

'Palliser J.'s Plan'

John Palliser sat on his horse and looked away to the north over the prairies. How far beyond the curve of the horizon did the rolling plains stretch on? What kind of country lay there? Rich grasslands? Dry, sandy sage-brush? Or sculptured bad lands? Where did the forests of the North begin? And where did the plains meet the shining mountains to the north-west? Was there any way through those mountains to the Pacific Ocean? And where did the boundary between United States and British territory run? He could not stay to find out. He had to go back to his home in Ireland after a long hunting trip in the prairies and mountains of the Upper Missouri. Ten years later, in 1857, patriotism and enthusiasm for exploration were to combine with his passion for buffalo-hunting and his zest for travel to bring him back, at the head of the British North American Exploring Expedition, to find the answers.

The prairies of British North America were then still a wild, sparsely peopled waste. From the single tiny settlement at Red River, where Winnipeg now stands, they stretched westward into dim, unimagined distances. Locked away from the nearest British settlements in the East by barriers of granite, swamp, and cascading river, they had only a tenuous connection with the outside world by the long, difficult river route to Hudson Bay and out through icy seas to the North Atlantic. On the west they were walled in by serried mountain ranges. The unsettled Indian lands in American territory to the south had, in the past, also cut them off effectively from the outside world, but now the western lands of the United States were beginning to fill up. The long isolation of Britain's prairie possessions would clearly soon be broken.

John Palliser, an adventurous, cheerful young Irishman, decided in 1856 that, failing any sign of official interest in the matter, he would constitute himself a one-man expedition to explore the British prairies to the north of the border and to find out whether there were practicable passes for a route through the wall of mountains at their western extremity and on to the Pacific.

A cheerful, light-hearted, handsome bachelor, sociable and accomplished, he was as much at home in Rome or Heidelberg as he was in Dublin or London, on a Scottish grouse moor or in the Swiss Alps as he was in the wild, beautiful Comeragh Mountains of County Waterford. He spoke French, Italian, German, and Spanish fluently, though his spelling in English was at times eccentric. He had a lively literary style and a good baritone voice. Once in New Orleans he sang both the bass and tenor parts at a charity performance of the oratorio *David*, when a professional soloist failed to appear.

The heir of a wealthy Irish landowner, he came of a family that had seen generations of Protestant piety and public service since William Palliser had come from Yorkshire as a lad in the late seventeenth century to become, in due course, Archbishop of Cashel and founder of the family fortune. At thirty-nine John Palliser had already served as High Sheriff of the County, Justice of the Peace, and captain in the Waterford Artillery Militia, with a prospect of succeeding his father, in time, as Colonel of the Regiment. He could look forward to a comfortable life of social importance and political influence at home, but he was possessed by the restlessness that drove so many young mid-Victorian men and women of rank and wealth from luxurious homes to the ends of the earth. They escaped from the unexciting ease and elaborate conventions of polite nineteenth-century society to the exhilarating and challenging simplifications of mountaineering or of travel in remote and primitive places. All five Palliser brothers and most of their friends and relatives succumbed to this fever. Ardent sportsmen, they spent much of their lives wandering about the world on big-game-hunting expeditions. Frederick and Edward Palliser, two of John's younger brothers, went with Sir Samuel White Baker (who later discovered the sources of the Nile) on shooting trips in Ceylon in 1847-8. There they visited a Scottish friend, William Fairholme, who was then running one of the pioneer coffee estates and who later married Palliser's older sister. Richard Wray Gledstanes Palliser, another brother, rescued a French lady from pirates in the China Seas. William Fairholme's brother George travelled in the Australian wilderness, and his youngest brother Walter was lost with Sir John Franklin on his final, disastrous polar expedition.

John Palliser's imagination had been fired by William Fairholme's account of a hunting trip he made in 1840 to the Grand Prairies of the Missouri, when on leave from military duties at his regiment's station in what was then the little eastern British North American province of Canada. Emulating his brother-in-law-to-be, John Palliser travelled in 1847 up the Mississippi from New Orleans by river steamer to Independence, on the site of present-day Kansas City, the jumping-off place for what was then the Far North West. There, in September 1847, he joined a trader of the American Fur Company with whose party he continued his journey up the Missouri and into the western wilderness far beyond the farthest limits of settlement.

He spent all winter and spring in the Indian country, staying at Fort Union and other trading-posts. He made a number of trips with the traders and their men as they moved about the country, and went off on independent excursions with his own guides and hunters; he even travelled and camped alone in midwinter with only his great white dog, Ishmah, for company. He made friends with half-breeds and with the Indians of the warrior Plains tribes; he had more than one narrow escape from war-parties and watched a battle between Minitarees and Sioux. He learnt how to run buffalo—a noble sport! He stalked cabri (the swift antelope of the plains); he tracked wapiti (alias elk, red deer, or wawaskeshu); he shot innumerable wolves and half a dozen grizzly bears, which in those days roamed the prairies.

Palliser left the Indians and the Upper Missouri with great regret in July 1848. When the American Fur Company's annual steamer left the Minitarees' (Mandan) Post, at the point where the eastward-flowing Missouri bends south, he embarked with a sigh and with all his buffalo robes, grizzly-bear and wolf skins, elk horns, and other trophies, and steamed away down for St. Louis while the last cheers of his hunting companions fell faintly on his ear.

He did not forget the prairies. Besides his hunting trophies, he had a more lively memento of his western adventures in the small menagerie of animals he had taken home. Among these were three buffaloes: Beauty, an enormous cow that later in Ireland had two splendid calves; a two-year-old heifer; and a tiny calf that he had captured himself and raised by hand. There was also an entertaining and amiable black bear, which was a particular friend of his exquisitely beautiful little *forcifer* antelope. As the party was on its way through New Orleans to embark for Ireland, the antelope was attacked by a large mastiff. The bear rushed to protect his little friend and a splendid fight ensued, with Bruin victorious. On another occasion, on the river steamer, the bear had been found in the pilot's bed. He had clambered into it after getting wet in a shower, and had rolled himself up comfortably in the blankets. Luckily the pilot was amused by the sagacity of the 'knowin' coon'. Besides the buffalo, antelope, and bear, Palliser had two Virginia deer and, his favourite, the faithful Ishmah—the half-wolf Indian dog he had bought from an ancient Indian woman. Ishmah had hated white men and Palliser had had a long struggle to overcome this rooted dislike. Then the dog had become his devoted companion. One bitterly cold night, when they were caught without shelter on the open prairie, he had saved his master's life, keeping him from freezing to death by huddling close beside him.

Poor Ishmah took to killing sheep in Ireland and had to be incarcerated in Lord Dunraven's private zoo; the buffalo all died of tuberculosis in the unaccustomed damp of the Irish climate, but, besides his ill-fated menagerie, John Palliser had the diary of his adventures in the Far West to keep vivid his memories of the prairies. When he got home, his family and a host of friends persuaded him to make it into a book. *Solitary Rambles and Adventures of a Hunter in the Prairies* was an immediate success when it was published in 1853, but as he worked on it, staying with a friend in London, Palliser must have been longing to throw down his pen and go back to the western plains.

He certainly went on wondering about the country in British territory to the north of the Upper Missouri. Going home from New Orleans, he had made a side trip to Panama, and crossed the Isthmus to the Pacific. On board the steamer to Havana he had met a Captain Ringgold, who had been a member of an official United States exploring expedition, which in 1842-6 had made detailed surveys along the Pacific Coast and up the valley of the Columbia. In 1853-6 the United States Government financed a new series of expeditions to look for possible routes for railways through the western mountains from the central plains to the Pacific. At least two parties from these expeditions had crossed the border into British territory.

By 1856 John Palliser had come to feel that it was high time the British, too, learned something about their prairie possessions. At a time when explorers were eagerly pushing their way through African jungles and arctic solitudes, there were still blank spaces on the maps of British North America along the international boundary where it crossed the great western plains, and no one was sure whether even such maps as did exist were accurate. Sir Roderick Impey Murchison, the great geologist, who was not only director of the British Geological

Survey and Museum of Practical Geology, but president of the Royal Geographical Society as well, wrote of the 'region along the southern frontier of our territory, between the parallels of 49° and 53° north latitude and from 100° to 115° west longitude, which, from various causes, remains almost unknown'.

It was known only to a few thousand wandering red men whose homeland it was, and to the handful of white men who had penetrated it in search of furs or souls. Even the fur traders and missionaries knew almost nothing of its southern reaches near the United States border. Only the proud, war-like, buffalo-hunting Indians of the plains—the Blackfoot and Bloods, Piegans and Sarcees, the Plains Assiniboine, Plains Cree and Sioux—really knew that sweep of country, each tribe its own wide range of territory. These Indians shared their knowledge with their cousins of mixed blood, the Métis, part Indian and part French or Scot, who also hunted the buffalo out on the plains. The knowledge of Indian and Métis alike was born of personal experience and communicated only by word of mouth, not committed to maps and written records. A handful of fur-trader explorers, notably Peter Fidler of the Hudson's Bay Company, had travelled across part of the plains. They had kept records and had even drawn maps of the country they passed through, but their work was little known to the public and in any case their findings might be biased; the fur traders did not want to encourage competition or settlement.

A few government explorers, soldiers, scientists, and missionaries had, it is true, travelled from Red River to the Far North West, but they had mostly followed the fur traders' highway along the north branch of the Saskatchewan River. None of them had examined the whole wide country that stretches south from the North Saskatchewan to the United States border. Only on its fringes had any detailed, objective record been made of the lie of the land, of its plants and animals, its soils and rocks, and the temperature and rainfall on the British side of the border. Without first-hand, dependable information, the public and politicians alike had only rumour, conjecture, and controversy as a basis for decisions as to policy. Was the whole vast country treeless, or were there woods and forests? What was the soil like? And the climate? Was there any fertile land? Or was it simply an extension of the great central desert of North America, which was thought to present such difficult problems in United States territory? Were there hills or mountains dividing the basin of the South Saskatchewan from the basin of the Missouri River? Did any big tributaries flow into the South Saskatchewan on its right bank? Could settlers establish farms and homes there? Were there any minerals? Could roads and railways be built?

Then there was the problem of possible routes from the British prairies through the wall of mountains beyond, to the Pacific Coast. Fur-trader explorers, notably David Thompson of the North West Company, had in the early years of the nineteenth century pioneered a route in British territory through the Rocky Mountains to the Columbia Valley, which was still in regular use by cross-continental travellers, but it lay far to the north. Fur traders, scientists, and missionaries alike, when they had occasion to travel between the prairies and the Pacific, normally went by this route. It was essentially a water route, with portages connecting the North Saskatchewan, via the Athabasca River and the Athabasca Pass over the Rocky Mountains, to the most northerly point of the Big Bend of the Columbia River at the Boat Encampment.

It was known that other passes existed farther to the south, leading from head-waters of the two branches of the Saskatchewan. The Indians used a number of these passes, and occasionally travellers used one or other of them when speed was essential. Sir George Simpson, for example, a fabulous traveller with all the resources of the Hudson's Bay Company at his disposal, had, when he was on his way round the world in 1841-2, crossed the mountains from the head-waters of the South Saskatchewan by a pass from Bow River, which is still called Simpson Pass. Two young soldiers had, in 1845, at the time of the Oregon dispute, used a pass a little farther south, probably White Man Pass, meeting Father de Smet, the Jesuit missionary, on his way by the same pass from Oregon to the prairies. Their secret report to the government on that territory's 'capabilities in the point of defence' described the pass as a defile impracticable for troops. It was therefore probably of little use for through traffic in British territory. Rumours of good Indian passes were none the less persistent, and in 1848 Palliser had met 'a very intelligent . . . half-breed gentleman' from Red River, James Sinclair, who had already crossed the mountains at least once with a party of emigrants from the Red River to the Columbia River. He described to Palliser another possible pass he hoped to try some day, which might or might not be in British territory.

Palliser wanted to go and see for himself. He decided that he would travel across the British prairies close to the border, due west from Red River to the Rocky Mountains, and then try to find the pass of which James Sinclair had spoken. As a student he had done some work in astronomy, and he could make observations for latitude and longitude, which would settle the question of whether Sinclair's pass lay in British or United States territory. He hoped he might perhaps find other passes, too.

He worked out a project for the journey that would give him a chance to get back to his beloved prairies and go buffalo-hunting again and would also be a useful and patriotic enterprise; it was high time someone collected what information he could about this little-known part of Her Majesty's North American domains.

Palliser had an idea that the Royal Geographical Society might be interested in his scheme. He had originally intended to pay his own way, but his family, wealthy land-owners though they were, faced, like many other Irish land-owners a hundred years ago, increasing financial difficulties. Already Colonel Wray Palliser, John Palliser's father, was finding that he had to sell some of his estates.

The Royal Geographical Society had organized a number of exploring expeditions and had persuaded the government to contribute to some of them. Perhaps the society would help him too. Professor Nicolay nominated him for election as a fellow of the Royal Geographical Society and he was duly elected on November 24, 1856. Then he put his proposal before the society. His idea was to travel by himself through the British prairies and southern Rockies, hiring local guides and *voyageurs* and living on what he could shoot as he went. He hoped that Boucharville, the splendid guide who had gone hunting grizzlies with him before, in the Upper Missouri country, would come with him again on this trip. For the information of the council of the Royal Geographical Society, he painted, on John Arrowsmith's latest (1854) map of North America, the route he intended to follow—a solid blue line running straight across the prairies westward from Red River and two lines of blue dots through the hypothetical southern pass through the mountains. In the Council Minutes for December 8, 1856, there is an entry: *'Palliser* J.'s Plan for the Survey of a large portion of North America, which was referred to Expedition Committee with power to act at once . . . ' The council referred the matter to the society's Expedition Committee, which summoned Palliser to London to answer their questions and explain his project.

Back in Ireland for Christmas, he waited impatiently at Comeragh House for the Royal Geographical Society to reach a decision about his great idea. He wanted to start in February, and it was already the end of December. He sent 'a trifle of Game' to the secretary of the society, asking anxiously how soon the 'big wigs' were likely to make up their minds about his plan.

CHAPTER TWO

'I leave London tomorrow . . . on my way to North America'

The Royal Geographical Society liked Palliser's plan, but they thought some scientists ought to go with him, men who were trained in accurate research and accustomed to the use of scientific instruments. Palliser was a fine shot and practised hunter. He was a hardy and experienced traveller, thoroughly inured to everything a man could suffer in mid-nineteenth-century travel in western North America. Tall and of a powerful build, he was a man of great strength and endurance, at the height of his powers. He knew something about the proud, warlike Indians of the plains and how to deal with them. He spoke French fluently—an important asset in a country where many guides and hunters were of mixed French and Indian blood. He knew how to take care of himself on the prairies—he had written delightedly of the pleasure of camping entirely on his own, without servants or gamekeepers to look after him, and having for dinner only what he could manage to shoot himself. But he was not a scientist. He had attended Trinity College, Dublin, intermittently for four years, but he had missed four terms, repeated a year, and in the end left without taking his degree. He was interested in every branch of science, but he was an imaginative and gifted amateur, not a professional man. The Expedition Committee of the Royal Geographical Society recommended that he should lead the expedition, but that he should have the help of two scientific assistants and two privates of the Royal Engineers. The president wrote formally to ask the Colonial Office to contribute £5,000 to finance the expedition on this basis. Palliser found himself contemplating, not the solitary adventure he had looked forward to, but the formidable task of organizing and directing a sizeable party of technical men. It was a prospect that might well have struck terror to the heart of anyone with his slight experience of administration. Nothing daunted, however, he stuck to his guns, and, as it turned out, the proposed scientists helped the project to gain government support and gave the expedition's work much of its ultimate great value.

The Under-Secretary of State for the Colonies at the time was another Irishman, John Ball, almost the same age as John Palliser and a great friend of the Palliser family. He was keenly interested in scientific problems and understood how much such an expedition might contribute, not only to fuller and more certain information about the country but to scientific knowledge in general. A keen amateur botanist, he was greatly interested in the work of men who were compiling systematic records of every possible species of plant all over the world and studying the conditions under which they grew. Sir William Hooker, the first director of Kew Gardens, was anxious that the expedition should make careful collections of plants and keep records of temperatures inside tree trunks and underground in the bitter cold of the prairie winter.

Physicists were laying the foundations of the international study of the earth's magnetic pull, which in our own day has been the subject of intensive world-wide study in the International Geophysical Year. A hundred years ago records were already being made at points scattered round the British Empire, and, indeed, all over the world, to provide a basis for new ideas in the infant science of terrestrial magnetism. General Sir Edward Sabine was eager to seize the opportunity the expedition offered to extend these records.

Murchison, the president of the Royal Geographical Society, as a leader of the band of pioneer geologists who were working out the classification of the earth's rocks and clays, sands and gravels, according to their character and age, fully realized, of course, how useful detailed and dependable information about the rocks and soils and fossils of the prairies and western mountains of British North America might be.

The climatologists wanted more precise information about temperatures, rainfall, winds, snow, and frost conditions, especially to compare with information published in 1856 by an American, Blodget, about climatic conditions in the central plains of North America. Observations made in these remote regions might help the astronomers, too, while zoologists as well as botanists wanted to know more about the wild life of the western plains and mountains.

John Ball immediately and strongly recommended that the government should finance the expedition. Within a week the Secretary of State, Henry Labouchere, gave his sanction, and a request went forward for Treasury approval of the £5,000 estimated cost. While the Treasury was giving the matter consideration, John Ball consulted a number of eminent scientists, among them Darwin, about it, and called a committee of scientists together, under the chairmanship of the president of the Royal Society, to discuss plans for the scientific work to be done, to recommend possible scientific assistants to do it, and to draw up the detailed instructions they should be given. In the end it was decided to send with Palliser a botanical collector, a magnetical observer, a geologist-naturalist-medical man, and an astronomical observer, who was also to be secretary of the expedition. The idea of taking along two privates of the Royal Engineers was dropped.

John Ball suggested that if Eugene Bourgeau was free, no better collector could be found; did the director of Kew Gardens think he should be asked to undertake the botanical work? Sir William Hooker instituted inquiries about the personal habits of this 'prince of botanical collectors', who had supplied Kew with a mass of specimens from distant lands. His work was undoubtedly first class, but had he perhaps in his long, solitary collecting trips, contracted an addiction to the bottle, or any other awkward habits? He had not. The quiet little French family man, whose career started with his love of flowers in the Alps, where he tended his father's herds in the Haute Savoie, turned out to be amiable, cheerful, helpful, conscientious, and efficient—a general favourite.

Sir Henry Lefroy, who had made a series of invaluable magnetic observations himself in 1842-53 at a number of stations in British North America, ranging from Toronto to Lake Athabasca in the Far North West, recommended Thomas Blakiston, a lieutenant in his own regiment, the Royal Artillery, for the job of magnetical observer. At twenty-five Blakiston had already seen distinguished service in Nova Scotia and in the Crimean War. He had volunteered to go with the expedition, writing to Murchison to ask him to support his application. It was arranged that he should travel to York Factory on Hudson Bay by sea with his delicate instruments, and so to the prairies by York boat, with the company's brigades that carried the yearly outfit of trade goods by river and portage from Hudson Bay to the remote trading-posts far inland. The instruments were in less danger of damage on this route than on a jolting, overland journey, and, on his way to join the rest of the expedition in its proposed winter quarters at Fort Carlton on the North Saskatchewan River, Blakiston would be able to make observations, which would be valuable for comparison with Lefroy's earlier observations, at York Factory and elsewhere along the route.

Murchison himself found a geologist and naturalist who was also a medical doctor—James Hector, from Edinburgh University. Hector had been outstanding among his fellow students on geological field trips and in excursions among his rugged native mountains. He had trained himself to take discomfort and hard travelling in his stride. Though only twenty-three, he was to make a magnificent contribution to the success of the expedition and the progress of geological knowledge.

Dr. Edward Purcell of the Naval College at Greenwich recommended young John W. Sullivan, who had been teaching there, as an efficient mathematician and sextant observer. He was to take charge of the expedition's astronomical observations and secretarial work.

It was a likely-looking team—but it had taken time to organize it, and time was precious. The Royal Geographical Society had written to the Colonial Office on January 13; the Colonial Office had not replied. Palliser had been back in London since the middle of January, getting more and more impatient. On January 17 he had written to his friend John Ball, the Under-Secretary of State at the Colonial Office, explaining how important it was for him to make an early start to allow time for slow travel and careful observation. The Under-Secretary had noted that there was reason in his urging and wrote to ask the Treasury for a decision, emphasizing that the matter was now pressing. By March it was still more pressing. Palliser anxiously awaited word of the government's decision.

Meanwhile neither he nor the Under-Secretary had been idle. John Ball had worked out a long list of questions for Palliser, who was busy gathering all the information he could that would help him to answer them, with a view to making detailed arrangements. He talked his project over with Sir George Simpson, the Hudson's Bay Company's North American governor, who had come over to London on a visit from his headquarters at Lachine, near Montreal. Sir George gave him a great deal of information and advice and undertook to give the expedition the help that only the Hudson's Bay Company, with its monopoly of trade and efficient transcontinental organization, could give travellers on the prairies and in the mountains of western British North America. He wrote to Lachine to arrange for two canoes to be placed at the expedition's disposal and to Red River to make sure that enough horses, stores, and equipment would be available for its journey over the plains.

Palliser also discussed the project with several other Hudson's Bay Company men who were in London and with the few available scientists who had ever travelled west of the Great Lakes. Sir John Richardson, the great naturalist, and Sir J. Henry Lefroy were especially helpful to Palliser in working out answers to John Ball's long list of queries about transportation, routes, and essential equipment and supplies. These ranged from paper for pressing Bourgeau's botanical specimens and red tape for correspondence with the Colonial Office, to scalping-knives.

Besides dealing with the scientific side of the project, John Ball had also been giving careful study to the proposed routes and costs. He now recommended an addition to the original plan. He wanted to know more about the route from Lake Superior to Red River. He thought that, instead of going up the Missouri through United States territory, the expedition should travel west by canoe from the head of the lakes to Red River, reporting on the route as they went. The Royal Geographical Society thought this would be a waste of time, as many travellers had already passed through what they considered a well-known and only slightly interesting tract of country, but Ball stuck to his point and this third job was added to the expedition's programme.

Again there was a long wait while the Treasury gave further consideration to the proposal. Murchison wrote to the Colonial Office once more, asking urgently for a reply. At long last came the welcome word from the Treasury: 'My Lords will not object to an expenditure not exceeding £5,000 in two seasons . . . ', provided that the Colonial Office itself took full responsibility for the expedition, instead of leaving it in the control of the Royal Geographical Society. The Colonial Office wrote to Palliser at the end of March appointing him to command the expedition.

It looked as though the decision had come too late. Palliser had suddenly been taken violently ill. For two days he was delirious and it seemed doubtful that he would recover. John Ball was away in Ireland, electioneering. Everything was thrown into confusion. Bourgeau had arrived in London from Paris and had to hang about waiting for the expedition to leave. What was he to live on? The Treasury was forced to sanction—grudgingly—a small payment to support him. Should Hector and Bourgeau go on ahead? Supposing Palliser could not go, what then? But Palliser's doctor was confident that he would recover and even that his health would be much improved after the attack. In due course, recover he did.

The party set off at last in good spirits and with high hopes. On May 14, Palliser wrote to the Colonial Office: 'Having engaged accommodation on board of Royal Mail Steamer *Arabia* I beg to report that in company with Doctor Hector, Mr. Sullivan and Monsieur Bourgeau I leave London tomorrow morning for Liverpool on my way to North America.'

They had a good crossing, but when the *Arabia* docked in New York there was trouble over the instruments. The customs officers wanted them all unpacked for inspection. It would be difficult to repack them securely for the long overland journey ahead. Happily, a chance friend whom they had met at their hotel, a Mr. Pompelly, intervened, and persuaded the authorities to let the expedition's baggage through undisturbed. As it was, one of the barometers had burst. The sudden heat in New York made it expand, and its metal bindings were too tight. Mr. Pompelly and a scientific friend arranged for the New York Observatory to lend the expedition one of its barometers until their own could be repaired and returned to them.

The party travelled on by train, visiting Niagara Falls on the way. At Detroit they had to wait for the lake steamer *Illinois*, which was to take them to Sault Ste. Marie, between Lake Huron and Lake Superior. There the two canoes, sent by Sir George Simpson from Montreal, were to meet them. There was still heavy drift-ice on the lakes, most unusually late in the season. It had damaged and delayed the steamer. The late start from London had not, after all, held up the season's work. Even Sir George Simpson, famous for the speed of his canoe journeys from Montreal to the West, with a picked crew of *voyageurs,* had been forced by the ice to wait. He was only eight or nine days ahead of them. At last the *Illinois* arrived and the party went on board for a comfortable voyage to Sault Ste. Marie. There was a good piano in the lounge, which Palliser tried. At night they danced in the forward cabin, but Hector commented that the ladies on board seemed a little stiff. When they reached Sault Ste. Marie, the sixteen half-breed and Iroquois *voyageurs* were waiting with two canoes to take the expedition on its journey across Lake Superior, and on from the head of the lakes to the prairies. Among the *voyageurs* was James Beads, a personal servant of Sir George Simpson; he had sent him with the crews as a very particular favour. Beads, as it turned out, was to go with the expedition all the way across North America to the coast.

Lake Superior was reported to be still covered with floating ice and time was pressing, so Palliser changed his plans. Instead of coasting along the north shore of the lake from Sault Ste. Marie in the canoes, in the normal way, he arranged with the captain of the steamboat to pick up the canoes and their crews and strike across the lake out of his usual course, to approach the western end of the Isle Royale as near as in the then knowledge of the soundings he could venture. This would save several days' travel and risk of further delays from ice. It was therefore on board the *Illinois* that they went up the grand canal that united the Sainte Marie River with Lake Superior. This had been constructed to avoid the falls between the lakes, and raised the ship thirty feet. In Lake Superior the scene was almost arctic, and the cold intense. There was floating ice everywhere. This broke up easily when the vessel forced her way through the glistening white masses, though some of the floating hummocks of ice were as much as five or six feet thick; Palliser congratulated himself on the change in plan as he listened to the steamer's paddles crashing and splashing through the ice, which would soon have done for their frail birch-bark canoes.

After coasting along the south shore of the lake the steamer turned north, crossing to the British side. At daybreak on June 12 it came within sight of Isle Royale. Four miles from shore—as near as the ship's captain dared go—the long, slender canoes were slipped into the water. The cargo had already been apportioned to each canoe, and the experienced *voyageurs* set about the difficult job of loading. No heavy, solid article of any kind could be allowed to rest upon or against any part of the birch-bark hull of the canoe. Long poles, reaching fore and aft, were placed along the bottom; on these the hard and heavy articles rested. A light wooden grating in the centre of the canoe kept the poles apart. On this the bedding of the two passengers was placed to make a kind of seat or lounge.

As the sun rose they parted company from the ship, which soon disappeared below the horizon. Off glided the canoes, the men singing the air of a Canadian boat song, 'Rose Blanc'. Half an hour's brisk paddling brought them to a small bay in the island, where they landed for breakfast. A strong wind suddenly blew up and kept them prisoners there till one p.m., so they had a chance to examine the rocky island, where the trees were not yet in leaf. While they waited, the *voyageurs* gummed the canoes, warming the gum at the fire, then rubbing it into the seams and using a piece of burning wood as a blow-torch to stop up all the crevices.

At last they set off again on the seventeen- or eighteen-mile paddle from their landing-place on the island to the main shore. Half-way across, they saw a new storm blowing up to windward and they worked furiously to reach the shore before it struck them. The canoes were heavily laden, so they would have been in serious danger if the storm had caught them out on the open water. Happily, it blew over; they were safe.

After four hours of paddling they reached an islet off the main shore in Thunder Bay. Everyone was relieved, as the *voyageurs,* not accustomed to starting from the point out on the lake where the steamer had left them, had not been sure of their bearings. Then, at last recognizing headlands to the north-west, they pushed on again to Fort William, which was sixteen or seventeen miles farther on. They paddled along shores thickly covered with pines, through a calm, lovely evening, passing under cliffs of dark basalt columns. The grandeur of the scenery, crowned by Thunder Mountain rising 1,300 feet above the lake, and the complete silence broken only by the sound of the paddles, made a deep impression on the new-comers. They passed a handful of Indian tents pitched near the entrance to Thunder Bay. It was dark when they paddled into the Kaministikwia River, and they landed at ten o'clock at Fort William, where they were most hospitably welcomed at the Hudson's Bay post. They had arrived at last at the starting-point of their explorations.

These explorations were to cover three distinct regions: the country between Lake Superior and Red River; the country between Red River and the Rocky Mountains; and the mountains themselves, with the territory stretching beyond them towards the Pacific Coast. The expedition was to map all three regions; to examine possible transport routes to and through them; and to appraise their capabilities for settlement, reporting on their agricultural, mineral, and other resources and keeping careful botanical, zoological, geological, meteorological, and magnetical records.

CHAPTER THREE

No Road by the White Fish River

To examine and report on the rugged country between the head of the lakes and Red River was the first of the expedition's three assignments. This had not been a part of Palliser's original plan. John Ball, at the Colonial Office, had insisted that the expedition should undertake it. He wanted an impartial opinion about the Hudson's Bay Company canoe route from Lake Superior to the prairies. Was this route as difficult as the Hudson's Bay men said it was? Sir George Simpson, the company's governor in North America, travelled west by it every year from his headquarters at Lachine. Other Hudson's Bay Company officers used it too. It linked a string of company trading-posts, but the company only used it for light express travel, not for freight, because the route by Hudson Bay from Britain was shorter and cheaper. Before the merger of 1821, though, the Nor'Westers had used the canoe route from Lake Superior to the West regularly for the fur trade; in the little British colony on the St. Lawrence there were those who thought it could—and should—be developed as a much-needed link between Canada and the West. Might it not be improved so that passengers and freight could use it?

The expedition was instructed to keep a careful record of the kind of country the canoe route took them through, laying down on the map and describing the rivers and lakes, the hills and forests, the rapids and swamps they passed. They were to study the rocks and the soil, the trees and plants; to find out how high the waterfalls were and how far travellers had to climb above Lake Superior, on their way west, over the height of land between the waters that drained into the Great Lakes and the waters that drained into Lake Winnipeg.

If the traditional route proved useless for settlers and freight, might there not be some other route which would offer an easier way through the rocky wilderness to Red River and the plains beyond? True, the Nor'Westers had carefully examined the various Indian routes to Red River from Thunder Bay when definition of the new United States border had forced them to move north from their old Grand Portage—Pigeon River route, but they had been thinking of the fur trade, not of settlement. It was worth trying again to find some way by which the little colony of Canada might establish effective communication with the huge western wilderness beyond the Great Lakes, over which the Hudson's Bay Company still reigned supreme.

Palliser was, therefore, instructed to examine another route that might perhaps be easier than the one the officers of the Hudson's Bay Company used. A tributary called the White Fish River was supposed to flow into the Kaministikwia River somewhere below Kakabeka Falls. Palliser was instructed to find out whether there was such a river, and, if so, exactly where it joined the main river. He was to send a small party up it, to find out whether it could be used as a through water-way and to study the country near its source and between its head-waters and the head-waters of the rivers that flow westward.

At Fort William, Palliser found a letter from Sir George Simpson suggesting that the party should get some lighter canoes for the White Fish River trip. These would be easier than the big canoes to carry past waterfalls and rapids and overland from one river to another. There would be many such portages to cross in the country of low hills that stretched away to the north-west, intersected by long, narrow lakes and innumerable watercourses, and broken by ridges of rock. The expedition accordingly secured three small canoes and three local Ojibwa (Chippewa or Saulteaux) Indians to help with the exploration of the White Fish. They repacked all the baggage in 'pieces', each weighing ninety pounds, for carrying over the portages. It was a blow to discover that some of the instruments had been broken in spite of all their care.

At Fort William they began their long series of astronomical observations, finding its latitude and longitude. They recorded the variation of the compass. They checked the chronometer rates, finding that these had been very uniform since they left England, as their results were only a few seconds different from those of an earlier party that had surveyed Lake Superior. Then they set off from Thunder Bay up the rich, forested valley of the Kaministikwia River. Two miles above the fort they passed an Ojibwa village near a Catholic mission. Their noses told them vividly that the occupation of these Indians was chiefly fishing; the atmosphere was redolent of the fish-oil used by them for dressing their hair and for cooking.

The explorers did not go far the first day, but next morning they set off at four o'clock, the usual starting-time. When they came to the Grand Rapid their *voyageurs* punted the canoes up it with long poles. After breakfast, at ten o'clock, they came to the Lazy Portage, where the baggage was landed and the canoes 'tracked' (that is, towed) up the rapids by their crews, wading up to their waists in the water. They came to the mouth of the White Fish River at 3:15 in the afternoon. It was easy to see why its existence had been in doubt: its mouth looked like a bay of the main river.

Torrents of rain now forced them to stop. Next morning the rain was still pouring down, but at last, at eleven o'clock, the weather cleared. Palliser left Sullivan to find the longitude and latitude of the mouth of the river and to measure its breadth and depth, and Bourgeau to collect plants, while he set off up the White Fish with Hector, James Beads, the three Ojibwa Indians, and two of the *voyageurs* in the three little canoes.

The first afternoon they passed twenty-six rapids, each

with only about two feet of water over the rocks. When they stopped for the night they constructed a shelter from the incessant rain and were soon rolled in their blankets and sleeping soundly. It was raining as hard as ever next morning. They waited till noon, but the downpour went on. The river, swollen by the unceasing rain, came rushing down with such speed and strength that they could hardly make headway. They had to force their way against the current, wading up one powerful rapid after another, hauling the canoes after them. Dr. Hector took half an hour to toil up one rapid. At the top, the current suddenly caught the canoe. It whirled round and round and shot off, away down the river. Doggedly he started the ascent all over again.

It was hard work, it was wet work, and it was discouraging work, as by now it was obvious that the White Fish River was not the answer to the riddle of a possible route to the prairies. Clearly it was not navigable, even for canoes. The whole party was wet, through and through, from the rain and from wading up the river. At five o'clock Palliser decided that the men could no longer withstand the continual soaking and stopped at the top of a more than usually powerful rapid to wait for Dr. Hector.

While Palliser was unloading a canoe, the men, in a desperate attempt to get warm, set fire to a large dead pine tree, which they then decided to cut down. A sudden gust of wind caught it as it fell; it swung round and came crashing down right on to the spot where Palliser was standing. He sprang aside; the smaller branches struck him, luckily doing him no injury, but the canoe beside him was dashed to pieces.

They were at the base of a high, steep bank, where the edge of the river flattened out for six feet or so—not a good place for camping with the river rising so fast. While they were considering what to do they nearly lost a second canoe. The swollen stream was so violent that it tore the canoe from the shore and was carrying it towards the rapid below when one of the voyageurs, noticing it, at once plunged into the river and caught it, at the risk of being swept down-river himself and drowned. It was bad enough to lose one canoe; to have lost another with its load would have meant serious trouble. Risking his life to save it was part of the strenuous and dangerous job a *voyageur* took as a matter of course.

After this misadventure the party camped at once, but spent an anxious night expecting all their provisions, clothes, and supplies to be afloat down the river before morning. By sunrise the river had risen to the edge of their camping-ground. They got away just in time. They were nearly ankle-deep in water as they broke camp, but only one coat was in fact washed away.

It was useless to try to go on with just the two little canoes they had left. Palliser sent James Beads back down-stream with one of the Ojibwa Indians and the two *voyageurs* to rejoin the main party. The canoes raced down the swollen river. It had taken the Palliser party two days to force their way up it; it took the four men three hours to go down again, running every one of the now-flooded rapids without stopping and at a fearful rate.

Meanwhile Palliser and Hector and the other two Ojibwa lads set off straight across country through the forest by compass-course to the Kakabeka Falls, where they were to meet the rest of the party. They climbed the steep bank, some 150 feet high, above their camping-place, to a plateau where thick forests of pine and larch alternated with swampy ravines full of black spruce. Fallen timber and dense undergrowth held them up. The streams, usually inconsiderable, were so swollen with rain that they had to cut down trees for makeshift bridges. For dinner they shot and grilled two grouse and a rabbit. After walking twenty miles they came on the Kaministikwia, about a mile below the falls. Following the bank up-river, through dense willow and cypress swamps, they found the main party already crossing the Mountain Portage. This portage meant a climb of 140 feet by a winding path up the rocky cliff, through which the river had cut a channel. The baggage and canoes had to be carried on another mile before it was safe to launch and load the canoes again. Palliser wrote:

> *It was here for the first time that we had an opportunity of witnessing what all travellers on this route had so justly admired, viz., that light spirit with which the voyageurs perform their hard tasks. They are mostly half-breeds of French and Iroquois extraction, and their cheerful French spirit is in happy harmony with the stern endurance of their Indian nature. The mode which they adopt for carrying their load [of two ninety-pound pieces each] is by means of a leather strap of about three inches in width, which they fasten round the load, leaving a loop which passes round the forehead. When all is ready away they run, and return until there is no more to carry, never resting on the road, and but rarely slackening their pace into a walk.*

Maddeningly, their last mountain barometer was broken on this portage.

Rain, thunder, and lightning without intermission kept them for two days and nights at Kakabeka Falls. At last, on the evening of the third day, the weather cleared, and, guided by the loud roar of the water, they walked over to look at the falls and the magnificent gorge the river had hewn for itself through the solid rock. Dropping stones and timing their fall, they estimated that the falls were 179 feet, 9 inches. Though not as extensive as Niagara Falls, the Kakabeka Falls were much higher, Palliser thought, and far wilder and finer than the falls at Niagara, which they had visited *en route* and which, on the American side, looked like an overgrown mill-dam, with shockingly utilitarian buildings crowded around them.

The weather had been so bad that they had not been able to make observations for latitude and longitude, while poor Bourgeau had been having a difficult time trying to dry his specimens of plants and flowers. There were even still hard-packed patches of snow about, though it was past the middle of June. Now Palliser ordered a general drying-out; large fires were lighted and soon the wild bush was steaming with reeking Manchester woollens and cottons.

When at last the weather seemed more promising, they packed their canoes and set off again, only to have to unpack everything after ten minutes, at the Priest's Portage. Altogether they crossed nine portages that day, with such sinister names as Portage of the Lost One and Bad Portage. They were not sorry when the evening camp-fire was lighted. When the weather finally cleared, after a week of solid rain, a new misery beset them; mosquitoes and bulldog-flies appeared in their myriads to torment them. The heat became intense. Portage followed portage. They measured the height of each one as accurately as they could, but the weather had been so unsteady that the barometer readings were not dependable.

They passed through magnificent scenery between rounded masses of granite and extensive swamps; they passed through tracts of luxuriant vegetation and through country ravaged by recent fires where nothing was left but dead trunks. They met a few small canoes, each paddled by an Indian and his wife.

At long last they camped at Prairie Portage, over the summit of the watershed that divided the rivers flowing to the Great Lakes from the rivers flowing 'down north' to Hudson Bay, and which was also the boundary between Canada and the territories of the Hudson's Bay Company.

At the beginning of this longest portage on the route was a tiny lake, enclosed by sandy hills and remarkable for the purity and coldness of its water. A quarter of the way across the portage was another small lake, where they camped. This lake was equally remarkable—for the warmth and impurity of its water! Here Hector climbed the highest hill they could see; he calculated that this was only 630 feet above the level of Lake Superior. It was not the altitude of the land between the Great Lakes and the Red River that made the journey so difficult and laborious; it was its rugged character and the alternation of rock and swamp and water.

CHAPTER FOUR

Down-Stream to the Prairies

O nce over the watershed separating the feeders of the Great Lakes from the rivers running west and then down into Hudson Bay, they would be going with the current, but first they had to struggle over the Savanne Portage between Savanne Lake and the Savanne River. The greater part of this desperate portage was over a dreary swamp, through which the men, loaded as they were—each with nearly 200 pounds on his back—had the greatest difficulty in struggling. When they reached the river, which was swift and deep, but narrow, they had to cut their way through barriers of drift-wood, besieged by mosquitoes even more virulent than usual, which left them with swollen hands and faces covered with bluish marks that in some cases did not disappear for many months afterwards.

By now they were running short of food, and when they met two Indians whose companions had decamped with all their stores, they could spare them only a very little to tide them over the emergency.

On they went, across more lakes, over more portages—including Deadman's Portage, where once a luckless *voyageur* had missed his footing and, in falling, had had his head almost severed from his body by the canoe he was carrying—and down more stretches of river. They suffered from intense heat, violent thunderstorms, and periods of steady drizzle. All this time they were making observations (some of which were upset by a derangement of the instruments), measuring altitudes, and recording the main features of the landscape and the geological formations. Bourgeau began to reap a rich harvest of flowering plants—and provided for his colleagues a feast of early strawberries.

They made a side trip to explore Sturgeon River, back towards the place where it had been hoped that the abortive route by the White Fish River might have joined the regular route. They found one lake beyond another and saw enough to satisfy themselves that they were in the heart of a wilderness of lakes, barely separated from one another by narrow and irregular ridges of granite, with densely wooded cliffs and islands. They decided that the best time to examine this country, where there was neither continuous land nor continuous water, would be the winter, when the lakes and swamps and rivers would be frozen and dogs and sleighs could be used. Careful but not entirely dependable calculation of the heights of the successive lakes—one of the aneroid barometers had become unworthy of reliance through the dial-plates' shifting—convinced them that little climbing would be saved by adoption of a direct route between Sturgeon River and the White Fish River, while the shorter distance to be travelled would be overbalanced by lack of any good water communication—unless, indeed, the old Pigeon River route was used, but that lay across the border.

From Sturgeon Lake to Lac La Croix they followed the aptly named Bad (Maligne) River; on Lac La Croix a fresh wind from the west blew up waves which, meeting the current of a river, produced at its mouth a sea that tried the strength of their bark canoes more than a little. They left the lake by paddling over flooded land, pushing their way among submerged trees to still another group of lakes. They threaded their way through a succession of rock-bound narrows where the placid water reflected the rich green of overhanging woods. Here there was splendid communication by water in almost every direction, but farther on the scattered waters joined in a broad river where there were more falls and rapids and portages. At one portage on Namakan Lake they camped on the top of a granite cliff, preferring a bed on hard rocks to one on soft herbage down below where the mosquitoes, their constant foes, carried on their unremitting attacks. They enjoyed wonderful views of waterfalls and rocky shores, though the steersman's steadiness was severely tested on occasion. In one lovely spot, something in the natural grouping of the trees and shrubs irresistibly called to their minds rural scenes at home; it was hard to realize that the hand of man had taken no part in producing the park-like effect. Here they found the remains of an Indian camp; in a secluded grove there were several coffins, raised above the ground upon posts to a height of five or six feet. They also found on a conspicuous point of land a solitary surveyor's post, perhaps connected, they thought, with the survey of the American shore on the other side of the lake. Possibly it had been left by David Thompson when, between 1816 and 1826, as astronomer to the International Boundary Commission, he had surveyed the international boundary from St. Regis, Quebec, to the Lake of the Woods. They had reached the part of their route that lay through the boundary waters.

When they reached Rainy Lake they were lucky; they shot some ducks, which were most welcome as by now they had hardly any provisions left. On the other side of the lake, Rainy River took them down still another rapid to the Hudson's Bay Company post, Fort Frances, named after Sir George Simpson's wife.

At the fort they made observations, as usual, to find the geographical position and the variation of the compass, for comparison with the observations made by Colonel Sir Henry Lefroy fifteen years before.

Two hundred Ojibwa were camped at the fort. When Palliser and his friends landed from their canoes and passed among the tents, many of the Indians pressed forward to shake hands with them, in such a manner as to leave it doubtful whether the honour was done *to* the visitors or *by* them.

Soon they noticed signs of excitement and consultation among the Indians:

... a loud beating of drums announced the signal of assembly to the tribe. Five long stools were arranged in a pentagon, and five chairs were placed in the centre of this enclosure. Here and there, at a very respectful distance, sat groups of women and children awaiting the commencement of the ceremony. The sound of the drum came nearer and nearer, and shortly the men of the tribe–upwards of two hundred of them, all highly excited–marched into the fort, in Indian file, with faces painted of every colour, heads decked with eagles' feathers, necks and fingers with brass rings, and many wearing very elegantly beaded dresses. The men were all armed, with the exception of the old or principal chief, who bore the calumet or pipe of peace, thus indicating that a friendly parley was sought. The principal men of the tribe seated themselves on the stools, and the young men either sat or stood behind. The drum ceased, and the old chief entered the house and demanded an interview with us. We assented, and forthwith repaired to the seats which had been placed for us. For at least five minutes after we were seated a profound silence reigned–a silence generally preserved for some time previously to the commencement of all Indian ceremonial speeches.

The chief commenced his harangue by assuring us that if we imagined that his tribe had assembled on this occasion for the purpose of begging we were mistaken; the reason of the present convocation was of a far greater moment than that. 'Perhaps,' said he, 'you wonder who I am that I should address you. My arms [heraldic arms] extend far back into time; my father and his father were the chiefs of this once mighty tribe. Their graves are in our lands, and not far from here. If you further question my authority for addressing you, look around me! These are my chiefs,–my soldiers,–my young men. It is by their wish and desire that I address you.' Here many voices grunted approbation. 'All around me,' continued he, 'I see the smoke of the pale faces to ascend; but my territories I will never part with; they shall be for my poor children's hunting fields when I am dead. But all they are poor now! our woods were wont to teem with animals, and our rivers and lakes to abound in fish; in those happy times our hearts were glad, but now my poor children often feel the pangs of hunger, and at those moments I think long (a favourite Indian expression), and my heart bleeds every noon to see my poor children nearer extermination. The Great Spirit causes the sun to give you light and heat as well as to us; you are our equals, so do not deceive us, but inform us of the true reason of your visit, and whither you are about to proceed to from here.'

[Palliser, a true Victorian moralist, made his reply,] briefly pointing out the advantages of agricultural pursuits and fixed habitations over their mode of life, with the chase as their sole dependence, and told them how provident foresight is the main reason of the more comfortable circumstances of the white man. We quieted all his anxieties concerning their lands by telling them that we were going a long distance from this place, and were only passing through their country on our route to much further lands, and that our object was neither to take them by force or even bargain with them for the sale of their territories; and moreover, if any body of people should wrest their lands from them, our great Queen would send her soldiers to drive those people back, and would restore their lands to them again.

At this point an Indian of a different tribe, who had been trading in United States territory, said he knew how his people had been treated by the 'Kitje Mohomans' (Big Knives, a word for the Americans) and urged the chief: 'Make him put that on paper.' 'Oh!' replied the old chief, 'there is no need of that, what he says he will act up to, for no one who came from the great Queen ever lied.' Palliser was much interested in this testimony, from the lips of an Indian, in favour of English honesty and good faith, both quite characteristic of the dealings of the Hudson's Bay Company towards them. The chief then asked Palliser to take a message to the Queen that his tribe were very miserable and wretched, their pipes often cold, and their tents melancholy. Palliser promised that he would give this message to 'the big men who were in the habit of giving good advice to the Queen'. When one of these 'big men', at the Colonial Office in London, read this report, he wrote in alarm in the margin: 'It is to be hoped that the writer will not compromise us with the Indians.'

After three hours and five speeches in the intense heat of the sun, the conference broke up. A gun given to the chief and tobacco distributed among the other Indians provided an amicable ending to the meeting.

The explorers got away from the fort that evening, and when they camped—on the American bank of the Rainy River—they caught some perch and some 'gold eyed carp', the now celebrated Winnipeg gold-eye. Here they encountered poison ivy for the first time, a plant that, they were surprised to find, produces a most intense itching sensation attended with considerable swelling and rash. These effects lasted for many days; some of the *voyageurs* suffered severely from them.

At the falls of the Rainy River next day they encountered more Indians. A number of the women came rushing down from their tents on the bank, to offer to sell them sturgeon, which they speared in great quantities. They met William Kennedy, a keen advocate of closer contact between Canada and the West, who was returning from Red River. They passed an Indian village on a large, green meadow. When they camped that night, they saw for the first time clouds of fire-flies illuminating the bushes as they flitted through them, reminding Palliser of Italy. There were also clouds of mosquitoes; all the way down lovely Rainy River their unremitting attacks kept the explorers and their men in a constant fever. Only when moving swiftly over the water did they have respite from the torment of their bites and horrid buzzing.

When they reached the Lake of the Woods, the men had often to get out of the canoes to haul them over the sandy shoals in the shallow water. Later, helped by a pleasant breeze, they sailed across the lake, but had to use their paddles again when they began threading their way among wooded islets. Next day they sailed right over one of the usual portages: unusually high water had flooded it. In the evening they came to Rat Portage, where they had to carry the canoes and their cargoes past a fall, leading into the Winnipeg River. They were surprised to find a wooden bridge over a wide tributary river. Here, too, Ojibwa Indians were catching sturgeon in great numbers below the falls, spearing them very dextrously. They stood on a projecting rock over some suitable eddy until a fish came within reach, when they secured it by a skilful thrust with a barbed spear.

After a day spent passing through scenery of wild grandeur, the explorers sat for a long time at night on the rocks and watched the surface of the water, which every moment was broken into phosphorescent circles by fish darting at the flies that hovered over the water.

Now they were in country that was a complete network of narrow lakes and swift streams. From 4:30 a.m. till after breakfast they did not have to make any portages; instead they enjoyed the exciting alternative of running rapids. One, known as the Spout Fall, was especially impressive: the river narrows gradually until it is not more than ten yards across, when the compressed waters make a leap of about four feet, with such force as to curve from the rocky ledge into the pool below. This dangerous-looking rapid both of their canoes ran in perfect safety, rushing at the leap with the speed almost of a railway train.

At the first falls of the Winnipeg River they stopped to take observations; the variation of the compass had suddenly increased sharply. Going on down the river they passed between cliffs of granite. Following the long bends of the river they came, suddenly and unexpectedly, on a little mission settlement, with a chapel and five small houses as well as cultivated land and cows and pigs.

Next day, father down-river, an Indian came to them in a canoe begging for medicine for his wife, who was lying sick. Dr. Hector could not make out what was the matter with her, but he gave the poor fellow some simple medicine, which would at least do her no harm.

The day was excessively hot. The explorers were amused at the manner in which the *voyageurs* flung themselves into the water without removing a single article of dress and after spluttering about for a while resumed their paddles, thoroughly soaked from head to foot. That afternoon the usual monotony of the voyage was broken by the appearance of two canoes rapidly advancing up the stream, their crews singing in full chorus. This turned out to be Sir George Simpson's party. He was returning from the annual meeting of the council of the Northern Department of the Hudson's Bay Company at Norway House. They were glad to hear from the governor that horses had been procured for the expedition, and that they were feeding up rapidly at a fine pasture ground in the neighbourhood of Lower Fort Garry.

After this meeting they had an accident: one of the canoes ran violently into one of the many blocks of stone that beset the river. They managed to keep going till they reached the next portage, but there they had to stop and wait for the *voyageurs* to gum the canoe where the bark was fractured.

Next night, after crossing the Seven Portages, where the Seven Sisters hydro-electric power station now stands, they camped on a granite island. They had scarcely made camp when a tornado swept through it.

A remarkably dense cloud approached us from the S.E. with very great rapidity, at a speed far greater than the mild breeze we experienced could account for. As soon, however, as the cloud arrived over our heads, we were assailed with a violent storm of wind, which instantly levelled the tents; down, also, came the rain like a waterspout, peal followed peal of thunder in rapid succession, accompanied with painfully vivid flashes of forked lightning.

Some time after this, although the wind fell, the thunder and lightning continued with unabated violence; the rain also ceased, and, although it was midnight, the heat became intense almost beyond endurance. This state continued for about an hour, when a breeze sprang up now from N.W., gentle at first, but in the course of half an hour reaching a maximum fury, and again laying our tents flat, but this time in the opposite direction. The rain, thunder, and lightning were also as bad as ever. This continued but a short time, when, suddenly, the wind lulled, the rain ceased, the thunder was heard no more, and nothing was left of the storm but the dense cloud now to N.E., and from which the lightning continued to play. This was evidently a circular storm, bearing a column of heated air with great rapidity from the southern parts of the continent towards the north, attended with the consequent violent electric phenomena.

As they went on down the Winnipeg River they came out of the granite country into marshy flats where grew the wild rice that the Ojibwa used to gather in great quantities. They could see the old banks left, when it receded, by the ancient, enormous lake that is now called Lake Agassiz after the great geologist. In the evening they arrived at Fort Alexander, just above the river's outlet into Lake Winnipeg. Here they found supplies thoughtfully left by Sir George Simpson: a cake, ten dozen eggs, a bag of biscuits, and a barrel of ale. Here, too, Dr. Hector found a great many patients, all suffering more or less from symptoms of intestinal worms, caused by an exclusively fish diet. He thought the oil from the liver of the plentiful catfish might be used instead of cod-liver oil in treating consumption, a common illness among the half-breeds of the country.

A favourable wind at first helped them on Lake Winnipeg, letting them set sail in fine style, but soon it grew too strong for the canoes, and they were glad to take shelter behind the projecting point of a bay. Looking out across the shores of the lake at the great expanse of water horizon and feeding gulls, they thought of the sea-shore at home. Small flocks of wild pigeons passing overhead gave them good sport while they waited for the wind to drop. As soon as possible, after making their usual observations, they coasted on along the lake shore. Next morning they made a very early start, buying some fresh fish from Indian visitors when they stopped for breakfast and, as always, making observations.

At 12:15 p.m. they entered the Red River, not by the main channel, but through a dense growth of bulrushes in a flooded marsh. Now, once more, they were going against the stream and found that the swift current slowed them up. They pressed on, and by evening were passing the outskirts of the settlement—a few log huts here and there, then the Indian settlement, then the Indian Mission on the other side of the river, with a very tolerably built church surrounded by trees, with the clergyman's house attached. At last, after dark, they came to Lower Fort Garry, where they were made welcome with the usual Hudson's Bay Company hospitality.

They had reached the edge of the prairies at last. They said good-bye to their *voyageurs* and the canoes that had brought them more than 600 miles from Thunder Bay on Lake Superior. One canoe went straight back to Canada; the other left for Norway House with two gentlemen of the company's service, bound for the Mackenzie River district. Palliser, Hector, Bourgeau, Sullivan, and James Beads stood and cheered as the crews set off, smart in the new fustian trousers and red flannel shirts Palliser had given them to show how pleased he was with their 'docility, cheerfulness, and stern endurance'. These had earned the explorers' golden opinions on their adventurous journey, a journey that had convinced them that neither a road nor a through water-way could be built between Lake Superior and Red River except with enormous difficulty and at enormous cost. The intervening country was neither all water nor all land. It offered little hope of supporting settlement. There was not even pasture for settlers' cattle in transit to the western plains; only mineral discoveries, they thought, were likely to make the region economically valuable and so justify expensive construction of a through transportation route.

CHAPTER FIVE

An Astronomical Boundary Line

*T*he explorers had arrived at Lower Fort Garry—'the Stone Fort', as the Red River settlers called it—late on a Saturday. On Sunday morning they went to church and there they found a very orderly congregation of about 300. While Archdeacon Hunter (who had translated the Scriptures into Cree) officiated, dozens of horses were tethered to the railings outside, all gaily equipped with beaded Indian saddles.

Their own saddles were in the bundles they had brought with them in the canoes. The horses Sir George Simpson had reserved for their use were grazing near the fort. It did not take them long to get their English saddles and bridles unpacked; it probably took the prairie horses longer to get used to such unfamiliar trappings!

Upper Fort Garry, nearly twenty miles south of the Stone Fort, higher up the Red River where the Assiniboine joins it, was the principal post of the Hudson's Bay Company in Rupert's Land, the huge territory drained by the rivers that, like the Red River, flow into Hudson Bay. The explorers therefore set off to pay their respects to the officer in charge, Mr. Swanston.

The ride gave them a chance to see something of the settlement, which clung to the banks of the Red River between the two company posts. A heavy thunderstorm gave them a chance to hear something of its history by driving them to take refuge in a house belonging to one of the original settlers, who in 1811 had been sent to Red River from Scotland by Lord Selkirk. This old-timer entertained them with an absorbing account of the troubles that the little settlement had struggled through since its establishment, and from which it had not even yet emerged. Though the explorers saw many signs of solid settlement and active cultivation—rich hayfields and fenced crop-lands, houses built along the brink of the river and even a water-mill busily at work on a small creek—they realized that the nomadic origins of some of its inhabitants of mixed blood still created problems. Many of them preferred the excitement of the buffalo-hunt to the humdrum drudgery of tilling the rich land of the Red River Valley. Palliser reported that 'the indolence of the people is truly wonderful . . . They hunt during three months of the year, and beg, borrow, and starve during the remaining nine.' All the same, he could appreciate their fine qualities and he must certainly have had a fellow-feeling for their love of hunting and of a wild, wandering life out on the plains. Was he not setting out himself on a journey across the buffalo plains—a journey that seemed sufficiently wild to some of his contemporaries at home?

It was evident that this journey was likely to have its excitements. The expedition proposed to travel through territory ranged by tribes to whom local report gave a most warlike character. Palliser knew enough about their cousins south of the forty-ninth parallel to take this reputation seriously. The tribes of the Blackfoot Confederacy—the Blackfoot themselves, the Bloods, the Piegans, and the Sarcees—roamed the far-western plains and the foothills of the southern Rockies. They were the enemies of the Cree, who lived along the North Saskatchewan. Horse-stealing raids into each other's territory often ended in war between them. The Plains Assiniboine—or 'Stoneys', as they were usually called—another fierce and independent tribe, who ranged from the Upper Missouri in United States territory (where Palliser had seen a good deal of them ten years earlier) to the South Saskatchewan country, were also enemies of the Blackfoot, while Sioux hunting-parties and war-parties roamed back and forth along the border where the Red River flowed north into British territory.

The Secretary of State for the Colonies had written in his official instructions to Palliser: 'I cannot too earnestly impress upon you the necessity for the utmost caution in the selection of the line of route to be taken by the Expedition, and in avoiding all risk of hostile encounters with any native tribes who may inhabit the country through which you may pass.' If Palliser's 'line of route' was to take him through the blank spaces on the map that he had set out to fill, it would take him through the heart of the country that these very warlike and warring tribes claimed as their territory. Could he go through them without getting into trouble with the Indians? He thought he could; he was going to try.

He discussed the problem with old Mr. Harriott, who, years earlier, had been posted successively at several far-western forts, including Chesterfield House at the Forks of the Red Deer and South Saskatchewan, and Old Bow Fort, the so-called Piegan Post, on the Bow River, thirty miles or so west of modern Calgary, just north of the Trans-Canada Highway. With his first-hand knowledge of the Blackfoot, Piegans, Bloods, and Sarcees, Mr. Harriott gave the explorers much useful information concerning them.

They were going to need all the information they could get. Palliser had counted on his old Missouri friend and hunting- and travelling-companion, the far-famed Boucharville, to roam the plains with him again, as guide and hunter to the expedition. Now Mr. Denig, another old Missouri friend, from Fort Union, brought him the disconcerting news that Boucharville was dead, killed the year before by the Sioux, along with another Missouri comrade, little Carifel. This was a sad blow. Palliser had to find a substitute—an untried guide. He picked John Ferguson, a Scottish half-breed, with old Henry Hallet as second guide. These guides, with the faithful Beads and ten more men, half-breeds and Indians, were to drive the carts, look after the horses, pitch and raise camp, hunt and cook, and, incidentally, make the expedition strong enough to discourage the attentions of casual war-parties, like the Sioux war-party that, it was rumoured, had the year before in United States territory decoyed Sir John Gore into a conference, and robbed him and his party of their baggage, horses, clothes, arms, and ammunition. Poor Sir John had just managed to get to Fort Union, without even a shirt.

Palliser hoped to do better than that, but careful plans and preparations must be made if his party was to examine the 300,000 square miles that stretched west from Red River to the Rocky Mountains, between the North Saskatchewan and the United States border, and to find passes through the great barrier of the mountains beyond—if they could. July was already half over. Clearly, what remained of that summer and the summer after would give them little enough time for the long journey through country that was still a little-known wilderness, without organized government or transport routes or settlements. From Red River, where Winnipeg now stands, to the tiny settlement on Vancouver Island, the whole huge territory was occupied only by wandering bands of Indians, a few hundred half-breeds, half a dozen missionaries, and the fur traders of the Hudson's Bay Company.

The expedition set about organizing transport and laying in essential supplies and equipment. It took them the rest of the week to get all the work done—repairing carts, organizing harness and pack saddles, and dealing with the innumerable other details essential for a protracted journey across the plains. They took with them plenty of ammunition, of course, and, as well as tea and sugar and enough pemmican and flour to last them until they were likely to encounter buffalo, they carried tobacco and an assortment of trade goods for presents for the Indians.

Palliser had thought it probable that, like the prairies of the Missouri, the whole of the Red River and Saskatchewan plains could be travelled in carts. The local people confirmed this idea; so they equipped themselves with two American wagons that Mr. Denig had brought with him from the Missouri, as well as with six Red River carts. These Red River carts were admirably suited to the exigencies of the country; they were remarkable in the total absence of iron or metal of any kind in their construction. Consequently, whenever a cart broke down it could be mended again, as long as any timber was to be found; even out on the plains, far from all timber, a breakdown was not an irremediable evil as long as there were buffalo to be had. A buffalo bull could be killed and the green hide used to lash together the broken shaft or wheel. It soon dried, with an iron pressure, securing all splinters and other damage. The two American wagons were less satisfactory. They looked very promising, as they carried three times as much as the carts and were handier, being wide enough to make it possible to get things out and put them back without unpacking everything else at the same time; but they were not a success. Any horses that were big enough for the wagons were buffalo-runners and, as Palliser soon discovered, had not been trained to draw; the tough little cart-ponies did not fit the wagons, and the wagon harness, designed for mules, was too big for them. One wagon soon broke down and the other sank in an unluckily deep part of the South Saskatchewan, while the Red River carts went creaking sturdily on, right to the Rocky Mountains.

Then there was the problem of horses. Travel on the plains and in the mountains was impossible without them. Palliser had hoped for mules, which he had seen used in the United States, and which might be cheaper, but no mules were to be had. The twenty horses that Sir George Simpson, true to his word, had procured for the expedition were not very promising. The winter before had been a particularly bad one and a great many horses had died. Anyone who was lucky enough still to have a good buffalo-runner was loath to part with it, and even Sir George had not been able to procure satisfactory animals. Such as they were, they would have to do, but they were still in poor condition after the long, hard winter, though the expedition's late arrival had at least given them a chance to feed up on the spring pasture and so regain some strength. But twenty horses were not enough for six Red River carts, two wagons, four explorers, their servant, the guide or headman, and eleven men. Palliser at last managed to secure nine more, but the expedition was never to be free from worry about horses all the way across the plains and through the mountains. Their plans had to be made with the greatest circumspection to conserve the horses' strength for the whole long journey ahead.

The first thing to be done, clearly, was to find out exactly where the United States boundary line might be. The Convention of London had settled in 1818 that the border from Lake of the Woods to the top of the Rocky Mountains was to run along the forty-ninth parallel of latitude—but no one knew just where that parallel was. It was not a line running along the crest of a range of hills or down the middle of a river, which could be easily identified; it was just an imaginary, invisible frontier, and no one had yet found out exactly where it ran—let alone put up a string of markers. Palliser was not to try to 'run a line'; that could only be done jointly by two parties of surveyors, one appointed by the United States and one by Great Britain; fifteen years were to pass before an official boundary commission was finally appointed to mark the forty-ninth parallel across the prairies. Meanwhile Palliser had been told simply to examine the region along the southern frontier of British territory; but to do this he must first satisfy himself as to its whereabouts. It was therefore settled that, with the three 'scientific gentlemen' attached to the expedition, he should travel due south to the limit of British territory, going up the valley of the northward-flowing Red River to the point at which it enters British territory; here the expedition planned to turn westward and travel along the border to Turtle Mountain.

Since this would mean a long, roundabout journey for the horses, Palliser divided the party into two. Ferguson, with James Beads and seven other men, went with Palliser to the boundary. The second guide, Hallet, and the rest of the men took eleven horses and the four most heavily laden carts, with provisions and articles not wanted for immediate use, due west from Red River Settlement, along the ordinary route, the Carlton Trail, direct to Fort Ellice, on the Assiniboine, where the Qu'Appelle River joins it. This would lighten the work for the horses and give them a rest and a chance of recruiting on the excellent pasture at Fort Ellice, while they waited for the second, boundary 'brigade' to arrive.

It took most of the day to get the two brigades under way. There was the usual scurry and bustle, swearing and shouting, attendant on a large party setting off from a fort. The road south, from the Red River Settlement to Pembina at the border, crossed the Assiniboine River quite close to its junction with the Red River. It was a deep and rapid river, with banks composed of soft, tenacious clay, the famous 'gumbo' of the prairies. It was quite a business getting the south-bound party across, but there was a ferry, run by one of the settlers, and they were all over before sunset and went on three miles before camping. Palliser and his three scientific colleagues went back to the fort for the last night they were likely to enjoy in civilized society for a long time. The civilized society in question included not only Mr. Swanston of the Hudson's Bay Company, who had received them so hospitably and helped them greatly with their preparations, but also Major Seton, who had come overland to Red River in advance of the troops then on their way from Canada by the Hudson Bay route, and Mr. Johnson, the Recorder of Assiniboia, one of the very few administrative and judicial officials in the whole enormous fur-trading territory in which the Honourable Company held sway.

These two gentlemen saw Palliser and his colleagues ten miles on their way next morning. Nine miles farther on, the explorers caught up with the slower carts, just as the men were pitching camp for the night. Five of the men were mounted, four drove the carts and wagons, and six horses ran bare as reserves in case any should tire. There was excellent grass for the horses, but the myriads of mosquitoes and flies gave them no chance to feed or rest. Fires had to be lighted and piled with green wood. In the dense smoke the horses instinctively took refuge from their tormentors.

Next day the party settled, as they hoped, into the regular routine of western travel, getting up at four in the morning for an early start, stopping for breakfast at 9:30, and making a midday halt to take observations for latitude and to rest the horses. Alas for their hopes! The flies and mosquitoes were so bad that their horses could not graze in peace except in the early morning between three and seven o'clock when the flies ceased their attacks; so they had to start later, breakfasting before they set off, instead of at a mid-morning halt.

The thunderstorms were just as impressive as the insects. The travellers had already experienced several tremendous storms, of which Palliser wrote: 'The lightning instead of descending from the sky flashes upwards from earth to heaven'—an observation confirmed by modern scientists. While they had been at Red River, a flash of lightning in a slight storm struck an Indian tent, killing one man, three women, and a cat. Palliser and Hector went at once to help, but the victims were all dead. There was nothing to be done but to take up a subscription and bury the bodies.

Now another thunderstorm, after a very hot day, brought out millions of insects, which infested their tents. The canvas was literally black with mosquitoes, and if they could have preserved the many species of moths their candles attracted they would have had a large collection. Travelling in the valley of the Red River was like passing through a tropical country, so numerous and plentiful was the insect life—and that in spite of slight frosts every night. At least there were no snakes except the beautifully variegated and harmless garter snake.

As they travelled south they noted the characteristic lie of the land: to the east the bends of the Red River, marked by clumps of wood, known throughout the prairie country as 'points', and to the west, open prairie. They passed several rivers, and at one, to their surprise, there was a ferry. The ferryman had come from the American side of the Lake of the

Woods by way of a swift little river, the Roseau, which provided a direct route, but only for small canoes. This was an ancient Indian way, known as the War Road. There were splendid meadows of natural hay, and many mowers were busily engaged in cutting and storing it. The grass for some miles around grew more than knee-high, affording excellent pasture.

At Pembina they found a tiny Hudson's Bay Company post, only important for being situated on the American frontier line. The country around awaited only the hand of the settler to render it productive and valuable, but it was still a wild waste; even so, a garrison of American cavalry had appeared there, at the border, the preceding October and had tried to stop the half-breeds from British territory from crossing the line on their time-honoured buffalo-hunt. There was talk of a permanent American garrison being established there. The American trading-post on the Pembina River just south of the border was an insignificant collection of huts, though it had for some years been worrying the Hudson's Bay Company as a competitor, buying furs in defiance of the Honourable Company's monopoly rights. There were also groups of settlers' houses and enclosed land and a post-office that handled mail for the Red River Settlement and other parts of the British territories, by routes through the United States.

River steamers on the Mississippi and Missouri, new stagecoaches, and railroads were bringing American settlement nearer and nearer; the explorers met a surveyor working for an American land company. He spoke of plans for rail connection with St. Paul, 350 miles away, itself then still 220 miles away from railhead. He showed them plans for two new American towns, which he had been commissioned by the company to survey and lay out at Pembina River, just below the border.

But where exactly was the border? Half a mile south of the little Hudson's Bay Company post they found a stake that marked one point on the boundary line, according to the observations of an American scientist and explorer, Nicollet, who had spent a good deal of time some years before tracing the head-waters of the Mississippi and their connections with other rivers. The Indians had destroyed the original post, but some Hudson's Bay gentlemen had planted another with great care on the same spot. Palliser and Sullivan now took observations to see whether the post was in fact on the forty-ninth parallel. They found that its latitude was 48° 59′49″N. It was a few yards within American territory, but they decided to give Her Majesty the benefit of the doubt. The American surveyor and Sullivan then took observations for a second post, 370 yards due east of the first post, to determine the direction of the frontier line. Years later, the official joint boundary commission of 1872-6 confirmed the accuracy of these observations made by Palliser and Sullivan and, although Palliser's posts could not be official, the presence of his expedition at the border made it clear to the American surveyor that the British had an interest in these western plains.

From the two little Pembina posts, the explorers turned westward. Straying horses delayed their start. While they waited for the men to recapture the horses, Hector tinkered with the aneroid barometers, which had not been working properly since they left Sturgeon Lake. At last he discovered what was wrong. The jolting journey had shifted the unstable dial-plates. He put them back and treated them most successfully by firmly sewing on their faces with brass wire.

When at last they got away, they made a forced march over fine, rolling stretches of prairie and arrived long after sunset at the little American border town of St. Joseph's, inhabited chiefly by Red River half-breeds. Everyone was asleep except one old French half-breed. He invited them to turn their horses into his yard, where they could go un-hobbled and have a good feed of hay while the members of the expedition regaled themselves on the celebrated gold-eyes, a particularly tasty fish.

Most of the young men were away on the great annual

buffalo-hunt, but they found a harness-maker to make over the wagon harness, which, in spite of alterations, still did not properly fit the horses. While they waited, they were visited by a ninety-one-year-old traveller who had just walked the seventy miles from Fort Garry. He had taken two days to do this, driving a young bull. He had been one of the American Fur Company's party that had crossed the mountains in United States territory in 1811, to go to Fort Astoria, at the mouth of the Columbia River on the Pacific. He came now to get the doctor's advice as to what he should do for his knees, for he did not, he said, 'find them so strong as they used to be'.

Everywhere they went, the doctor found patients. Another man who came to see him had lost parts of both feet when he had been frozen, out on the plains, in the very cold winter before their arrival.

The doctor had other work to do, too. He went off searching for geological sections, in cliffs or valleys, where the different kinds of soil and rock that made up the plains would be exposed layer on layer to his scrutiny. He reported that the valley was the eastern edge of a prairie level that sloped abruptly down to the Red River plains by a succession of terrace-like steps. He found enormous landslips at a very sharp angle, displaying the structure of this terrace from summit to base; it consisted almost altogether of coarse, loose sand with beds of rounded shingle and gravel. From the top of the terrace the plain stretched westward as far as the eye could reach. From its foot the lower country stretched to the north-east as far as they could see from the top of the hill. This level plain, they thought, had formed at one time the bed of a sheet of water, with Pembina Hill its western shore—Lake Agassiz again.

The continual haziness of the weather prevented them from making any astronomical observations, but they had to go on, crossing again, as they calculated, into British territory north of the forty-ninth parallel. They passed a great many fresh and salty marshes and small lakes abounding in ducks, waders, and other aquatic birds. They came to a creek that their guide had told them would be very hard to cross. While the horses rested and grazed, they sent men ahead to find the best fording-place. Even this was bad indeed. Here the fertility of resource of their prairie *voyageurs* was well displayed; in a few minutes they had felled trees and extemporized a rough bridge, over which the wagons, carts, and horses passed in safety, although crossing the place seemed at first sight to be quite impracticable. The men told them to their surprise that the stream lost itself in an extensive marsh; it did not flow on into any other stream.

All day they had been skirting the bottom of Pembina Hill. As they moved on, the steep escarpment gradually changed to a wooded slope. They camped by a small well, only one foot in diameter, the only water to be found in the neighbourhood; they had to draw a supply from it for their animals, not allowing them to help themselves for fear that they would trample the place into a puddle. This was their first encounter with what was going to be one of their chief difficulties: lack of water.

They climbed the hill next day to the higher prairie level. They could see the wooded slope stretching on far to the north-west. Next day they turned southwards again. They could see the cone-shaped Hill of the Great Medicine Dance, Paquewin, ten or twelve miles to the west, not far from the valley of the Pembina, which they soon reached. Half-breed hunters, travelling every year to and from the big hunt out on the plains, had made a fair, winding road; otherwise it would have been very difficult to get down the steep, wooded sides into the wide valley through which the little river winds. This valley marked the edge of *la grande prairie*. To the east the country was wooded and irregular; to the west, at the higher level, there was nothing but bare prairie lands. They had to load the carts with enough wood for two days, as they were now leaving trees behind, but they began to find plenty of dry buffalo dung. Its glow, as it burnt, somewhat resembled that of coals, so that it was a great acquisition for a camp-fire. They also carried a cask of water with them. They were lucky in reaching a swamp, beside which they camped. While they were having dinner a strong wind blew up. With the wind came what seemed at first to be a low, brownish-black cloud, but soon they discovered, by the aid of a telescope, that it consisted of myriads of grasshoppers. A breeze springing up from the east met this cloud, and suddenly the insects began to fall as thick as snow, causing the party much discomfort from the blows they gave them on their faces as they pelted down. The ground was soon grey with them.

They were now close to the country of the Sioux Indians. These Indians were wonderful horse thieves, as Palliser had observed ten years earlier. To be esteemed an accomplished horse thief was the summit of their ambition. Late in the night, a dog barked and put them all on the alert. Then they heard a shot, probably a blank shot fired at some dog trying his chance of stealing food in a neighbouring tent; this told them that there were Indians about somewhere, but no horses were stolen that night at least.

Another noise in the night gave the scientists a chance to disprove a superstition held universally by the half-breeds. They said that a mysterious sound in the swamp was from a poisonous plant that muttered to itself continuously, falling silent only when a man came near. Bourgeau and Hector set out with a dark lantern to examine this plant gifted with a voice. Several attempts failed, but at last a stealthy approach and quick work with the lantern shutter revealed a noisy little frog in the midst of his croaking.

From the Pembina River on, the soil was everywhere very poor, and what little grass there was had been eaten by the grasshoppers. The unhappy horses found it hard to get enough to eat. The party passed scattered granite boulders, some of which had been polished by buffalo rubbing against them, wearing deep trenches about them, as they walked round and round. Detouring to the north, they camped in the wide, well-wooded valley of Long River. Night-hawks (birds like whip-poor-wills; Palliser called them goatsuckers) startled them at dusk as they swept close by their heads, giving their booming call.

Next day was very hot. They found numbers of garter snakes, and in the noon-hour halt, while Sullivan was making observations, one of the men wounded a large prairie wolf; after a long run he succeeded in killing it. They headed for some woods to make their evening camp—only to find they had been deceived by a mirage; there were only small poplars. Luckily they found a broken cart, which gave them some fuel. They could now see Turtle Mountain in the distance. When they reached its outskirts they found a fine rich prairie studded with clumps of bushes and small poplars. On the sides of the mountain itself, the woods were so dense they had trouble getting through them. Pathless thickets made hunting very arduous, much more so than it had been on the Turtle Mountains farther south, to the east of the Little Missouri River, where Palliser had gone hunting grizzly bears on his first trip to prairie country. From a distance, the mountain (as it was called, in common with every little rise of ground in this flat prairie country) looked impressive, but when they came up to it they found it was only a dense forest covering a gentle swell in the prairie. It had once had a great name as a hunting-ground, abounding with moose, wapiti, and bears, but, as the buffalo resorted there every winter and brought in their train numerous camps of Indians and companies of half-breed hunters, the game had been either exterminated or driven away, though Palliser tracked an elk and got a shot at him, but missed.

So far they had seen no buffalo, but they felt this might be a good thing: there was less risk that they would run into bands of Sioux Indians. As the carts and wagons made their way westward along the northern base of the mountain, Palliser and his scientists made trips up it, to examine it and to see all they could, from its summit, of the country spread out before them. Looking down just before sunset from a little height above the camp, they watched a fog rising from the hollows where there were lakes. It looked like a flood flowing up round the curved knolls, which became islands. Then only the tops of the trees were visible. Soon the explorers themselves were enveloped in a fog so dense that they had no small trouble in retracing their steps to the camp, where the men were making huge fires to combat the chill.

Among the many lakes teeming with waterfowl on the high land they shot a number of bitterns and two cranes, one a large white crane measuring five feet eight inches in height, the other a grey crane measuring five feet, with a wing-spread of six feet. Both bittern and crane were excellent eating, and were common in this part of the country, but the cranes were very wild and shy. (Its shyness has not saved the large white crane, the whooping crane, from near extinction, nor has its fierceness when attacked, which another explorer, Hind, described the following year: 'It is a dangerous antagonist when wounded, striking with unerring aim and great force with its powerful bill. When the bird is wounded, the best way to avoid its attacks is to present the muzzle of the gun as it approaches, it will fix its bill in the barrel and may then be destroyed without danger. Instances have been known of this bird driving its bill deep into the bowels of a hunter when not successful in warding off its blow.')

Early one morning they received a visit from three wapiti, which had noticed two of their chestnut-coloured horses feeding on the opposite side of the lake, and had immediately swum across to where they were grazing. This visit helped fill their larder, as they killed one of the does and set to work slicing and drying the meat.

The delay gave them a chance to take observations at noon. There had been a thunderstorm with several showers of very large hailstones, lasting almost continuously for nineteen hours and followed by daily storms, so that it had been difficult for Sullivan to get observations. A few days earlier he had managed to get one, which showed that their camp was then almost on the boundary. Now, at last, he managed to get another observation. This showed that while the greater mass of Turtle Mountain was within United States territory, the boundary line passed directly through the lofty, conical mound standing out from one end of the hill, which the half-breeds called the head of the turtle they thought the mountain resembled; thence it passed to the north of another point termed by the half-breeds the heart of the turtle. Here was one place, at least, where a well-defined natural feature marked the imaginary astronomical boundary line.

CHAPTER SIX

Buffalo

*A*t 'the head of the turtle' the explorers swung away from the border, which they had now examined for some 200 miles westward from Red River. First, though, after a long, round-about ride, Hector succeeded in gaining the highest point of the mountain, from which he could see far to the north and away to the south and west over American territory. In contrast to the lovely country immediately around the mountain itself (today the setting of the International Peace Garden), nothing was to be seen at a distance but a bare and barren prairie stretching in every direction.

The expedition now headed north-west towards Fort Ellice at the junction of the Qu'Appelle and Assiniboine rivers, just east of the present Manitoba-Saskatchewan boundary. Here they were to meet the men and the horses in the charge of old Henry Hallet. Hallet's party had travelled by the direct, regular route connecting Red River with Fort Carlton and Fort Edmonton on the North Saskatchewan. They arrived at Fort Ellice two weeks before Palliser's party, so their spare horses had had a chance to rest and graze and were in good shape again. Now the tired horses that had brought Palliser and his party on their roundabout route needed a chance to recruit their strength after their long, hard journey, made harder by the torment of horse-flies and mosquitoes and by very heavy going, especially over some sand-hills between Turtle Mountain and Fort Ellice. Palliser therefore decided to let them rest while he made a 'branch expedition'—

one of the innumerable side trips that make it so hard to keep track of the expedition's travels.

Angling across the plains on their way to Fort Ellice from Turtle Mountain, the explorers had crossed the Souris River, not far from where it joins the Assiniboine. At the crossing Hector had come on some lumps of coal, which he thought had been washed down-stream from coal-beds higher up the river. He was anxious to find and examine these.

Besides, they had heard curious accounts of rocks of a peculiar shape near the border on the Souris River, a few miles south-east of the twentieth-century town of Estevan. Hector wanted to examine these strange appearances and hoped to find the coal he was looking for in the same part of the valley of the 'Mouse' River, as he usually called the Souris—translating its name into English.

By great good fortune the Hudson's Bay Company interpreter at Fort Ellice was the celebrated James McKay, a remarkable member of a remarkable family. He was one of the best men the Hudson's Bay Company had on the prairies—fearless and knowledgeable, a splendid guide. He was detailed for many especially difficult and dangerous jobs. When Sir George Simpson in 1859 travelled to the prairies for the first time by the overland Mississippi route, instead of by the canoe route, it was James McKay who was sent to escort him. The rare travellers and big-game hunters who visited the prairies all wanted to have him as guide and interpreter. Lord Southesk described him when he first met him in 1859 in St. Anthony, on the United States side of the border:

> *A Scotsman, though with Indian blood on the mother's side, he was born and bred in the Saskatchewan country, but afterwards became a resident near Fort Garry, and entered the Company's employ. Whether as guide or hunter, he was universally reckoned one of their best men. Immensely broad-chested and muscular, though not tall, he weighed eighteen stone; yet in spite of his stoutness he was exceedingly hardy and active, and a wonderful horseman.*

His face–somewhat Assyrian in type–is very handsome:
short, delicate, aquiline nose; piercing dark grey eyes; long
dark-brown hair, beard, and moustaches; white, small, regu-
lar teeth; skin tanned to red bronze from exposure to weather.
He was dressed in Red River style–a blue cloth 'capot'
(hooded frock-coat) with brass buttons; red-and-black flannel
shirt, which served also for waistcoat; black belt round the
waist; buff leather moccasins on his feet; trowsers of brown
and white striped home-made woollen stuff.

I had never come across a wearer of moccasins before, and
it amused me to watch this grand and massive man pacing
the hotel corridors with noiseless footfall, while excitable little
Yankees in shiny boots creaked and stamped about like so
many busy steam-engines.

With McKay, Palliser and Hector set off for Roche Percée,
leaving Sullivan at Fort Ellice to take a series of observations
for latitude, longitude, and variation of the compass, and
Bourgeau to classify and preserve his specimens and pack
them for shipment to England, where some of them can still
be seen in the museums and herbarium of the great botanical
gardens at Kew.

After two days' travel they came within sight of Moose
Mountain, away on the horizon to the south-west, just such
another long, low, tree-covered hill as Turtle Mountain. The
country round it, too, was studded with clumps of wood,
while on Moose Mountain itself the pattern of woods was an
exact counterpart of that on Turtle Mountain; there was even
the same sharp conical peak at the west end of the hill, and to
the south and west a boundless sweep of plain, unbroken by
even a single tree. Journeying on, they came out on to these
treeless prairies; once more they had to carry with them the
wood they needed and use buffalo dung for fuel.

There was buffalo dung, but they had not yet seen a single
buffalo, though they had now been journeying for some
hundreds of miles in buffalo country. Palliser was feeling
frustrated: the only animals they had met since leaving Fort

Ellice were bands of antelope, which were so fleet that they could seldom be shot, except by trading on their curiosity. The hunter would flap a red or white blanket; the antelope would try to get the wind of the unusual object, to find out what it might be, and the hunter, running round to the lee side, might then get a chance of a shot.

That was all very well, but Palliser had for months been looking forward to running buffalo. Now at last his hopes were raised. Two half-breeds, from a hunting-party encamped near Moose Mountain, chanced on them while they were at dinner. They had not found any buffalo yet, either, but they were confident that next day the explorers would fall in with some bulls. Their forecast proved right. At long last the explorers sighted two bulls. It must have been a tense moment for Palliser. Had he lost his old skill? Could he, after ten years, live up to his reputation as a fine buffalo-hunter? He could and he did. The report says simply, 'we had not proceeded far after breakfast when we came in sight of two buffalo bulls, which I killed'—a laconic record of a triumphant feat.

The hunt had delayed them and they pushed on late that night, having trouble getting the cart past boulders that so covered the ground that they could hardly get it along. Just as they came to the edge of the Souris Valley, a most terrific thunderstorm came on and they camped hurriedly.

When day broke, they discovered a large camp of Indians on the opposite bank of the river, the white tents glistening in the rising sun. They made off up the valley to examine it, but soon saw a number of Indians crossing the river towards them. From the open manner in which they came it was clear that their intentions were friendly. The explorers chose a good position and waited for them. A few had guns, but the majority were armed with bows and arrows. They turned out to be a party of Stoney Indians. McKay knew most of them and went back with them to their camp on fur-trade business. The Indians had come from the Grand Coteau of the Missouri in American territory, half a day's journey to the south of the Souris. They were keen for the explorers to go to their camp

to trade horses, but McKay soon discovered that all they
wanted was rum.

They had a prisoner, a little Ojibwa boy. He managed to
escape from his captors' camp and hid till the explorers' party
was on the way back. Then he joined them. He proved very
useful but was a thorough adept in all sorts of mischief.
Meanwhile the explorers had been examining the river
valley carefully. Hector went to see the far-famed Roche
Percée, the great rock pierced through by an enormous hole.
The Indians never passed it without making some offering to
the Manitou that, to their minds, it represented. They rubbed
vermilion on it or deposited beads, tobacco, or other offerings in the crevices. They had carved rude designs with their
knives all over the soft surface of the stone. The sandstone
weathered in such a way that there were many such curious
shapes, which the Indians regarded with superstitious dread.
Big lumps of hard rock, which had not broken down under
the effects of wind and weather as quickly as the softer rock,
had become isolated and perched on natural pillars. These
were grouped as if they formed the ruins of ancient buildings.
Hector made sketches of this grotesque natural architecture
along the river-bank.

He was disappointed that he did not find any high-quality
coal, nor, indeed, any great quantity even of the lignite that
he did find. Today Roche Percée stands in the great coal-min-
ing district of south-eastern Saskatchewan, but the deposits of
lignite coal lie under many feet of soil and over-burden, so
Hector did not find them. He could not foresee the mines and
electric-power plants of present-day Estevan and Boundary
Dam!

On their way back to Fort Ellice, Hector and McKay
climbed to the top of Moose Mountain, making their way with
difficulty up through the dense woods on its sides. The climb
was worth the trouble. From the summit they had a splendid
view of the country for miles on every side. Hector was
beginning to get a comprehensive impression of the character
of the southern prairies in British territory, which helped the

expedition to work out the extremely useful and comprehensive description that was later published in a thick, official blue-book.

Back at Fort Ellice, Palliser found that the horses, though in better condition, were still not fit to travel. Besides, the party needed more ammunition, a supply of which McKay was every day expecting from Fort Pelly, the principal post of the district, some distance farther north. They had to wait.

Palliser took advantage of the delay to send a messenger back to Red River Settlement with mail. He had sent some letters off from the American post-office at Pembina, but had doubts about their safety. Though the post-office was described to him as 'a very lucky one', it was run by a half-breed who was frequently away, leaving everything in the care of an Indian wife who could neither read nor write nor even speak any language but her own. When anyone asked her if there were any letters for him, she simply handed over all the letters in the post-office, so that the inquirer could appropriate the one he wanted! That was the last post-office of any kind. Beyond Pembina the conveyance of letters was entirely a private act at the expense of the Hudson's Bay Company and formed no part of any postal system, as Palliser found, to his cost. He had to pay his messenger £5 to go to Red River—four days' journey there and four days' back, with one horse worn out and exchanged at the settlement for a fresh one—and in the end he brought only three letters!

While they were waiting, still within the shelter of the company post, trouble blew up that very nearly ended the expedition before it had got fairly out into the true, untravelled wilderness. From Fort Ellice the much-frequented Carlton Trail swung north-west to the north branch of the Saskatchewan and then westward up the river. The officers and employees of the company normally kept to this trail on overland journeys, as did most of the rare non-company travellers; heavy traffic and most passenger traffic still went by boat by the North Saskatchewan itself. Palliser proposed to leave these well-known routes and travel due west to the

'Elbow' of the South Saskatchewan, where the river, flowing north-eastward, turns suddenly to the north-west. From the Elbow, Palliser hoped to travel up the South Saskatchewan to the Forks of the Red Deer River. This would mean a journey not only through trackless wilderness, where even the fur traders seldom ventured, but through the heart of the country ranged by the warlike Plains Indians. John Ferguson, the chief guide and interpreter, had become thoroughly alarmed at the idea of penetrating a region so full of dangers. He soon stirred up the other men employed by the expedition into an equal fever of apprehension. He set to work to organize among the Indians at the fort some testimony that the course the expedition had planned was impracticable. He gave Palliser false information about the proposed route, saying that the carts could not cross the Qu'Appelle River, and proposed that they should go west instead, along the north branch of the Saskatchewan River through country that was already well known.

McKay discovered the 'conspiracy' and told Palliser about it. Palliser asked him to come with the expedition in Ferguson's place as guide and interpreter. The idea pleased McKay, but he had to get permission from his superior, Mr. Christie, at Fort Pelly, the chief factor in charge of the district. A messenger was sent off on the 200-mile return trip to Fort Pelly.

Meanwhile the horses were at last judged fit to travel again and the anxiously awaited powder, ball, and shot arrived. At once Hector started off on a due-west course to the Qu'Appelle Lakes Post with most of the men and the carts and horses. Palliser waited at the fort until the messenger should return from Mr. Christie.

Hector's advance party recorded the usual detailed description of the country-side as it went along. The road, though evidently a much-used track, was very bad, and sorely tried the strength of their carts; only Red River carts could have stood the strain, and even one of the Red River carts broke a wheel and another upset in a swamp. The first morning out they were delayed by a fog so dense that they could not find their horses. The second night they camped by a pretty little lake. This was the last water they expected to see for many miles. As it turned out they had difficulty, not from too little water, but from too much. They found innumerable swamps and lakes, among which they had to wind their way. One lake with a stony shore made an agreeable change from the usual marshy sloughs. They found choke-cherry trees laden with fine ripe cherries, which, though slightly astringent (and, of course, consisting mostly of pip) were very pleasant to the taste. They killed so many wildfowl that one evening they had no fewer than forty ducks, besides several geese, roasting at the same time round their campfire. The avocet, which they saw here for the first time, amused them. Its long delicate bill, turned upwards as if the wrong way, gives the bird a most comical appearance.

They were to wait for Palliser and McKay at the Qu'Appelle Lakes Post. This post was right out on the plains, actually some eighteen miles south of the Qu'Appelle Lakes, but it had kept its old name when it was moved south from the lakes, where it had originally been established. It was then the farthest south and west of all of the Hudson's Bay Company posts. In 1822-4 the Hudson's Bay Company had sent a flying expedition of ten officers and a hundred men to examine the country along the upper South Saskatchewan, where the Red Deer joins it. Earlier there had been several trading-posts on the river. The company had withdrawn from the south-western prairies when it was discovered that they had little to offer in the way of furs, and after a number of lives had been lost in trouble with the Indians.

Even so, the prairie country was important to the fur traders. It was the source of their food supplies. Pemmican, made from the meat of its teeming herds of buffalo, provided the staple diet of the company's officers and employees living at the trading-posts and for the *voyageurs* who carried the furs out of the country in the annual boat brigades. This pemmican, harvest of their buffalo-hunts, was brought in for trade by the Indians of the plains and the half-breeds of Red River, who, organized with military discipline under their leader, the Warden of the Plains, went out on the prairies every year on two tremendous buffalo-hunts. The Qu'Appelle Lakes Post was an important supply depot.

The prairies along the South Saskatchewan had a second important role in the Hudson's Bay Company's trading operations. They insulated the rich, fur-bearing regions farther north from possible competition from American fur traders. Empty, apart from the wandering bands of buffalo and warring Indians, these inhospitable plains rolled off, south to the American border and west to the Rockies, into unknown distances, the distances Palliser meant to examine.

While Hector was waiting for Palliser to catch up with him, he went north to visit the Qu'Appelle Lakes. He procured a guide and a note from the Hudson's Bay officer in charge to Charles Pratt, at the Church of England mission on the Qu'Appelle Lakes. Hector described this hospitable catechist, who had been educated at Red River, as a pure Stoney Indian by birth; Palliser said he was a pure Cree Indian; and Hind (the Canadian explorer who visited the Qu'Appelle region the next year) called him a half-breed. Whatever his derivation, he had a very comfortable little house and an excellent garden in which he grew corn, barley, potatoes, and hops.

Mr. Pratt took them across the river next day in a skin canoe, the led horses swimming after them. They rode downstream to see a great slide of the bank. Here Hector had hoped to see something of the basic geological structure of the plains, but only found red and yellow clays exposed, together with sandy drifts. Poor Hector! He was having a difficult time. So deep were the beds of clays and sands and gravels left behind by the ancient lakes and rivers and glaciers that he could not get at the underlying rocks to see what kind they were. He had to study the earth dug by badgers from their holes in the hope of finding out something about the rock structure below the surface of the plains. Neither in the sides of steep coulees nor even in the so-called mountains could he find anything but accumulations of sand, clay, gravel, and soil, though he suspected that the hills might have a rocky core.

The party consoled themselves with a breakfast of pelican and fish. The fish they had caught in the lake, and the pelicans had been part of a flock gliding majestically upon it.

When they got back to the Qu'Appelle Lakes Post they found that Palliser and McKay had arrived. Mr. Christie had himself made the three days' journey from Fort Pelly to Fort Ellice to meet Palliser; he had willingly given McKay leave to go with the expedition. Sir George Simpson was annoyed with him for doing so, when he heard about it, and made sure that it would not happen the next season. Christie had brought with him a replacement to take charge of Fort Ellice while McKay was away. Riding hard, Palliser and McKay covered the 125 miles from Fort Ellice to the Qu'Appelle Lakes Post in two and a half days.

They arrived to find a large camp of Plains Cree had come for trading. While the Indians were there, the catechist paid Hector a return visit. He told the explorers that these Cree were getting very worried because they thought the buffalo would grow scarcer and scarcer. He said they were anxious to try agriculture. He thought they would make a start on it if they only had spades, hoes, and ploughs.

Among them there was a great chief who was a remarkable exception to the generality of the Plains Indians. Though he had been a noted warrior in his youth, he was now called the Peacemaker. The Cree and Blackfoot were deadly enemies, but twice within the last two or three years he had pushed his way alone into Blackfoot country and walked into the enemy's camp, unarmed, peace-pipe in hand, exhorting them to peace and offering them the alternative of killing him. The result, on each occasion, was a treaty of peace with the Cree and a present of horses to the Peacemaker. Palliser engaged him as a guide to the Elbow of the South Saskatchewan, for which service he was to have a horse and a suit of clothes. They called him 'Nichiwa' (meaning 'friend'). His Indian name was Maskepetoon.

Now they were ready to start off into the trackless wilderness they had come so far to see. Here, at last, as Palliser stood looking to the west, he could say, 'westward of this . . . is unknown, and the whole country in this latitude is untravelled by the white man.'

The first night out they camped in the Squirrel Hills, where they had good wood, water, and grass, but there were signs that they were getting into arid country again with poor, stony soil, where there would be difficulty in finding pasture. The next day the Peacemaker counselled them to load the carts with wood; there would be no more wood, except in the valleys of the rivers. Their course lay due west; as far as the eye could reach, nothing but desolate plains met the view. These 'desolate plains' are the Regina Plains, where now so much first-class wheat is grown. They came to a little creek called the Creek-before-where-the-Bones-lie and, in the evening, to another creek, the Creek-where-the-Bones-lie. The Indian name was Wascana creek; on it the city of Regina stands today, with its fine buildings, beautiful lake, and tall trees. Then, a hundred years ago, there was little water and very little grass; some small willows, but no wood fit for fuel. The nearest inhabitants were an old man and some women and children, in two Indian lodges on the first of the two creeks. The young men were all away hunting buffalo.

The next camping-place of the expedition was on Moose Jaw Creek. Here they found a number of Indian tents, among which, right in the middle, stood a large medicine lodge covered with hierographic characters, birds, and animals of various designs. Again there were only women and children. The women asked leave to come and see the wives of the men of the party, and expressed considerable surprise when they told them they had none. No Indian could survive for long without his wife, who did so much of the work that was essential for survival. Only war-parties travelled without women.

On Moose Jaw Creek there was wood, water, and grass, but once again the Peacemaker told them to load the carts with enough wood to last for five days. There was no more to be had east of the Elbow.

The next day they had great difficulty in getting over Moose Jaw Creek. The steep banks of what seemed an insignificant stream made it impossible to get the carts and wagons across, and they had to make a long detour to the south before they could find a possible crossing-place. They got to 'Thunder Mountain Creek' (Thunder Creek), where there was no wood at all; so they cooked their supper with buffalo dung and some of the wood they had brought with them.

They were now near the Missouri Coteau, the long, low hill that is the edge of the next upward prairie 'steppe'. Hector and McKay, who had gone off to explore to the south, did not catch up with the main party when it made camp. Palliser delayed the start next morning, hoping the doctor's party would come up with them. He was disappointed. When his party stopped for dinner they could see Indian tents; before they had finished their meal they were surrounded by Cree, who had at first thought they were a herd of buffalo. The Cree had seen nothing of the doctor. He still did not arrive next morning. Palliser waited; he was worried. Perhaps Hector and McKay had got ahead of the main party, not knowing of the delay caused by the trouble over crossing Moose Jaw Creek. At last they set off again. Twenty-five of the Indians went with them.

There was still no sign of Hector and McKay the next night, and again Palliser delayed the start of the main party in the morning; but at long last they arrived, with a large contingent of Cree. They had slept the night before in one of the Cree lodges and were very hospitably treated, having received many invitations to the festivities in various tents. In the tent in which the doctor slept, a Blackfoot scalp was hanging. The women danced around it, forcing the captured wife of the dead brave to join them in the dance. Hector's party had had to spend the night previous out on the open plain without food, fire, or blankets, after riding over seventy miles.

They had met an Indian travelling on foot, returning from burying his relatives who had died of smallpox the year before. According to Indian custom he had thrown away all his clothes to celebrate the event and as a sort of sacrifice to the Manitou of the prairies. The doctor gave him their only blanket.

This was the party's first encounter with the dreaded smallpox, a disease of almost yearly occurrence and fearfully fatal among the Indians. McKay told them that half the Indians tenting round Fort Ellice the year before had died from it. They had heard rumours there that there was an epidemic of it at Fort Carlton, where they were to spend the winter. It looked as though sick Indians might be a more serious danger than Indians who were fighting fit!

They began to hear a good deal about Indian wars and to see evidences of conflict themselves. One of the Indians who came in with the doctor had been scalped by the Blackfoot not long before. He lay wounded and insensible from loss of blood, and left for dead; but after his enemies had departed and his consciousness returned, he made his way back to his friends. He wore a handkerchief bound tightly round his head and did not wish to show it to the doctor, nor did he like that his misfortune should ever be talked of. Nichiwa told them the story:

> . . . *he was one of four young men who had escaped from a massacre of his friends by the Blackfeet in a ravine near the elbow of the south branch of the Saskatchewan last spring. It appears that the Crees and Blackfeet had been at peace, and were tenting together, but after the return of the former 25 young Crees formed a horse-stealing party, and having previously constructed rafts succeeded in stealing the Blackfoot horses, and by crossing themselves on the rafts succeeded in leading off the horses swimming in their wake. When the Blackfeet missed their horses they set off in pursuit, and*

following up the track came to the bank of the river whence they had been taken across. While they were still there one of the young Crees actually had the hardihood to reveal their position by glancing a small looking glass, and as it were chaffing the Blackfeet. The season being so early (just after the breaking up of the ice), the water was intensely cold, and the river very high, wide, and rapid, so that these young Crees never dreamt of the possibility of the Blackfeet pursuing them without rafts across the South Saskatchewan, and during the time consumed by the Blackfeet in the construction of these they thought they had abundance of time to escape with their stolen horses far beyond the fear of pursuit. The Blackfeet, however, turned about, and departed as if returning to their camp, and then made a detour to a point higher up the river where, concealed by a bend, they swam their horses across. At sunset they fell upon the Young Crees, surrounded them in the coulee in which the men encamped, and killed 17 of them on the spot with bows and arrows, and by rolling large stones on them. A few got away wounded under cover of the night, and only three or four ultimately recovered.

Such tales, which lost nothing in the telling by the Cree, some of whom were still in mourning, alarmed Palliser's men very much. One old man, who had thrown away almost the whole of his attire and was now clad in a very old robe, with his head plastered with mud, implored them to go no further among these 'wicked men'. Undeterred, they were still determined to press on.

Palliser had, at the Qu'Appelle Lakes Post, secured a fine mare from Mr. Pratt in exchange for two of his worn-out horses, and now he seized the chance to get two more fresh horses from the Cree. He would have exchanged more but for the extreme soreness of the Indian horses' backs.

They were now verging on the neutral ground between the Blackfoot and Cree. The Indians said that there were plenty of buffalo two days' journey to the westward, but as this was in enemy country they did not like to go so far. As the explorers travelled on they began to see buffalo, single bulls at first, then bands of bulls. Palliser encouraged Sullivan to run one of these and reported, ' . . . he acquitted himself very well, rushed in boldly, and bowled over his bull at the first shot.' One of the men also killed a young bull. They were glad to be able to eat a little of the meat, but they were hoping soon to find cows, which would be much better eating.

The Peacemaker was now expecting to meet Blackfoot any time; he smartened himself up considerably, having obtained from Palliser an old shooting-jacket, from the doctor a pair of corduroys, and from Sullivan a waistcoat and neckerchief. The explorers did not think that his European clothes improved his appearance; on the contrary, they made him look like a monkey.

Next day they sent scouts ahead, who reported a band of cows. They saved most of their remaining firewood for what they hoped would be a fine supper, and after a hurried breakfast Palliser set off with McKay and two of the men, Hallet and Morin, who were two of the best buffalo-hunters in Red River Settlement, in hopes of fresh meat for supper. The ground was full of badger holes. This made running the horses very dangerous, rather like riding a steeplechase over a rabbit warren. Palliser was riding his own horse, Pharaoh, a big grey. Coming up behind some sand-hills, they got very close to the herd. 'When the race began [Palliser wrote] the pace was tremendous, because early in the day the cows are far swifter; in less than five minutes we left the bulls floundering in the rear, and were ahead among the cows, Hallet and I riding neck and neck.' Palliser fired the first shot but missed. He slackened pace, and, riding knee to knee with Hallet, asked him for his loaded gun, saying: 'You cannot come up!' Hallet, piqued at being asked for his gun, swerved away, but McKay, whose horse was not as good as Pharaoh, rode up saying, 'Captain, my horse cannot do it, I shall injure the horse, and do no good; take my loaded gun, give me your empty one.' Palliser got a second shot and killed a fine cow. McKay gave Palliser another loaded gun, but it missed fire.

Palliser was wondering whether Pharaoh, fresh as he seemed, could stand still another race, when another of the men, Beauchamp, a very good hunter and a lightweight, came up on a slower horse. Palliser, calling him, leaped off Pharaoh; Beauchamp jumped on and very soon picked out and brought down another fat cow. Morin bagged a third. Hallet's horse put a foot in a badger hole, and horse and rider got a fearful fall.

The buffalo-chase carried them westward. At the end of the race they could see the cliffs of the South Saskatchewan. Their goal was in sight, but they had to stop to cut up the meat. While they were doing this the carts caught up with them. The task accomplished, they camped on the banks of a creek where they found wood, water, and a little grass. They also found sage-brush for the first time, so they called the creek Sage Creek.

CHAPTER SEVEN

The South Saskatchewan

At last the expedition had reached the great, mysterious river that had for so long been its object. Open plains sweep up to the high banks of the South Saskatchewan; lofty, sandy cliffs fall steeply to the river-bed. From the top of the river-bank, the explorers could see ten miles up the deep valley, with all the windings of the river laid out below them. In spring and early summer, when mountain snows are melting, its waters come down in spate; when Palliser first saw it, at the end of summer, there were still deep channels and a strong current, but very noticeable, also, were sand-bars, with a heavy growth of young willows, and, projecting into the stream, points of land on which grew woods of willow, birch, and poplar.

Sixteen miles above the Elbow, where the Coteau crosses the river, the valley is wide and the banks are very high. Below the Elbow the valley narrows. It is here that the South Saskatchewan Dam is being built; soon the scene that Palliser saw will be drowned in a huge, new lake, which will bring water to the dry lands bordering the river, which Palliser reported were arid and sterile.

Buffalo and locusts between them had swept away what little grass there had been; once again the unhappy horses went hungry. The horses were also in danger from Indian war-parties. They had to be carefully guarded, especially just before daylight, the favourite moment for an attempt to steal them.

The Indians came here only in war-parties, never to hunt, so game was plentiful. The explorers found great numbers of buffalo, always dogged by wolves prowling round them ready to attack any worn-out or wounded straggler or straying calf. Sometimes the buffalo fed close to the expedition's horses at night, while the wolves howled piteously out on the plains and moved restlessly about on the heights above the camp, clearly visible in the moonlight. Wildfowl, too, were very abundant. Geese surprised them by starting up from a tiny slough that seemed much too small for so big a flock.

The South Saskatchewan proved a happy hunting-ground not only for the sportsmen of the party, but for the geologist as well. At last Hector had some luck. He studied the cliffs to great advantage, finding interesting cretaceous strata and fossils.

He was also interested in the odd interconnection between the valleys of the Qu'Appelle and of the South Saskatchewan. Palliser sent him off to explore the country to the east of the Elbow. He found a small stream which, at the Elbow, runs into the South Saskatchewan from the east. Swampy lakes at its source also drained to the Qu'Appelle River, flowing in the opposite direction. The summit level dividing the South Saskatchewan and the Qu'Appelle lies in a valley more than 100 feet deep, with steep sides. This valley runs right through from the Qu'Appelle valley to the Saskatchewan. The Indians called the creek that runs from this valley to the Saskatchewan, Aiktow, 'the river that turns'; at high water it flows east as well as west. Palliser, always interested in water-ways, suggested that an engineering investigation should be made with a view to establishing communication between the Saskatchewan and Assiniboine, should the progress of population ever warrant this. Hind, visiting the Elbow the following year, suggested that the waters of the South Saskatchewan should be dammed up and diverted into the Qu'Appelle, to provide a more direct water route to Red River than the South Saskatchewan itself could provide. Today the dam on the South Saskatchewan is being supplemented by a dam across this connecting valley to the Qu'Appelle, which Hector explored a hundred years ago.

While on his branch expedition up the Aiktow, Hector nearly had his horses stolen, but the Peacemaker raised the alarm when in the night he heard Indian signals, which sounded like chirping birds. In the morning they found the tracks of their unknown visitors and one of the horse cords had been cut, but, thanks to the Peacemaker's vigilance, the horses were safe.

On Hector's return the party travelled on up the South Saskatchewan, finding, beside the river, cottonwood trees such as Palliser had known in the Missouri country, as well as sage-brush everywhere and cactus plants with thorns which were sharp and poisonous, causing pain and irritation in the sole of the foot when trodden on. They killed a fine stag wapiti, but it was not an unusually big specimen. There were still plenty of buffalo and they could stalk them easily in the broken country along the river, so they had no need to tire their horses further by running buffalo out on the plains.

Summer was drawing to a close. The flowers were all dead, killed by the frosts at night, so Monsieur Bourgeau had now only the seeds to collect. A violent gale blew their tents down twice in one night, for the tent-pegs had a bad hold in the loose sand. (This was not the only problem caused by the sand: it blew uncomfortably into their blankets, and, on the march, the carts sank into it up to the axles.) The next day was fine. A large grizzly bear came out of a clump of willows and lay sunning himself on the side of a hill on the opposite side of the river, just near enough for them to be able to see that it was a bear and not a buffalo. As they had no means of getting quickly across the river, they had to content themselves with viewing him through a telescope.

The grizzly was calm, but the men from Red River were not. They were getting more and more excited and worried as the expedition went deeper into Blackfoot country. When they learned that Palliser hoped to push on still farther, up the South Saskatchewan to where the Red Deer joined it, they were horrified. They had not forgotten that thirty-odd years earlier the Hudson's Bay Company had abandoned its post at the Forks of the Red Deer and South Saskatchewan as being too dangerous and too costly; this had given that part of the country a bad reputation. The men tried hard to persuade Palliser that the party was not sufficiently numerous and that to proceed any further into Blackfoot territory with such a small party was too dangerous. They thought they had done wonders already in having gone as far as they had. Wisely, Palliser discussed the matter with McKay, who knew the country and the men. He had a pretty shrewd idea of the risks involved. He was, besides, a man of undoubted courage and strength of character. He replied: 'Captain, if you say the word go, I will say, hurrah, let's go; but if you ask my advice, I will tell you plainly that I think it is too dangerous, and more than this, if you press it, your men will break up, and beyond Beads, John Foulds, and old Hallet I could not say who would stick to you.'

Palliser took his advice. Most unwillingly, and unconvinced, he abandoned the project of pressing on farther west. He prepared to cross the Saskatchewan and make tracks for winter quarters at Fort Carlton. It turned out to be a wise decision. The horses very nearly gave out as it was, before they reached the Fort. Even another few days' work might have been disastrous.

Crossing the river was a problem. The stream was wide and deep with a sand-bar midway across, beyond the deep main channel. Palliser gives a lively account of how they crossed. After taking the body off one of the wagons and converting it 'into a skiff by lashing oil-cloths about it, so as to make it as nearly water-tight as possible, we then fastened together all the horse lines and cords, both of leather and hemp, which we could collect, and made them into one long rope, one end of which we fastened on the shore where we stood, and then with the assistance of our waggon skiff paddled over to the sand-bar and secured the other end by means of a strong post firmly driven into the ground, thus establishing a communication by which we crossed the carts in safety'.

They were not so lucky with the undercarriage of the wagon. As they were trying to get it over, their rope broke, and the wagon sank in about twenty feet of water in the middle of the channel. They got all the horses over safely by collecting them together into a band and with long willow sticks driving them into the water, the men and the Peace-maker shouting all the while and assailing with sticks and stones any frightened animal that attempted to turn back. The rapid current carried the horses quite a distance downstream before they could get a footing on the opposite shore.

Again the men paddled into the river in their wagon-skiff; they succeeded in fishing up and lashing together the broken extremities of the line and, with its assistance, crossed all the luggage and instruments to the sand-bar. Beyond, the water was shallow enough for wading. They caught the horses and reloaded the carts before they camped near a marsh, where at last there was very fair grass for the horses.

Again they saw the grizzly wandering slowly along the base of the valley, but when some of the party went after him he vanished into the thick growth of willows on the border of the river. Buffalo were plentiful here, too, on the north side of the river, and they found a beaver dam. For the last golden days of September they stayed in camp to rest their horses. They tried hard for a whole day to get the wagon up again out of the deep water, but they could not move it from the sand in which it was deeply embedded. Going through a thicket, Palliser started two grizzly bears, and fired at one without success. The bears made for the plain and were followed by the doctor and Hallet on horseback, over very bad country. After a hard run Hallet succeeded in killing the female, who had turned to make a last fight. They felt Hallet deserved great praise, as he was very badly mounted and had had a fall during the run. The he-bear, much the larger, handsomer, and more grizzled of the two, got away. They had other good shooting, as well, getting some very fine specimens of wapiti, deer, and cabri. They took the antlers and skins to Fort Carlton with them in the carts and on their arrival sent them off to England.

Now they struck off to the north-east, at first following down the left bank of the river and then moving off north-ward. Though the plains were still for the most part bare and arid, and the lakes were fringed round the edge with thick encrustations of salt, bespeaking rapid evaporation, the explorers began to find clumps of trees and patches of pasture, and there was rich grass on the slopes of the deep gullies running down to the river valley.

As the carts went slowly on, the mounted men scattered to hunt. One man set off to run buffalo with his pipe in his mouth. He had fired and missed, and commenced to reload the gun in the ordinary manner, by pouring out powder from his horn into the palm of the left hand, when a spark fell from his pipe and set the powder alight; the fire jumped to the powder-horn and blew it to pieces. The man, astonishingly, escaped without a serious burn, but lost his whiskers, eyebrows, and eyelashes. The Peacemaker, too, ran buffalo that morning. He killed a good cow, but complained of having lost his ramrod. He went back some distance to look for it. When at length he abandoned his search and returned to cut up his animal, he found the remains of his ramrod in its body. He had loaded with the ramrod and, in the excitement of the chase, had forgotten to withdraw it before firing. Later a large band of buffalo ran right across the party's line of travel, just ahead of the carts; without any exertion they killed three fat cows.

By now many of the horses' hooves were worn so thin and sore as to leave signs of blood in their tracks. The men tried to relieve them by wrapping their feet in dressed buffalo skin. One horse got so weary they had to leave him behind, but the next day McKay went back for him and managed to bring him on, rescuing him from all the wolves in the neighbourhood, who were hungrily watching his movements.

Once they had left the river, they again encountered a

familiar problem: difficulty in finding water. Many of the swamps were quite dried up.

A new danger threatened, as well. The grass was like tinder. To the north and east they saw that the prairie was on fire: ' . . . a spark from a pipe may be sufficient to set 200 square miles of prairie in a blaze. The Indians are very careless . . . and frequently fire the prairie for the most trivial reasons; frequently for signals to telegraph to one another concerning a successful horse-stealing exploit, or in order to proclaim the safe return of a war-party.'

Fires had killed all the trees in huge stretches of country which had once been wooded. Besides, they sometimes cut off the buffalo from a whole district, thus causing great privation and distress to the Indians. Their own fire 'ran' after breakfast, but they quickly extinguished it, beating it back with blankets and saddle-cloths.

The prairie fire they had seen was still burning next day. Dense smoke warned them to camp in a swamp in case the fire should move in their direction. A storm came on, blowing in turn from every point of the compass, because the fire had disturbed the equilibrium of the atmosphere. The whole horizon glowed from north to east.

The following day they came to the burnt-over ground, travelling half stifled with heat and dust for about ten miles and halting for breakfast at a stagnant marsh, the only place which had not been burnt and where there was any grass for the horses. The poor things found it very painful to travel over the charred soil with hooves worn down nearly to the quick. The whole sky was overcast with a dense canopy of dirty smoke that made everyone as black as a sweep.

They now came on patches of scrubby wood and young poplars. They were leaving the open prairies of the south and coming into the park-lands of the North Saskatchewan. One morning Palliser found the men smartening themselves up and putting on their best clothes. He asked why. The guide, Ferguson, now back on safe ground, said they would be at Fort Carlton by noon. Palliser knew from their observations for latitude that they could not yet be so near, but the men insisted that they recognized the landmarks. Palliser began to be afraid he must have made a mistake and was out in his reckoning, as the men were so certain that they knew where they were. They could hardly be persuaded to make camp that night; they were determined to go on for one more hour, which, they were sure, would bring them to the fort. They said to Palliser, 'How can you know, when you were never there?' He finally prevailed on them to make camp. Even after a more than usually early start next morning they still had not sighted the fort by breakfast-time; either the men or the fort were altogether out of reckoning. When they stopped at a fine lake at ten o'clock, the men recognized it, realized they had been wrong before, and began to entertain very exalted notions as to the powers of the sextant. They travelled all day and when they camped that night could see the high banks of the north branch of the Saskatchewan away to the north.

Next day, when they really were only five miles from Fort Carlton, they all busied themselves getting out their best clothes and razors. The whole party made as elaborate a toilet as possible, preparatory to entering the fort. They did not see it until they were almost on it, lying close under the south bank of the North Saskatchewan. When they arrived, Richard Hardisty, the Hudson's Bay factor in charge, was making preparations for their accommodation there during the winter months—not an easy matter at a trading-post designed only to accommodate officers of the Hudson's Bay Company, half-breed *engagés*, and Indian visitors. Palliser was not impressed with the condition of Fort Carlton, but later came to understand and appreciate all the extra work that Hardisty had had to do and the difficulties he had had to resolve to make it possible for the expedition to use the post as their winter base.

CHAPTER EIGHT

'Silently as an Indian'

The first season was at an end; winter would clearly soon be on them. The night before they reached Fort Carlton there had been a violent thunderstorm followed by snow and a heavy fall of sleet, with frosty fog in the morning. It was now early October. Evidently this storm was a warning; though they might still expect a short return of genial weather in the Indian summer, it was clear that the season when horses could be used for long journeys was coming to an end. The horses needed what little good weather remained before the onset of winter to feed up, so they would be fit to withstand its rigours. They would be needed again for the next season's work and, as usual, their welfare was of paramount importance.

Palliser had seen enough to realize that the time allotted was too short for the work to be done; the country was far more extensive than anyone had imagined. They could not hope to cover its whole enormous breadth and width in two seasons. Palliser knew that he must try to persuade the government in London to let the expedition stay out for a third summer. So far he had not had one line from the Colonial Office since he started out. He decided that he must travel to Montreal or New York to send off an urgent dispatch asking for an extension of the expedition's time. He must have a reply before the next season's work should begin. Writing to the Colonial Secretary, he even offered to make a quick trip back to London to discuss the expedition's future plans.

Not only did he have to communicate with the government; he had also to settle the expedition's accounts with the Hudson's Bay Company. Sir George Simpson had decreed that the bills for all the supplies the expedition purchased at Hudson's Bay Company posts—and that meant everything they needed that they could not get by hunting—were to be sent to Lachine to be priced, so Palliser did not know exactly how much had been spent. He had to see Simpson in Lachine to settle these financial matters.

Then, too, there was the problem of the instruments needed for the scientific observations. Many of these could no longer be used; hard usage, accidental breakages, and the jolting journey had ruined them; they needed expert attention. Only in New York could they be repaired.

For all these reasons Palliser decided that he must make the arduous journey to Montreal and New York. Most of the men were to go back to their homes at Red River for the winter. Palliser had planned to go down the Saskatchewan by boat with the men. At the last minute they refused to go by water, on the ground that their contracts did not include boat service. Palliser re-examined the agreements Mr. Swanston had drawn up for him in Red River and found that the law was in the men's favour. The custom of the country, the unwritten law to which everyone held, forced Palliser to change his plans; he had to arrange for supplies and transport for the men, as well as for himself, for the overland journey: dry meat and pemmican, two carts and three horses.

The scientists—Hector, Bourgeau, and Sullivan—were to spend the winter at Fort Carlton or travelling from it as a base. Leaving them to their winter's work, Palliser started off in a heavy snowfall with McKay, John Ferguson, Pierre Beauchamp, and a young Indian from whom they had hired horses for the trip. After a sharp ride of twenty miles they reached the south branch of the Saskatchewan, where they camped. At sunrise they crossed in a skin canoe and had breakfast on the south bank with some traders they found there, who were distant relatives of James McKay. They travelled steadily on for three days to the Touchwood Hills Post, a ride of 146 miles. Another three days' ride across country brought them to Fort Pelly, the chief post of the district. Here they hoped to get fresh horses. The working horses were all away, but they got permission to use two of the brood mares kept at the fort. The mares were unbroken, but after a day's hard work and a few falls they finally succeeded in making them carry not only a rider but also packs.

They crossed the Assiniboine and again struck off across country. They had a struggle to get over the Qu'Appelle River, when they reached it, on account of its steep and muddy banks, the horses sticking and floundering and re-crossing the river several times before they finally succeeded in getting up the other side. They spent a miserable night in a swamp, but at last arrived at Fort Ellice.

From Fort Ellice to the Red River the two branches of the Carlton Trail were so strongly marked by carts that Palliser felt the tracks deserved the name of roads. At 'the Manitoba portage' (Portage la Prairie, where long ago the French traders used to cross from Lake Manitoba to the Assiniboine and so to the Missouri), Archdeacon Cochrane received them most hospitably. He had built the church there with the help of the boys in his school. With an axe over his shoulder, he used to take them to the near-by woods to get timber for his building operations. Though close to seventy years old when Palliser met him, he was still said to be hard to beat at either chopping or ploughing, and gave his pupils both a fine education and an interest in agriculture.

Back at Fort Garry, on November 1, Palliser set about getting horses and an outfit for his trip south by the route through American territory to St. Paul. Horses were expensive and hard to find, and it appeared that they would be still harder to sell at St. Paul; so he hired an intelligent young fellow named Robert Tate to supply him with three horses and provisions for the trip, Tate undertaking all risks, for £60. One horse pulled a cart carrying provisions, such essential equipment as kettles, and the instruments; a second was packed with the bedding; the third was for Palliser's use.

They got to Pembina on the third day, but there the mare Palliser had been riding had a strange accident. Tate tied her up and left her with a feed of barley; a starving cow, attracted by the barley, attacked the mare viciously, and gored her so severely that they had to leave her behind, giving up all hope of her recovery. They went on, Palliser now on foot like the others; the route was a good one, the snow was unusually late, and they were all in excellent wind and travelled fast. Twenty-four miles in a day was not unusual. At last, at Ottertail City, they reached the watershed of the continent, which divides the waters that flow into Hudson Bay from those that flow into the Gulf of Mexico. This 'city' consisted of the wooden house of an old Scotch settler with a stable and cowhouse attached. The stable contained a horse and the cowhouse contained an ox. These, with the settler's old half-breed wife and their daughters, made up the entire population! Here they stayed over Sunday to rest the horses, and three days later arrived, on a tremendously cold night, after a run of forty-five miles, at the American Indian Agency of Crow Wing. It had taken them eleven days (allowing one Sunday to recruit the horses) to complete their journey on foot from Red River Settlement to the terminus of civilization on the Mississippi, a distance of some 520 miles.

The two *voyageurs* hurried back to Red River, but first Robert Tate agreed to come down again with another hardy young fellow the following March, from Red River, to meet Palliser on April 1, on his return from the settlements, to help him carry out a scheme for crossing the watershed of the country by canoe.

From Crow Wing, Palliser proceeded by a series of conveyances, mostly without springs, to St. Paul and Prairie du Chien. He had one more adventure before he got back to civilization. At Saulk Rapids he left his travelling-desk in his hotel room; someone broke it open and stole from it his rings and some watches (including one belonging to a Mr. Taylor, the Hudson's Bay Company officer at the Touchwood Hills

Post, which Palliser was taking out for repairs). Luckily, the thief missed the money that was also in the desk. On his way back in the spring Palliser recovered the stolen articles through the good offices of the hotel-keeper, for whose wife he immediately ordered an impressive ring as a token of his gratitude. With characteristic open-handedness, he had already ordered a new watch for Mr. Taylor.

From Prairie du Chien he went on by train to Chicago, Detroit, and Montreal, where he speedily dispatched his business with the Hudson's Bay Company. Then he had time for some sociability. Sir George gave a dinner party at Lachine that must have been in the tradition of the old Nor'Westers' banquets. Palliser referred to it more than once afterwards in his letters. He dined with the Solicitor-General, John Rose, a rising politician in the little colony of Canada, who was to play an important role in Confederation and in the Dominion of Canada after 1867. At his country house, 'a very good one quite in the English style', Palliser met a number of men who were to be candidates in the forthcoming election. He must have had a chance to size up some of the ideas current in British North America, east of the Great Lakes, about the destiny of the vast country west of the Great Lakes which he was exploring.

From Montreal, Palliser went on to New York with the instruments that were to be repaired. These were becoming a great worry to him. He decided that it would be useless to buy any more new ones. The old ones had already cost more than he had expected, especially the complicated magnetical instruments the Royal Society had had ordered for Blakiston's work. Knowing by now how hard it was to avoid breakages when travelling over rough country, he was very much concerned about the safety of those in Lieutenant Blakiston's care on the long trip up from Hudson Bay to Carlton.

At last he had nothing more to do but wait for a reply to his dispatches to the Colonial Office. He had not been summoned back to London, so while he waited he went off to New Orleans to see his old friends there again.

No dispatches from the Colonial Office followed him. He became anxious. When he got back to New York in February there was still no reply. The Treasury and the Colonial Office were involved in a discussion of the question of a further grant to make a third season's work possible. If Palliser was to be back at Fort Carlton by the time the weather was again fit for exploring, he must start. He wrote again to the Colonial Office, saying that he assumed that since they had not replied they meant him to use his own judgment; and that, without any hesitation, he determined on passing another winter in British North West America. He sent off his letter and left for Montreal via Boston. At last, on February 18, the Colonial Office wrote. When the letter reached New York Palliser had left, but the contents were telegraphed after him. He had been given permission to spend a third season exploring.

His worries were not over, all the same. When the letter caught up with him he was astonished to find how much the expedition's bills came to already. He thought he had settled up all the accounts in December with Sir George Simpson, but there were unexpected accounts for supplies—especially instruments—purchased in England, and more accounts began to come in from outlying Hudson's Bay Company posts. At Lachine he went carefully over his plans with Sir George, who wrote to the Governor of the Honourable Company that he thought that now things were arranged so that the costs would come within the sum of money available. Sir George gave Palliser another of his celebrated dinners. Then Palliser set off again for the West.

At Simpson's suggestion, he stopped in Toronto to call on the Governor General, Sir Edmund Head. It turned out that Sir Edmund was an old friend of John Palliser's father—in fact, Colonel Wray Palliser had taught Sir Edmund to box! Sir Edmund gave Palliser a great deal of information and got him a retrieving dog. This was a very welcome addition to the party, as ducks and geese were often the only procurable food; when shot, they usually fell into the middle of a marsh or lake.

Back at Prairie du Chien, Palliser boarded the first steamer of the year for St. Paul. There was doubt as to whether it would be able to get through the ice, but it crashed through triumphantly, the engines at every turn driving the paddles against the ice with a noise like thunder. When they arrived at St. Paul they were cheered by an immense concourse of people, tumultuously welcoming the first steamer of the season. When he arrived at Crow Wing, Palliser had reached the extremity of civilized—or rather, public—modes of conveyance. Here Palliser witnessed a fearful fight. One man was shot, another wounded, and a great ruffian was taken off, handcuffed, to St. Paul.

Palliser was deeply interested in the possibility of using the Red River as a water-way. Ten years before, when he had made his journeys on the Mississippi and Missouri, he had been much impressed by the usefulness of steamboats; he thought it probable that they could be used on the Red River as well as further south, to open up easy communication between the little Red River Settlement and the outer world. When the expedition had travelled from Fort Garry up the Red River to Pembina the year before, the river had been in flood, its waters five feet above the normal level, so it had not been easy to judge its possibilities as a water-way, but Palliser had noted that, though there were many bends in the river, they were long bends with gentle curves. He thought they would not be a serious obstacle to navigation by steamboats or other craft of moderate length. Now he proposed to cross the short divide between the Red River and the Mississippi and travel all the way down the Red River from its head-waters to the Settlement, to find out whether his idea was sound.

He succeeded in purchasing a tolerable canoe and collected the bedding, kettles, and other gear he had left at Crow Wing to await his return from the East. Robert Tate arrived on April 1, true to his promise, with a young Scots half-breed, both looking fearfully worn and haggard. They had had a desperate journey. The snow had all melted, much earlier than usual. Throwing away their snowshoes, they had walked through half-frozen slush from morning till night; the ice had broken up on the rivers shortly afterwards and they had had to wade many of them.

A young American joined the party; he wanted to go up the Crow Wing River to superintend the cutting and floating down of some pine lumber. He was to prove both an excellent hand with a canoe and an entertaining companion, regaling the party till a late hour with stories of the Californian gold diggings. But first, while some Indian women were caulking the seams of the canoe, he went home for supplies, soon returning with a capital cheese and a bag of biscuits.

In spite of the caulking, they found, after only two and a half hours' punting up the river, that the canoe was leaking. They put ashore at an old deserted hunting-camp and discovered that the women had not been able to resist the temptation to eat the grease, instead of mixing it with the gum, which all cracked off again. They were busy the rest of the evening making the canoe staunch. The weather suddenly became very warm and their old enemies the mosquitoes were very troublesome.

They reached the mouth of the Leaf River (a tributary of the Mississippi) and stayed there with some American squatters. Here the American lumberman left them and a snowstorm held them up. Ironically enough, the heat had, meanwhile, turned their pork rancid, but ducks and geese, very numerous and in excellent condition, provided the food they needed. The retrieving dog must have been useful. Leaf River turned out to be a terribly tortuous river, so that after hours of work they had not proceeded more than a mile or two in a straight line. Snow-falls continued and the water froze on the poles, which made punting sometimes painful to the hands. They spent a night at Leaf Lake with another settler. A Frenchman undertook to take the canoe on his ox-wagon across the seven-mile height of land to Ottertail Lake, but he lost his way and took them to another lake on another river instead. They found Ottertail Lake at last and the Misses Macdonnel—presumably the daughters of the settler at

Ottertail City—harnessed their ox and, with dispatch and efficiency, brought over the canoes and all the gear.

The ice was bad on Ottertail Lake. Once the canoe was nearly crushed, but they jumped out into water up to their armpits and managed to throw everything onto the ice. They mended the canoe thoroughly and set off again. Another snow-storm held them up for three days, but they made themselves very comfortable, building a shelter of branches with the canoe at the back. None of them had travelled by that route before, but at last they found the entrance to the Red River and began their descent again to the north.

For more than two weeks they travelled down the Red River. At one portage they found a settler who had been robbed by Indians. They encountered other settlers who treated them hospitably; they were, in turn, able to help a party who had been stripped very bare indeed by the Indians, who burnt their homes down. The ruins were still smoking when Palliser passed by. He himself had been shooting ducks and did not cease doing so, not wishing the Indians to conclude that they were a party so small as to fear them. All this took place on the United States side of the border, where serious trouble with the Sioux Indians was soon to flare up.

On May Day, at sunset, they arrived again on British territory, at Pembina. They came to Fort Garry two days later.

The canoe journey down the Red River convinced Palliser that it was indeed navigable by steamboats, and he reported his findings to the British government. The report was published. Next year an enterprising Minnesotan, one Anson Northup, carried a steamboat in pieces over the height of land from the Mississippi and assembled it on the Red River. The vessel, called after its first owner, plied the Red River from south of the border to Fort Garry and became such a powerful rival to the time-honoured inland navigation by York boats from Hudson Bay that the Hudson's Bay Company acquired a share in it in 1859.

After this brief boating interlude, Palliser returned to overland travel, and at once he found himself in difficulties about horses. He had left five of them at Fort Garry in November in the care of Pierre Beauchamp, but three had died. He had to buy two new horses. There was other business to be transacted and stores to be laid in, but he set off at last with three men (including last year's guide, John Ferguson), three carts, and four horses. The fourth horse was a spare in case, as seemed all too likely, one of the others gave out. There was still very little grass, and what there was proved violently upsetting for the horses, which had been accustomed to the dry frozen stuff of the previous season. They got new horses at Fort Ellice and again at Touchwood Hills, but even so they had great trouble getting to Fort Carlton. It was difficult going over muddy ground and through swamps and there was heavy snow and cold wind on the last two days of May.

While Palliser was plodding on towards Fort Carlton, Dr. Hector and Mr. Hardisty were hourly expecting him back; they started out in the hope of meeting him, taking fresh horses with them. They were resting their horses at the point where the trail strikes off from the Carlton–Touchwood Hills trail to Fort à la Corne (situated just below the Forks of the North and South Saskatchewan), when, as Hector wrote: 'Captain Palliser suddenly walked in upon us, silently as an Indian. He was walking in advance of his party, as the horses had all broken down, and they were bringing them slowly on, while he kept ahead in order to have a better chance of killing game . . . They had travelled pretty much in this style all the way from Red River, a distance of 550 miles.'

CHAPTER NINE

The Magnetical Observer

ll this time, while Palliser had been on his long journey to the East and back again, the other members of the expedition had also been very busy. Among the busiest was a new member of the party, the magnetical observer, Lieutenant Blakiston of the Royal Artillery, who had been left behind in England to bring out, by the long sea and river route via Hudson Bay, the delicate instruments he would need to record the pull of the earth's magnetism.

While Palliser, Hector, Bourgeau, and Sullivan had been struggling across the granite wilderness between Lake Superior and Red River and ranging the southern plains in the summer of 1857, Blakiston had been hard at work learning how to use these complicated instruments.

The scientists of the world—Frenchmen, Russians, Germans, and Italians—had been working for several decades, with help from their governments, on the problem of the earth's magnetic force. Von Humboldt, a German, had in 1836 suggested to the Royal Society that Great Britain, with its 'extensive dominions in all parts of the globe', should set up observatories in a variety of suitable places. The Royal Society and the British Association for the Advancement of Science had taken the matter up with the British government and in 1839 General (later Sir) Edward Sabine, Royal Artillery, was appointed to superintend a series of stations at Toronto, St. Helena, the Cape of Good Hope, Van Diemen's Land (now

Tasmania), and in the territories of the East India Company, in addition to the observatories at Greenwich and Dublin, established in 1837. Sir Henry Lefroy, then still simply Lieutenant Lefroy, had in 1842 been sent to the observatory at Toronto. From there he had made a trip to Lake Athabasca by the Hudson's Bay Company canoe route from Lachine to Fort Garry and so down to Norway House, which was his base station for his northerly observations. He visited York Factory and travelled up the North Saskatchewan and over the Methye Portage to the Mackenzie River system. At Fort Chipewyan on Lake Athabasca he spent more than four months in 1843, taking observations, with the help of Bombardier Henry, R.A., every hour, and at times of special magnetic disturbance, every two minutes. In early 1844 he went on to Fort Simpson on the Mackenzie River.

Palliser's expedition offered a chance of getting an additional series of observations in north-western British North America, both at new positions and at some of the old positions, after the lapse of time, to compare with those Lefroy had recorded. Sir Edward Sabine (later president of the Royal Society) was keen to seize this opportunity.

The necessary instruments were prepared at Kew Observatory, and Blakiston, whom Lefroy described as 'one of our most promising young officers', put himself under instruction to make himself competent to use them, and look after them—itself a problem, when delicate equipment had to be carried for hundreds of miles by boat and portage, Red River cart and pack-horse. He spent his army leave at Kew and was given special leave of absence to finish the preparatory work before he sailed out of the Thames on June 21 on board the Hudson's Bay Company ship *Prince of Wales*.

After a seven weeks' voyage he reached York Factory on Hudson Bay, at the mouth of the Hayes River. Here he spent a week making magnetical observations; then, on August 31, he set off with a brigade of six boats by the usual 'inland navigation' to Fort Carlton. The boats travelled 400 miles in three weeks, making thirty-five portages, to Norway House, north of Lake Winnipeg. In all that distance the travellers saw only one building. At Norway House, Blakiston spent a day making magnetical determinations from sunrise to sunset.

As the Hudson's Bay Company brigade was going on to Red River, Blakiston's baggage was now transferred to a boat going up the Saskatchewan. With a fair wind, they ran across the greater part of the north end of Lake Winnipeg. A heavy sea then forced them to put ashore; the water rose during the night, so they had to take the cargo out of the boat and haul her up in the dark. No harm came to the magnetical instruments, which Blakiston had packed with particular care in boxes and secured with strips of rubber, but two mountain barometers, which had to be carried loose in the stern sheets, were broken. The costly magnetical instruments that Palliser had been worrying about were safe, but the expedition was getting very short of barometers.

Next day Blakiston's party camped at the foot of the Grand Rapids, on the Saskatchewan, just above the point at which this river flows into Lake Winnipeg (where today a great hydro-electric power plant is under construction). It took the whole of the following day to get boat and cargo to the upper end of the rapid. This was accomplished in the usual way by hauling the boat on a line to the carrying-place, thence transporting the cargo in 'pieces' over the mile-long portage and towing the empty boat by rope up the rapid under the cliffs along the south side. It sounds straightforward, but what exhausting labour it meant for the *voyageurs!*

On they went up-river, past The Pas, to Cumberland House—established by the Hudson's Bay Company in 1774, the first permanent fort on the Saskatchewan—where they spent a Sunday of the most lovely Indian summer weather; past the Forks, where the south branch of the Saskatchewan joins the north branch. At last, on October 23, after a trip of fifty-three days, they came to Fort Carlton, where Blakiston was thankful to be installed in comfortable quarters. They were just in time. Ice was already forming along the shore. The river would be frozen before the boat could reach the next fort up-river, so the crew had to be sent overland.

Fort Carlton, Blakiston knew, was the expedition's winter quarters, but the only member of the expedition there when he arrived was M. Bourgeau, the amiable and hard-working botanist. Hector was off geologizing; Sullivan had gone to Jack Fish Lake to see about some horses; and Palliser had already left for the East. In making the last-minute change of plans for land travel in place of river travel, Palliser had forgotten to leave a letter for Blakiston, though he sent an apology for his oversight at the first opportunity. Not having seen Blakiston's instructions, he had no idea what help he would need and so, in any case, could not have left directions as to what assistance the other members of the expedition were to give him.

Blakiston was naturally upset. Something of a stickler for etiquette and accustomed to clear-cut, precise army routine, he wrote: 'My position on the expedition was not defined; I had work to be done in which assistance was required, and yet no authority to procure it.'

He did not need authority, as of course Palliser well knew, in that friendly and co-operative group of explorers. When Hector and Sullivan returned, Blakiston showed them and M. Bourgeau his instructions, in which a hope was expressed that he might be able to make observations every hour for three or four months, to complement Lefroy's observations and those made in 1853-4 on the arctic coast. At once the three other members of the expedition expressed their desire to aid in the work, and construction of a rough but useful little observatory was begun without delay.

It was still warm enough for Blakiston to make outdoor observations, which he started as soon as the instruments were set up and adjusted. On November 12 the four scientists began a series of hourly readings of changes of the magnetic declination, the temperature of the air, and state of the weather, together with six-hourly readings of the barometer and hygrometer, besides the daily self-registering thermometers. M. Bourgeau was at the same time making daily observations of the temperature of the ground at a depth of two and three feet; these he conducted with uninterrupted regularity.

The hourly series was carried on by a system of watches, each watch being six hours during the day and four hours during the night; the observations were made at the exact minute of time according to a chronometer, which Blakiston kept regulated by astronomical observations. For the first month the work was by no means pressing, as four observers took their regular turns, though, even so, the observations kept them all prisoners at the fort three days out of four. On the fourth day they each had, in rotation, a most welcome holiday, when they could go hunting. In December Hector had to go off to Fort Pitt and Fort Edmonton to make arrangements for horses and men for the next season's work. That left only three observers.

The next two months were trying ones. Only Bourgeau came through them unruffled. The work was heavy for three observers. Food was scarce and grew daily scarcer. Blakiston began to think that Sullivan's observations were not always accurate. Sullivan was working hard on the expedition's journal and its complicated accounts; he was making other observations; and he was ill for eleven days. Blakiston had not an easy temper; he and Sullivan quarrelled. They both wrote to Hector explaining what had happened, each giving his own side of the story. To make matters worse, Blakiston thought that the expedition's stores were being used too freely. He considered his position by no means enviable and had decided to carry out his special instructions and interfere in no matters concerning the expedition. Accordingly he refused to take any responsibility about the stores, but remained critical, in public as well as in private. He described as 'pilfering' what Sullivan regarded as allowing the men sufficient supplies. He asked M. Bourgeau, the ever dependable, to take charge of the stores. So did Sullivan, handing over his keys to him.

Meanwhile the food situation had gone from bad to worse. All the families at the fort and all but one or two men had been sent away to the plains, where they could hunt, or to lakes, where they could get fish. At last Mr. Hardisty, the Hudson's Bay Company officer in charge, asked Sullivan and the expedition's cook, Sir George Simpson's old servant, James Beads, to move to Jack Fish Lake, where at least they could be sure of enough fish to keep them going.

Blakiston wrote furiously to Hector that Sullivan had 'taken on himself to desert'. He had already written that, because of what he considered Sullivan's undependability, he 'could not be justified in making any use of him [Sullivan] to carry out the hourly observations', but he was very angry when Sullivan went off with Beads, at Mr. Hardisty's request, to the fishery. He himself was finding things dull, and the increasingly heavy, unremitting work very trying. He was longing to rejoin his regiment, which had been ordered to India for active service in the Indian Mutiny, but he did not feel that he could leave the duty on which he was engaged. He grew more and more irritated and resentful at what he thought were Sullivan's shortcomings. The situation between the two men had become impossible. As so often happens when men are isolated through a long, monotonous winter of arduous work, little things grew into serious issues and bred bitter antagonism.

The observations had now been made uninterruptedly for three months, but Blakiston was not yet satisfied. He reported: 'I consulted with M. Bourgeau, who immediately expressed his willingness to devote himself to the work as long as I thought proper for the good of science. For two months, consequently, were the observations carried on by M. Bourgeau and myself, the instruments being registered every hour, day and night, and it was not until five months were completed, and the spring botanical collecting commenced, that I brought the series to a close.'

The ambitious five months' series was brought to a successful termination on April 16. Blakiston wrote: 'Considering that the use of the magnetic instrument employed was entirely new to the observers, I cannot but say that the greater part of the observations were made in a manner most creditable to themselves . . .'

He generously put his obligation to his colleagues on public record, praising particularly the untiring zeal manifested by M. Bourgeau during the whole period. Even so, Sullivan's inaccuracies had not been forgotten; the bitter quarrel that had sprung up between them still rankled. Blakiston realized that he had perhaps caused himself to be looked upon by some as an unwelcome addition to the expedition, but wrote: 'I have the satisfaction of knowing that in making all private feeling succumb to the requirements of duty, I have carried out that which possibly others more yielding might have failed to accomplish.'

Science had been served 'with exemplary zeal and assiduity', as General Sabine wrote later, but at the sacrifice of harmony and good feeling. Hector on his return found that both Bourgeau and Hardisty regarded Sullivan 'as an object of commiseration and pity'. Blakiston's unbending sense of duty had overflowed from the discharge of his own responsibilities into constant and public complaints about the shortcomings of everyone else on the expedition—excepting always M. Bourgeau. Hector had hard work keeping on good terms with him. He recognized and appreciated his splendid abilities and driving energy, but felt that his rectitude was of the rigid sort that made it difficult for him to have any understanding consideration for others.

But quarrels or no quarrels, no matter what the feelings of the party might be, the meteorological observations went on even after the magnetic observations came to an end, until the expedition left its winter quarters in June, and even then Blakiston had left a thermometer behind. Its readings were registered by the Hudson's Bay officer and men at the fort all through the summer and autumn of 1858, and for six months after Blakiston had left the fort. As he wrote: 'The climate, therefore, of this station is likely to be well determined.'

Chapter Ten

'A jolly little cariole'

While Palliser was away, Hector was to make preparations for the next summer's work, arranging for the men, horses, and supplies that would be needed. This meant visits to Fort Pitt and Fort Edmonton farther up the North Saskatchewan. Although the north branch of the river was already fairly well known, the doctor welcomed the opportunity to examine it, and the country round about, himself.

But first he had to get things organized at Fort Carlton, where Bourgeau and Sullivan were to stay on with James Beads as their servant and old Hallet and two other men to take care of the precious horses and to hunt. John Foulds was to travel with Hector. The first problem was supplies. Hector made an inventory of the stores they had left, deciding that, without waste, they had enough tea and flour to see them through the winter. He added that they would be well off if they could only secure a supply of buffalo meat. At this point Indian hunters arrived with supplies for the fort—fresh meat, dried meat, grease, skins, and cords to trade. Trading involved consumption of a considerable quantity of liquor. The fort was in a dreadful state of riot as a result; the noise of Indians drumming, howling, and brawling never stopped. This did not keep the children from their games; Hector was amused to see them playing with tops, toys that he thought must have penetrated from the haunts of civilization.

The horses were still a problem. Palliser had left very

careful instructions about their care, especially about seeing that they had enough to drink. He did not think much of the idea that they could eat snow. Sullivan went off with one of the Hudson's Bay Company officers and one of the men to Fort Pitt to collect some more horses. The others were sent to the company's 'horseguard', ten miles down on the other side of the river, where there was plenty of rich pasture. Hector went to see them there. Already some of them had picked up wonderfully. He brought back four he needed for a trip to the Thickwood Hills, but first he went in search of a missing mare. He rode forty-six miles without finding her, getting back two hours after dark, after a long struggle against a bitterly cold wind and driving snow. Two days later, astonishingly, it was very hot! Hector was often to notice, that winter and the next, the sudden changes in temperature brought about by the surprising chinook wind.

The house the explorers were to occupy at Fort Carlton was being repaired, so Hector and Bourgeau went off to study the different kinds of trees along the river, shooting grouse, and visiting the horseguard. Swarms of wildfowl, very fat and very shy, were migrating southward. Hector's dog, Hero, had been used as a retriever all summer, which rather spoilt him as a pointer!

They heard about epidemics of hydrophobia, which sometimes made the numerous wolves especially dangerous in the spring. If a mad wolf bit someone, the Indian cure was 'to sew the patient up in an old buffalo robe and to fling him on a large fire until it is well singed, when he is considered *done'*. The doctor thought that, if the patient survived the treatment, the fright and violent perspiration might help to cure him.

Wolves were troublesome even when they were not rabid. They killed a foal one night. The next night they took a great piece out of its mother and, the night after, killed her outright.

Then there was the problem of meteorological and other records to be kept all winter. Hector helped Bourgeau and

Sullivan arrange the thermometer and other instruments for the meteorological observations; they also sank a metal tube nearly a yard into the soil, to test, as Dr. Hooker had directed, how cold the ground became, deep down, during the winter.

Now Hector had a chance to go off geologizing. He hoped that he would be able to get a lot of useful information at the Thickwood Hills, lying to the north-west, on the other side of the river from Fort Carlton.

Crossing in a boat, the party made for a cone-shaped hill called by the Indians 'Manitou's Rest'. On the top was a figure cut out where the great spirit was supposed to have reclined. Hector commented that 'the Indians always touch [it] up every time they visit the place; but if the cutting in the turf be the impression he left, as they say it is, he must have been a most rectangular spirit.'

Now they began to find thick, green pine-woods—a welcome change after the treeless prairies—and clear lakes, though on the first day's journey they found one lake that was saturated with salt, with large, beautifully formed crystals of sulphate of soda lying heaped up on the shores. Here, too, they came on marshes again, the deep, dense marshes they had encountered between Lake Superior and Winnipeg, which were (and still are) called 'muskegs' after the Muskegoes or Swampy Cree, who lived between Lake Superior and Hudson Bay.

They had been told that they could not get close to the Thickwood Hills with the cart, but they succeeded in forcing a passage through the broken country, after some upsets and a lot of hard work chopping down trees. That night they cut poles and put up a leather tent that Hector had acquired, camping in true Indian fashion, all in great spirits at having got on so well.

Next day they had considerable difficulty in getting to the top of the hill, so dense were the thickets of poplar. At last they came on a track cut through the woods by some Indian moose-hunter, which led them up onto what turned out to be not a hill but a lofty tableland, with an irregular surface, covered with swampy lakes and thickets. Returning to camp, they were enveloped in dense masses of smoke, which rolled in volumes from the west, where the woods seemed to be on fire, the dismal gloom filling them with a feeling of depression difficult to shake off. All night the sky to the south-west was brilliantly illuminated. Going on next day, they struck the trail of some Thickwood Cree, who were following the old route Sir John Franklin had taken to Great Bear Lake in the winter of 1819. These Cree had killed five wapiti and offered Hector some meat, but the horses were too tired to carry any extra load. The Cree and other Indians in the area used to take their furs to the company at Fort Carlton, but lately they had been carrying on a considerable trade with 'free-traders' from Red River, who brought them American goods and wretched, poisonous whisky. A party of free-traders had left their comfortable homes and travelled all the way from Red River to spend the winter in this wild country, more from love of a wandering life than from any hope of bettering their condition by the pittance of profit they made in their trading as middlemen between the Indians and Americans. They were extremely hospitable; they gave Hector's party a dinner of fresh buffalo meat and pressed them to stay, but, as they had plenty of trader's whisky with them, Hector was glad to get away before nightfall for the sake of his men. It was this party that had let their camp-fire run and so started the fire that was still rapidly advancing over the Thickwood Hills.

Finding he was foiled once more by want of sections where he had expected an interesting field for geology, Hector went back to Fort Carlton; there he found both Sullivan and Blakiston waiting on the bank of the river. Blakiston had arrived from England via Hudson Bay, and Sullivan from Fort Pitt.

Once more the horses needed attention. It was the custom to tie their fore legs together with a soft leather band to keep them from wandering, but at the company horseguard the band had been kept too tight; so Hector took the horses away—all but one that was ill and could not swim the river—

and put them in the charge of the expedition's own men south of the river. There two horses were killed by wolves, and two strayed off and could not be found. Eventually the men discovered a fine feeding-ground beside a large lake, about nine miles off, and soon the horses' condition improved greatly.

Once the horses were satisfactorily settled, Hector sent off Hallet and Morin, with hunters from the fort, to try to get some meat. The scientists also did some hunting in what spare time they had, as food was none too plentiful. The hunters from the fort, going out after the buffalo, had started a prairie fire, which gave them some new excitement. It swept very close to the fort; everyone went out to burn the grass around the hayricks to keep them from being destroyed. Next day, luckily, the wind changed and the fire turned off to the south.

Besides hunting, geologizing, and taking his share of the hourly observations, Hector had plenty to do as a doctor. One night he was called to treat a violent case of hysteria in an Indian girl. She had been shot through the shoulder some years before by a Blackfoot. The Indians thought she could foretell the future. Another day a man was brought in from the buffalo-hunt dangerously hurt from having been thrown from his horse when an old bull charged him; he had burst a blood vessel and injured his chest very seriously.

Now it was November. The river was blocked with ice, and by the middle of the month was quite fast set; the snow on the ground was permanent, though not very deep. Hector tried walking on snow-shoes; then, with Mr. Hardisty, he went out dog-driving for the first time and found it delightful. He described the experience:

> *We had four dogs dragging a light sleigh, or 'sled' as it is always called, made of two birch planks lashed together by cross bars, and turned up at the point; the whole shaped like a Norwegian snow shoe, but 10 feet long and 14 inches wide. As the dogs were fresh, and had no load, they went very fast, sometimes we ran behind, time about, and when out of breath*

would jump on for a ride, a feat not very easily accomplished by a beginner, for, as the least unsteadiness in planting your feet on the sled caused it to dodge from under you, a fall headlong among the deep snow on the side of the track was the general consequence, followed by a frantic race to make up with the dogs again, who of course had made off with redoubled speed.

The cold was now intense. The whole party settled down to a routine, each taking his shift at the observatory, working on maps and reports, visiting the horses, and hunting when there was time. The Hudson's Bay Company hunters came back from the plains and the fort was again the scene of riot and drinking. Some Indians arrived with a young Englishman called Vidler, who had come to the country to hunt. He had been living with the Indians on the South Saskatchewan for two months and was dressed as they were. He was destitute, and they fitted him out again. A few days later, he left with the Indians, with a dog sled he had got from Mr. Hardisty.

Hector was planning a trip to Fort Edmonton in December, so he sent Hallet and Boucher off to trade for dogs with the Indians. All travel about the fort, called 'tripping', was now done with dogs. When the new dogs arrived, Hector went out every day with them. They were very savage and did not take kindly to their harness. Mr Hardisty fitted Hector up with 'a jolly little cariole' that would do for passenger or goods traffic.

This cariole is only a sled with parchment sides, sustained on cords that pass over a back-board standing about a foot from the end; it resembles much a coffin-shaped slipper bath. The harness consists of a collar made of an iron ring, with a pad on it, which passes tightly over the dog's head, but fits his shoulder well; to this is attached two long straps of dressed hide, kept up by a band across the dog's back; to the collar and back band are generally attached rows of bells, the merry jingle of which enlivens the journey, and gives spirit both to the dogs and drivers. Favourite trains of dogs are dressed up in very jaunty style, with ribbons and brightly-coloured saddle cloths. Four dogs are attached to each sled, and they are driven solely by the voice, no reins being used. On a river where there is no decided track it is of course a difficult matter to keep them straight, and then a man generally runs before, whom they follow; but in a track where other sleds have passed, or where snow shoes have been used, there is no difficulty in driving them, as they never have any wish to turn aside [into] the soft deep snow that is on either hand. Where snow shoes have been used, or where a dog sled, or train, as the whole turn-out is called, has passed over the snow, the track hardens so as to remain all winter, and even where more snow falls, always affording a hard regular bottom much easier to travel upon than it is to beat a fresh track. Some of the dogs are wonderfully sagacious in discovering and keeping on old tracks, so alive are they to the additional ease it gives them in dragging their load.

The Edmonton party set off on December 14. Hector had been up all night; he lay in his cariole, rolled up in robes, enjoying a snooze until it was broad daylight. They had been travelling up-river on smooth ice, but now struck off across the plains to the west, towards Redberry Lake, in sight of which Hector made his first real winter encampment. He enjoyed the novelty very much and described it in detail:

The first step on halting is of course to untackle the dogs, which for to-night were all tied to trees, lest they should return to the fort, as it is no use tying an Indian dog by a cord. The method is, to tie a stick about four feet long close under its neck by one end, while the other is attached to the tree, so as to prevent him gnawing either cord, and so making his escape. One man then busies himself clearing away the snow, and cutting willow twigs on which to lie, which he spreads out in a square space just large enough to hold the party, who lie side by side with their feet to the fire; another employs himself cutting firewood, tree after tree being cut into logs six or eight feet long, the great secret of a comfortable winter camp being to have good firewood and plenty of it. Accordingly a smart look out is always kept as evening approaches for a good camping place, the requisite for which being a bluff of dead wood, whereas in summer it is always water that determines the choice. In travelling in winter water can be procured anywhere by melting the snow as soon as the fire is lighted; in half an hour after the halt the kettles are generally on the fire, and all are busily engaged changing their moccasins, a good voyageur being as particular about damp feet in camp as any anxious mamma could wish her darling boy to be. The penalty of travelling with damp feet next day might be the loss of some of the toes by frost-bite, so that one has good reason to be careful. Besides care on this point, a great secret in making your feet last you on a long trip, especially with snow shoes, is to have large moccasins, and instead of attempting to wear knitted socks, wrap your feet in a square piece of blanket, as is the fashion of the country. Too much covering on the feet only increases the chance of their being injured by pressure, without increasing the warmth, for keeping up which exercise should alone be trusted to.

There was one wide stretch of bare, open plain, but they covered this dangerous traverse comfortably, after waiting a whole afternoon to give themselves a clear day in which to do it. At sunset they came on a large camp of Cree Indians, who pressed them to sleep in their lodges. Hector thought it better to camp at a little distance. He traded for some meat for his dogs. The Cree came trooping down in great numbers, and stood gazing idly at them while they were busy getting their camp in trim. They had heard that Hector was 'a medicine man' and watched all his doings with great attention.

That night there was a magnificent display of northern lights, forming a high arch from which rose streamers of light, bright crimson-lake in colour, which after fifteen minutes were replaced by flashes of pale green light; after this the arch split into three parts and disappeared.

By tempting her feminine nature with some bright blue and yellow beads, Hector got a new dog from an old Indian woman, to replace one of his that was too slow. The new dog was huge, a beautiful black and olive-grey colour, nearly a pure wolf, and quite as savage as any wild one. The only way of getting his harness on was to watch for a chance and give him a sharp blow across the nose, which for a few minutes produced the same effect as a dose of chloroform.

They passed several Indian camps, each near a buffalo pound, and spent a night at the company's winter post on Jack Fish or Pike Lake. Coming down onto the ice of the lake in dim twilight, they could hardly see the western shore, but they held on across the slippery expanse on which neither men nor dogs could get a proper foothold (the wind had swept all the snow away), towards a small twinkling light they could see through the deepening darkness. This proved to be the fire in the Hudson's Bay man's tent. He had been so busy trading with the Indians, in competition with free-traders from Red River, that he had not had time to build anything except a small storehouse and was still living in a leather lodge, in Indian fashion. It was astonishing how comfortable he had made himself. Notwithstanding the contrary interests, the party of free-traders who were on their way to Red River with their booty spent the evening pleasantly around his fire laughing, joking, and playing on the violin, everyone making an evening of it before they parted.

The free-traders went off next morning with nine dog sleds, all seemingly well laden, though the loads might have been fictitious, to deceive the company's people. Competition had been keen. The company had decided to meet the threat of free trade, not by trying to enforce its monopoly rights, but by meeting competition with still more energetic competition, and had managed to drive off the free-traders, who had originally planned to winter at Jack Fish Lake.

There the Indians could be sure of a constant supply of food. At the north-east corner of the lake, where a large stream flowed in, the water stayed open all winter. Here they could spear an immense number of pike, which actually crowded the open water. They caught other kinds of fish, as well, in nets under the ice.

The ice itself made a slippery trap for buffalo. The Indians drove a band of cows out onto it; of course they fell and stumbled helplessly, while their pursuers, on foot, easily killed all fourteen of them.

The party travelled on towards Fort Pitt. At long last they found immense herds of buffalo—a welcome sight, as their provisions were at a low ebb. They saw a herd of bulls feeding in a swamp, a strategic spot where the hunters could easily get close to them. They shot one, and the dogs, for once, got a good supper. Hector realized when he reached the Saskatchewan again that he had come to another of the 'steppes' by which the great plains climb up from Lake Winnipeg to the foothills of the Rocky Mountains. Hills, or buttes, like Red Deer Hill and Horse Knoll, standing by themselves, were detached outliers of the next higher level. Beyond the river he could see other high, conical hills, like Frenchman's Knoll (now Frenchman's Butte) which were clearly outliers, in their turn, of a still higher prairie level, at the top of yet another upward steppe.

Working their way through thick, low brush and having great difficulty with the many deep, steep gullies that cut across the plain, they lost their way among the many buffalo tracks in the deep snow. At last the guide recognized the hill that overhung Fort Pitt and they headed for the Saskatchewan. When they had clambered down to the river, Hector was interested to find bits of fossil in boulders of soft grey limestone; as well, he found fragments of coal in considerable quantity in the sandbanks along the river.

It was difficult to travel on the frozen river; the water had overflowed the ice and formed a thin, treacherous upper film. After a few miles of this hard going, they climbed the high bank again and swung off to the west, cutting off another big bend of the river, this time on the north. At last Fort Pitt came into sight. Again they had to climb down the steep cliffs into the deep valley of the river and cross it. The company officer at the fort, a Mr. Simpson, and everyone else who lived there turned out when they saw a strange party crossing the river, to extend the usual hospitable welcome.

Fort Pitt was small, but it was important. It was one of the best posts in the whole Saskatchewan district for trading provisions. The buffalo were never far distant even in summer, at this point, as the true bare prairies extend very far north; there were no trees at all within sight of the fort. Plains Cree traded at the fort, bringing in pemmican, dried buffalo meat, grease, buffalo robes, and wolf-skins; when there was peace, the Blackfoot came to trade as well. Hector reported: 'Sometimes, when there is war, smart skirmishing goes on close to the fort, and not infrequently the Blackfeet attack the place itself.' When he arrived, the trade goods at the fort were all used up and its storehouses were full of provisions.

This was a business trip. Hector was busy making arrangements for the horses and men needed by the expedition for the next summer, but he found time to do some exploring. M. Chastellain, another of the Hudson's Bay officers, took him to a hill across the river, from which he was able to learn the names and get the bearings of all the prominent points.

He also took hourly observations for a twenty-four-hour period for comparison with the hourly observations he knew were being taken at Fort Carlton at the same time. Here, too, he experienced another chinook, that extraordinary warm wind that blows down from the mountains, bringing sudden, midwinter thaws to the far-western plains. He noted on December 23 that he was surprised by a sharp fall of rain, accompanied by a sudden rise of the thermometer for a few hours.

The day before Christmas, at daylight, he started for Fort Edmonton in company with the Hudson's Bay factor. The four sleds set off across country, until at another bend they came back to the river, which here as elsewhere was hemmed in by high, almost precipitous banks. They made their way down to the river along the bed of a small creek, and travelled on over the ice to the Vermilion or Paint River. Here, to avoid another enormous detour to the north, they had to leave the river again; so they camped for the night before striking off across the plains. They had come thirty-three miles that day; the men as well as the dogs were rather tired, but as it was Christmas Eve they did all they could to enjoy themselves! The night was bitterly cold. Sub-zero weather had followed the brief thaw. The thermometer at sunset—which was at four o'clock—stood at nine below zero.

On Christmas Day they crossed the wide stretch of open prairie, passing many herds of buffalo on their way. They camped early to kill a bull for the dogs. They, at least, were to have a Christmas dinner. The travellers were entertained by well-marked sun-dogs and at night by another magnificent display of northern lights.

Next day they came on an immense camp of Indians, all bawling and screaming and all in a high state of excitement. Having succeeded in driving a large band of buffalo into their 'pound' during the night, they were engaged in slaughtering them. More than 100 buffalo bulls, cows, and calves were crammed into the pound, which was made of stakes, with boughs interlaced, and was about fifty yards across. Hector did not think the space would have held all the buffalo alive, without some being on top of each other. The terrified beasts had been driven down an inclined plane made of rough logs leading to a gap through which they had suddenly to jump about six feet into the ring, so that they could not return. To the entrance of the pound, lines of little heaps of buffalo dung or brush converged from several miles out on the prairies around the clump of wood in which the pound was concealed. These lines served to lead the buffalo in the required direction when they had been driven into the neighbourhood. When first captured and driven into the pound, the buffalo ran round and round violently and, the Indians affirmed, always with the sun. Crouched on the fencing were the Indians, even mere boys and girls, all busy plying bows and arrows, guns and spears, and even knives, to compass the destruction of the buffalo. After firing their arrows they generally succeeded in extracting them again by a noose on the end of a pole; some had even the pluck to jump into the arena and pull them out with their hands, but if an old bull or cow happened to observe them they had to be very active in getting out again. The scene was a busy but a bloody one; the slaughter had to be carried on until every animal was killed to enable the Indians to get the meat. Hector took a hand by trying the penetrating power of rifle balls on the thick skulls of the animals, with invariable success; it was the least cruel way of killing them, as they dropped at once.

There were many superstitions connected with the whole business; the Indians always considered that their success in procuring buffalo in this manner depended on the pleasure of the Manitou, to whom they made offerings, which they placed under the entrance to the pound. Here Hector saw a collection of Indian valuables, among which were bridles, powder-horns, tobacco, beads, and the like, placed there by the believing Indians, only to be stolen by the first scamp in the camp who could manage the theft adroitly. In the centre of the pound, also, there was a tall pole on which they hung offerings, to which piece of idolatry the doctor felt he made himself an accessory by giving them his pocket handkerchief to convert into a flag.

Meanwhile the Hudson's Bay factor had been busy trading with the Indians for an additional dog for Hector. Then they set out again to the west. When they stopped for dinner, Hector shot one of the oldest bulls he had seen; he regretted having to leave behind the magnificent shaggy head and battered horns. A plain enclosed by hills stretched before them, ten miles across; it was covered with immense herds of buffalo. The afternoon was bright and fine, with just enough frost to keep the snow crisp. It was an enlivening scene, reminding the travellers of a huge cattle-fair at home. The snow was deeper now. Some of the men had always to go ahead to break a trail on snow-shoes.

Nearer Fort Edmonton this was no longer necessary.

Large parties with horse sleighs had made an excellent track, along which Hector and his companions travelled in the dark at a brisk run. On the last day they had started out at three in the morning and, just at daylight, had come back to the Saskatchewan. Round a bend they came in sight of Fort Edmonton, standing on a most commanding point about 100 feet above the river, just in front of the place where the Legislative Building stands in Edmonton today. They were soon up the bank and within the palisades, enjoying the hospitable welcome of Mr. Swanston, who had entertained them the previous summer at Fort Garry. He was now in charge of the company's Saskatchewan district. The doctor and his party joined the great gathering of people who had come long distances for the Christmas and New Year festivities. In all they had come 393 miles from Fort Carlton in thirteen days, a quick trip, which Hector knew would have been impossible without Mr. James Simpson as his experienced fellow traveller.

Fort Edmonton was quite as large as Fort Garry, built of wood and furnished with strong bastions and palisades, though these last were rather rotten. Hector spent some time examining the country round the fort. Again he was surprised by the singular weather produced by the chinook, and he was very pleased when Mr. Swanston volunteered to keep 'a meteorological register' of temperature changes.

Not only the weather, but the method of feeding the people in the fort, surprised Hector. Boats were built there to take each year's harvest of furs down the Saskatchewan; so about fifty men were employed, and usually there was a population of about 150. All these were fed on buffalo meat, with a few potatoes, if the crop was good. Among them they ate two buffalo a day, on the average. In a windmill on a hill behind the fort, with home-made granite millstones, they managed, when they got a gale of wind, to grind some tolerable flour, but so little that most of the flour they used came from Red River or even all the way from England. Hector felt that it might be less laborious to grow food than to haul it in from the hunting-grounds, and in many years there was a scarcity of food, and even starvation; on the other hand, it was sometimes difficult to keep crops safe from visiting Indians, who trampled them down.

At last Hector was able to find some good exposed sections where the river sweeps close under high banks. In the beds of clay and sandstone he found coal, which seemed to be of a very useful quality and was in fact used for the forge at the fort. The women of the fort used pipe-clay from a near-by deposit for washing blankets, working it into a lather. No use had yet been found for the 'black unctuous mud'—presumably oil—that oozed from the round hole not far east of the fort, which they had never been able to fathom with the longest pole they could find.

Hector had come to Edmonton to engage half-breeds from Lake St. Ann's to work for the expedition the following summer, but they were all away out on the plains, hunting buffalo. While he waited for them, he made a trip to Rocky Mountain House, six days' journey farther up the Saskatchewan. He took John Foulds with him and two of the company's men. Each man, like Hector, had a dog train.

This was wooded country, where the trails were cut through the bush. Everywhere there were beaver, and the beaver had brought about immense changes in the appearance of the country: 'Wherever there is a hollow in which water could collect, this industrious animal seems to have applied his instinctive ingenuity to create a lake. Some of these beaver's dams are of extraordinary size, stretching for hundreds of yards, and sometimes 6 to 8 feet high.'

The trail wound about to take advantage of every possible opening, to diminish the amount of cutting necessary. Hector found that he got quite bewildered by this bush travel. On some patches of country there was no snow. They set fire to the grass, just to be able to say that they had done so, on the tenth of January. All the same it was bitterly cold. One night they had to light two fires and lie between them to counteract the keen, biting north wind which continued to blow very hard, although the thermometer fell to twenty below zero.

Cutting across the plains, they passed lakes and streams that drain into the South Saskatchewan. They steered by the 'Medicine Lodge Hills' where the Indians held great festivals in spring. At last Hector got his first sight of the Rockies, under rather unfavourable circumstances, as the sun had already set behind them. He climbed a hill while the men were making camp, and made out the outline of the mountains, bounding the horizon from south to west-by-north, but still at a great distance. He was struck by the fact that though the plains were white with snow the mountains seemed black, having snow on them only in streaks and patches, notwithstanding the season and their great altitude.

Next morning they started some hours before daybreak, crossing swampy plains by a well-beaten track in full view of the mountains:

> *The effect was quite exhilarating as they became lighted up rapidly by the pinky hue of morning, and then I found that the black appearance which they presented the evening before arose from the immense proportions of abrupt cliffs which they present, on which the snow cannot rest. We got quite excited with the view, and went on without halting for about 30 miles, when my men said we were about seven miles from the fort, and they must halt and wash; so they made a fire and spent fully an hour dandifying themselves to appear before their friends.*

Rocky Mountain House was a very different sort of place from Fort Edmonton. It was a roughly constructed group of log huts consisting of a dwelling-house, stores, and workshops, all surrounded by a palisade. The woodwork was very old and rotten, and the whole place was tumbling to pieces. A great many Indians were camped round the fort, waiting for Mr. Brazeau, whom Hector had met on his way to Edmonton, to come back with a supply of rum. The fort was occupied only in winter. In the autumn when the company people came back each year there were plenty of moose, wapiti, and caribou (which Hector called 'reindeer') and other deer. Now, though, in the depths of winter, the residents of the fort (mostly women at that time of year) were badly off for food; supplies were nearly used up and all they had to live on was little better than the sweepings of the stores. Before leaving in the spring, the company people planted potatoes, barley, and turnips. What the Indians had left of the crops when they got back in the autumn suggested that the soil and climate were favourable to agriculture, if it could be carried on.

Again Hector climbed a hill to get a view of the abrupt and bold outline of the Rocky Mountains, of which he made a careful sketch, taking bearings of the different peaks and noting the lower, wooded range in front of the main range. Some Blackfoot who had just arrived at the fort watched his proceedings very curiously, as they thought he had gone up the hill to have a medicine dance. Medicine or no medicine, he had a geological field-day, at last finding plenty of places where he could study geological formations, and again discovering coal.

His own dogs being tired out, he borrowed another train of dogs from the fort to make a trip up the Clearwater, which flows into the North Saskatchewan at Rocky Mountain House. Travelling on the ice, he studied the cliffs and the forest trees. When he got back he found still more Blackfoot Indians. They had brought badly needed provisions, though they were short of food themselves, as the buffalo were so far out on the plains that on the journey to the fort they had used up their supplies. They wanted rum so much that they traded some of the scanty supply of meat and pemmican they had left, and soon there was another dreadful scene of riot and disorder. Even though the rum was mixed with water—eleven parts of water to one of spirit—it still easily made the Blackfoot violent, so that the trade was always one of great trouble and even danger to the company's servants.

When the Blackfoot were at a fort, one chief always remained sober, to keep the peace—a very sensible precaution. Hector thought the sober chief of this band, Petope, the Perched Eagle, a fine fellow. He insisted on sleeping on the floor in Hector's room, partly as a compliment, but more because he considered it an honour to brag of among the others afterwards.

Rumour always travelled quickly through the Indian country, and the Blackfoot had already heard of the expedition and were making the most absurd guesses as to the reasons for its intended visit to their country. Hector decided he should tell the chiefs the facts to gain their goodwill. Only a few of them came, the rest being still the worse for their debauch, but that night one of the chiefs who had heard what Hector had to say harangued the other Indians from the palisades of the fort on the necessity of behaving well to the white men, reminding them that they got nothing but good at their hands and not to confound the explorers with the 'Big Knives', the Americans, who, he said, did not treat them well, but were deceitful. This was an allusion to the Missouri traders, whose disturbing competition in the fur trade put the poor Indians on a very false footing. The chief then repeated to his tribesmen all the doctor had said about the expedition.

Next morning ten or twelve of the principal Indians, sober once more, came crowding into Hector's little room, to hear what he had to say. On Mr. Brazeau's advice he gave them papers, with their names and a statement that they had promised to help the expedition. He himself kept a note of what the Hudson's Bay traders thought of each chief's character, so they would know later who could be trusted as guides and so that they could be sure of recognizing the chiefs at once when they met them on the plains. Hector distributed presents of tobacco and trinkets with the papers and sent others to some of the principal chiefs who were not there. He trusted to Mr. Brazeau and the Hudson's Bay Company interpreter, Felix Munroe, who was related to the Blackfoot tribe, 'to discriminate the proper persons'. In addition to Petope, the Blackfoot chiefs were the Main Tentpole, the White-calf-that-ran-up-the-hill, the Swift Wolf, the Old Swan, the Ancient Sun, the One-that-sits-in-the-tent-and-never-goes-out, the Bear's Hip-bone, and the Chief Mountain, besides the medicine-man, Natoos, the Sun. This was the name they always called Hector by, as they knew that he, too, was a medicine-man. The Little Chief was a Sarcee, the Swift Ermine a Piegan, and the Great Rain a Blood Indian.

Petope was the great war chief of the Blackfoot. He made a long speech contrasting the Cree unfavourably with the Blackfoot who, he said, had large hearts and could show hospitality. Hector observed that their men were finer and more powerful and their women (who were fond of handsome dresses) prettier than the Cree. Hector promised to take Petope on as a guide the following summer.

He also tried to find a Stoney Indian who was said to know the Rockies well, but in a two-day trip into the forest to the west he missed him, only to find on his return to the fort that he was there, having come in to report that he had killed two moose. This man promised to act as Hector's guide in the mountains the next summer.

Hector decided to go back to Fort Carlton on the ice of the river, as there was so little snow on the prairies, though this of course meant a longer journey. There was so little food at Rocky Mountain House that they could only get enough for three days for themselves and for one meal for their dogs, to last for a distance of over 200 miles. Hector felt that there must be no loitering.

As they travelled, Hector mapped the river, taking bearings with his compass from each bend to the next. He kept notes of the geological formations they passed. At one point lofty precipices of sandstone 150 feet high hemmed in the river; Hector named this 'Abram's Gates', after his guide who had been talking about this wonderful place ever since they started. False ice near rapids gave them some trouble the same day; the dogs broke through it several times.

By the third day, the dogs were like a pack of wolves from hunger, so they pressed on several hours after sunset and, next night, as they had nothing to eat, they made only a short stop, going on at nine o'clock and reaching Edmonton at 7:30 next morning after a ninety-mile run, so completing the 212-mile trip from Rocky Mountain House to Fort Edmonton. They were, of course, all played out, but hunger and fatigue soon disappeared under the kind attention of Mr. Swanston, an old and experienced traveller who knew the proper mode of treating such cases.

At the fort, Hector studied prevalent ailments, including goitre and influenza. The return of eighteen hunters from the plains with forty horse sleighs loaded with buffalo meat was a welcome and lively event, especially as the horses were only half broken; they had been brought from the mountains the summer before.

Hector joined one of the Hudson's Bay Company men, another Sinclair, on a trip to the Lake St. Ann's (Lac Ste. Anne) Mission. They used a horse sleigh and slept out one night on the way. That night, the coldest night that Hector ever camped out, the thermometer at Edmonton fell to -47°; the mercury thermometer he had with him was quite frozen. The same night at Carlton, 400 miles to the east, Blakiston recorded a temperature of -54°. Crossing six miles of frozen lake next morning, both Hector and Sinclair got their faces frozen. Within two weeks the temperature had gone up to 65° and the snow had all disappeared.

Father Lacombe, the celebrated Roman Catholic missionary, and his 'coadjutor' were nearly alone, as the people of the two villages were away on the plains hunting buffalo. They carried on little cultivation but caught thousands of whitefish in the lake. Next morning it was still so cold that the priests had to wear greatcoats and mittens while they held the service in the little wooden chapel. Father Lacombe lent Hector his dog train to explore the lake in fine style; then he took leave of the kind and hospitable priests to return to Edmonton in a single day.

Now Hector had to go out on to the plains to find the Lake St. Ann's half-breeds he needed for the next season's work The Wesleyan missionary's interpreter, Peter Erasmus, wen with him. Travelling was awkward. In the morning the ground was hard frozen, but there was no snow for sleighs, and by the afternoon the ground was slushy. They used horses, with a spare one to carry blankets and a kettle.

They found the hunters' camp that night and slept in one of the tents. More of the hunters came in next day, a motley troop with loaded horses and dogs, travelling in a style hardly different from Indians. There were about 200 men, women, and children in the band, with forty tents, which were merely Indian wigwams of buffalo skins sewn together and stretched over poles. The men were generally handsome and well built, but very few of the women were even comely. They wore clothes of European manufacture, but even those of the men who could speak French preferred to speak Cree. They were very hospitable and feasted Hector on buffalo meat and the delicacy of the season, muskrat, which they speared through holes in the ice. Hector found this mousy-flavoured and oily, though scarcely more so than beaver flesh. He spent the rest of the day persuading the half-breeds' old chief, Gabriel Dumont, to consent to act as guide for the expedition. This was an uncle of the Gabriel Dumont who became Riel's general in the 1885 rising; he had repeatedly crossed the Rocky Mountains and could speak Blackfoot. As soon as Dumont consented, Hector got all the volunteers he needed from among the young men, though they all seemed to consider the service a dangerous one and were very particular in stipulating that the party should be sufficiently numerous and well supplied with ammunition. The information Dumont gave Hector about the country to the south and about the mountains was very useful in working out plans for the second season's work.

At last, in the middle of March, Hector started back for Fort Carlton with his own man, Foulds, and a company man who was returning to Fort Pitt. Each of them had a dog train. They hoped to travel on the river. Hector borrowed a pair of skates, so he got along with great ease, while his companions were slipping and tumbling on the smooth, snow-free ice. A new fall of snow gave them trouble farther on. There had been so little snow when they left Edmonton that they had not thought of bringing snow-shoes. Now the sun made the deep snow soft during the day and the dogs could hardly drag the sleds over it. In the end they travelled at night when the cold set in and froze the snow again, and rested by day—or, rather, the men rested; Hector found that he could not sleep in the bright sunshine and so spent the days exploring and geologizing. Coming back to camp along a beaten buffalo trail, he encountered an old bull, which he shot; he carried a load of fresh meat back with him.

The party was glad to see a snow-shoe track which led Hector to two Indian tents, where he got a pair of snow-shoes in return for a little tobacco and ammunition. After that they could at least beat down a track for the dogs. This made things much easier, but when they came to some rapids there were holes in the ice through which water had overflowed to a depth of several feet. A new, thin skin of ice formed on this water and on this they had to travel. The dogs kept popping through. The men had to lie on their sleds, which presented enough surface to bear up their weight. Doing this, Hector fell asleep while he was in the lead. (He had broken trail on the snow-shoes from seven p.m. to two a.m.) The other men, thinking he was keeping a look-out, followed boldly, running behind him in the dark. Suddenly the ice gave way. Hector was awakened by their cries to find that he had escaped sharing a ducking. The water over the lower, sound ice was only four feet deep; so with a little scrambling both men and dogs soon got out again. A big fire and a few hours' halt put them all to rights.

At Fort Pitt Hector found that an Indian carrying important letters for him to Edmonton had missed him. While he was waiting for him to return, the first goose arrived, flying down the river, and the Indians saw some ducks out on the plains—decided signs of spring. With the problem of next season's travel always in mind Hector did some horse-trading, securing seventeen animals for the use of the expedition.

When he started again, the ice on the river had become rotten and unsafe, and he and Foulds had to take to the trail. Even so, they had to fling away the dog sleds and make the dogs carry the things on their backs, as the snow failed them altogether on the second day.

At Jack Fish Lake they found Sullivan where he had been with Beads since they had been obliged to leave Fort Carlton in the winter, when provisions became short. Since Hector had passed in December, Mr. McMurray had built a comfortable little house of two rooms. Green poplar had been used in the construction of the roof; the warmth indoors had opened the buds, and the inside was in full leaf.

At Jack Fish Lake they got Indian *travails* (as Hector called the more commonly spelt *travois*). These were two poles ten feet long, joined together at an acute angle at the end that rested on the dog's neck, the other ends trailing on the ground, kept apart by a few cross-bars close behind the dog's tail; on these the load was strapped. With ten dogs accoutred in this fashion, they went on down to Carlton. Sullivan and Hector now rode, but Beads, Foulds, and the others went on foot. At least, Hector started out on horseback, riding his new horse, a beautiful young animal that had been brought across the mountains from the Kootenay Indians and had not been perfectly broken. They had only gone about four miles when the horse became restive, threw Hector over his head, and got away. He was soon out of sight and it was not until after some weeks' searching that he was found, forty miles from Jack Fish Lake. They had to pay twenty beaver skins to the Indian who brought him in.

Following a new trail over the south end of the Thickwood Hills they travelled twenty-five miles a day and reached Carlton after three days. It was ticklish work getting across the river on the rotten ice, but they arrived safely and found Lieutenant Blakiston and M. Bourgeau both well and tolerably hearty, considering the short commons they had been on and their hard work in carrying out the magnetical observations by themselves for the past six weeks.

Hector had one more trip to make. Provisions were so scarce that he realized that the men from Edmonton and Lake St. Ann's must not come to Carlton to wait for the start of the new season's work. He went up to Fort Pitt to stop them as they came down with the Hudson's Bay Company boats of the Edmonton brigade. This time he made the trip in three days with a good strong horse, getting to Fort Pitt just a few hours before the first boat arrived.

He sent the men and the horses out to the Eagle Hills, the nearest point to Fort Carlton where they could support themselves by hunting buffalo, until the rest of the expedition was ready to join them. It took Hector another eight days to come back down-river to Fort Carlton by boat with the brigade, a very pleasant trip in the company of the gentlemen of the Hudson's Bay Company's service—more like a picnic than hard travelling in a wild country! Moreover, it gave him a chance to see and map the last lap of the river from Rocky Mountain House right to Fort Carlton.

By June 2 the brigade had gone on down the river from Fort Carlton, carrying off nearly the whole civilized population of the Saskatchewan, except some of the women and children. After the bustle of mustering the company's brigade and starting the thirty boats down-river, things were dull at the fort. Hector and Chief Trader Hardisty, who had been left in charge at Carlton, set off along the Red River trail in the hope of meeting Palliser on his return from his journey to the east. They rode south-east along the Carlton Trail towards Red River. The South Saskatchewan, unlike the North Saskatchewan (which, through lack of snow in the winter, was still very shallow), was in full spring flood. They constructed a rough skin canoe to carry their saddles and blankets and swam across the river with their horses. Next day, while they were resting twenty-six miles south-east of their crossing-place, Palliser walked in on them, striding on ahead of his party.

CHAPTER ELEVEN

'Little Bourgeau is a Brick'

N ow, for the first time, the entire party was together, including Blakiston whom Palliser had not seen since their brief meeting in England fifteen months earlier. He found that the relations between the magnetical observer and the other explorers were far from happy, but for the time being their differences were apparently smoothed over. By the middle of June the expedition was ready to start on the new season's work. The men from Red River and the half-breeds from Lake St. Ann's, whom Hector had engaged during the winter, were waiting out on the plains; only the supplies ordered from the Hudson's Bay Company at Norway House, a supply post on the route from Hudson Bay, had not yet arrived. Blakiston wanted to make some more magnetic observations up-river, farther west, to compare with those made earlier by Lefroy; so Palliser sent him off with a small party to Fort Pitt and Edmonton. The brigade of boats with the supplies would probably arrive at Fort Edmonton before Blakiston had finished his observations. He could get a guide there and rejoin the main party where the Medicine River runs into the Red Deer, bringing the supplies with him. The main party, meanwhile, set out to explore the country between the north and south branches of the Saskatchewan.

The Peacemaker, the Cree guide who had travelled with them the year before, came to see them, but this time he would not come with them; in spite of all his efforts war had broken out again and he could not travel in Blackfoot country. The Cree had started the trouble by stealing Blackfoot horses. These were always a temptation, as the Blackfoot devoted themselves to rearing horses and had much better mounts than the Cree.

No sooner had they set out than the explorers encountered difficulties about food for their own horses. The pasture was poor over large areas, partly because spring was late and partly because there had been bad fires the year before. Indeed, Palliser came to the conclusion that much of the country that was then open prairie had once been wooded; the trees had been destroyed by frequent fires.

Palliser went off with one of the men to fetch the Lake St. Ann's contingent from the Eagle Hills. A Cree Indian with his wife and child arrived. He had gambled away everything he owned and was entirely naked except for a buffalo robe wrapped loosely round him. His two miserable dogs were virtually starving and snapped up every scrap of leather they could steal. This Indian told them that a large Blackfoot war-party was on its way into Cree country. Farther on they met another Cree, a chief, who told them a Cree had already been killed by the Blackfoot.

All this was not likely to make it easier for the expedition to explore the rest of the South Saskatchewan River and the country beyond, to the border, but Palliser was still resolved to try. A large camp of Cree sent a deputation to wait on the party, demanding 'presents of all kinds, among which a little *ishcoley wapoe* (fire-water) stood prominent'. Since the party had always made it a rule not to carry any liquor on the plains, there was no chance of the Cree getting any. To escape from other demands they changed their direction.

They were now among buffalo and could replenish their scanty stock of provisions. This gave the men enough food, but made it all the harder to feed their horses. In some areas the buffalo had stripped the prairie almost bare of grass. In spite of frequent, violent storms with drenching rain, and some with hail, water was also a problem. They found small swamps, stagnant marshes, and a few lakes and pools, but most of these were intensely salty. A draught of water from one of them was like a dose of salts.

One of the best horses disappeared. It was tied to a dead buffalo's horn, in the usual way, while its rider cut up the meat. A sudden storm broke, with violent wind and rain. When another member of the party came over the hill with a load of brushwood, the already frightened horse panicked, snapped its halter, and galloped off. Horses, as usual, were all-important; so four of the smartest men instantly set off after it. They had great difficulty in following it, in the teeth of the storm, but they chased it till dark. Then they had to spend the night out on the open prairie without even a shrub to shelter them from the savage weather. As soon as day dawned, they mounted, took up the horse's track, and started after it again, but all in vain. They came back at last without the horse, cold and drenched. One of them took ill as a result, with acute inflammation of the lungs, which held them up for several days.

The halt at least pleased M. Bourgeau, as the spot was a good one for botanical researches. All the winter he had been pining for spring to come, so that he could get on with his collecting. Unfailingly cheerful, obliging, and hard-working, he had done efficiently whatever needed to be done, diverting himself, after he had made his meteorological and magnetical observations, by snaring hares or enjoying an occasional game of whist. All the same, he found that time went slowly. He was not a sportsman and could not amuse himself by hunting. He waited anxiously and endlessly for news from home; no letters had come from his wife. He wearied, too, for a sight of the mountains. Born in the Alps, he did not feel happy on the open, rolling plains. He wrote miserably from the flat expanse of prairie: 'J'aime les montagnes.'

Now, at last, the long, dreary winter was over and he was having a field-day; his work took his mind off his troubles. Trees were scarce, but in the valleys there were a few white birches, and low-growing willows, aspens, hawthorns, and

Manitoba maples (the sugar tree of the Cree). They found the remains of an Indian camp, which showed that a party had been there that spring to make sugar from the maples. There were many shrubs, too; one, which the report called 'shepherdia' (*ostea argentea*), in full flower, smelt delicious.

Bourgeau worked enthusiastically. Palliser wrote to Sir William Hooker at Kew: 'Little Bourgeau is a Brick his collections seem to me (who know nothing of Botany,) very pretty and the colours as vivid after the specimens are saved, as they are in life—He is most indefatigable and always at work.' He wrote again, later: 'He has been a most active energetic and excellent companion, always hard at his work in which his whole soul seems engrossed and no matter what his fatigues or privations may be, his botanical specimens are always his first care.' He was indeed the 'prince of botanical collectors', as Sir William Hooker called him.

He was so keen that everyone else in the party got interested in botany too. Sullivan undertook to make the 'thermometrical observations of the soil' for him, as his time was wholly taken up in collecting and drying his botanical specimens. Palliser helped too. Bourgeau wrote to Hooker: 'Thanks to Captain Palliser, who has taken much interest in the success of my labours, and who has greatly assisted me in preserving the specimens from damp during the journey, I have about 22 packets of dried plants, and 110 of different sorts of seeds. The herbarium contains about 460 species, and about 60,000 specimens.' Some of these are in the museums and herbarium of the Royal Botanic Gardens at Kew to this day, the colours of the flowers still bright after a hundred years.

Bourgeau must have needed all his devotion to botany to get him through the summer. A shocking horseman, he had to travel wearily in the jolting carts. There was an odometer fixed to the wheel of one of the carts to measure the distances traversed. Sometimes Bourgeau got excited when buffalo appeared and dashed off after them, cart and all, upsetting their careful measurements.

There was other cause for excitement. They were now very near the Blackfoot country. When their scouts one day reported that they had heard shots, ammunition was served out and the whole party remained on the alert, especially as the buffalo were moving across the plains as though they were being hunted. Next day they came on the site of a very recent Indian camp. Indians or no Indians, the explorers continued to hunt buffalo, to make observations for latitude and longitude, and to take the temperature of the soil at a depth of three feet.

Near the Battle River they crossed 'Ambush Coulée', called by the Cree 'the place where we were surprised while sleeping'. Many years before, a war-party of Blackfoot had trailed a hunting-party of Cree. Guided by the sound of the women cutting wood, they had silently surrounded the camp in the dark of the night. When all was quiet in the Cree camp, they rushed with one loud yell upon their sleeping enemies and killed all but one old man. Hector, making a short trip to the north, came on the recent track of a war-party and found the shelter they had made, of interlaced branches of poplar, against one of the frequent storms. Hail had completely stripped most of the trees of their foliage. The next day they came in sight of the Neutral Hills, to the south. These were the recognized boundary between the Cree and Blackfoot tribes.

At night sheet lightning played in the northern sky, while fire-flies lit up the surrounding coppice. The Indians believed fire-flies to be the spirits of their departed friends, holding their great feast on the plain when the nights were quiet and warm and the buffalo were in the best condition.

Impressed with the fertile soil, the explorers were confident that this part of the country was fit for immediate settlement and wanted but little culture to yield splendid fruits.

They came on the site of a medicine lodge, where a great ceremony was held. For this, a tree chosen by the woman who was selected by the majority of the other women as the most virtuous in the camp was decorated with curious characters painted on pieces of bark and other offerings to the Manitou.

Once in Blackfoot country, they had to make rules about buffalo-hunting, both to keep the men from straying away from the main party and because buffalo were so plentiful that they had to economize ammunition and prevent useless slaughter.

By following the buffalo roads they escaped getting mired. To cut off a long bend to the south, they crossed the Battle River, though Hector and two men followed the curve of the stream while the main party took the shorter route. When night fell he had not returned. They were uneasy, as they were near an assembly place of the Sarcees (allies of the Blackfoot), called 'the Flag-hanging Hill'; moreover, they had found a dead buffalo cow, still warm, with an arrow through her heart. Clearly there were Sarcees about. Next evening, as night advanced, they saw two riders coming at full speed; hopes that this was the doctor were dashed when, as they neared the camp, the riders gave at intervals a yell which certainly did not come from any Scottish throat. The riders proved to be two Sarcees who said that the doctor and his party had spent the previous night at the Sarcee camp; he was now on the road with some Indians coming to join the other explorers. They also said that a large party of Piegans and Blood Indians had just left for the Red Deer River; having killed a Cree Indian, they wanted to reach a safe encampment, as no doubt a war-party of Cree would soon be on their trail. The doctor arrived shortly with twenty of the Sarcees, an advance party of a larger deputation that they intended to send next day. The explorers sent word to the Sarcee camp that they wanted to trade horses. The larger deputation duly arrived, a body of about seventy men headed by the chiefs, richly attired in dresses ornamented with porcupine quills and trimmed with ermine. Sullivan reported:

> We invited them to sit down and smoke. The chiefs were pleased with their reception, and inquired all about the

purposes of our journey; they remained with us the whole night. We observed that several of them had lost a joint of one of their fingers. This we learnt was the consequence of a custom common to them with many other kindred tribes, of biting off the joint of a finger when unsuccessful in the performance of a vow. Among their women also, as among those of the Blackfeet, it is not uncommon to find many without a nose, or minus an ear, bitten off by their husbands in a fit of jealousy.

The Indians proved troublesome and the explorers thought they meant mischief. They managed to get rid of them, and travelled a long way before camping next evening. The mosquitoes were even more troublesome; even the half-breed *voyageurs* suffered severely from them.

Food was getting short again; so Palliser went after buffalo with two of the hunters. They killed six cows. Others in the party went after beaver, as they had seen a number of beaver dams. A halt was called to collect provisions and to slice and dry the meat. The hunters brought in eleven buffalo. By nightfall the meat was arranged on poles with small fires around it in order to keep off clouds of bulldog-flies which, for the first time this season, attacked the party. Hundreds of wolves, drawn by the scent of the meat, lurked around them at a respectable distance; they killed a few, but their skins in the summer were not worth the ammunition expended. Apart from the buffalo needed for food, only such prizes as the giant moose they had brought down a few days earlier were worth shooting. With his leg broken by Palliser's first shot, this moose, which stood six feet four inches at the shoulder, turned at bay and put up a gallant fight, though riddled with shot and arrows; he so terrified the horses that some of them threw their riders and stampeded off, but at length, surrounded on all sides, he fell, game to the last. He provided the camp with a splendid feast of moose meat, moofle (the tender nose), and gut sausages—delicacies the hunters prepared with great skill.

As the hunters ranged the country after buffalo, they came on a beautifully clear lake to the south covered with water-birds, but many of the swamps and lakes were brackish; wherever the water was sweet and fresh, their old enemies the mosquitoes were a horrid torment. The heat was intense.

Coming out of a valley, they crossed the trail of a Blackfoot war-party which had clearly passed two or three days earlier on its way to Rocky Mountain House. Gaining the summit of the ridge, they saw smoke from the direction of Red Deer River. They did not answer it, for fear of bringing a large party of Indians down on them, though they thought at first that it might be a signal from the doctor, who was off on a side trip. However, they decided—rightly—that Hector could not be lost, as he had with him one of the best hunters.

Palliser, too, had been off on a side trip, to Bull Lake and the Red Deer River. They met him again on a tributary of the Red Deer in company with a small party of Rocky Mountain Stoneys, with whom he had been hunting after a chance meeting. Though they belonged to the same tribe as the warlike Plains Assiniboine, this band lived in the mountains. Unlike their relatives of the plains, they were peaceful and inoffensive. They were very poor, and went about almost naked, suffering great misery through want of food despite the fact that they were expert hunters. Occasionally they made excursions onto the plains after buffalo, but as a rule they stayed in the thick woods, hunting moose, wapiti, long-tail and short-tail deer, big-horn sheep, and bears. They were Christians and unusually attentive to what the missionaries had taught them. They would neither hunt nor travel on Sundays, and every morning and evening devoted a short time to religious duties.

Moving south-westward, the explorers had now come to the upper reaches of the Red Deer River, where they hoped to find coal-beds reputed to be on the river-banks. Sure enough, they found coal—and found that it was burning! The Indians told them that it had been on fire for as long as they could remember. They tested the coal and found that, if lighted at night, it would keep a fire going till morning.

To cross the river they had to make rafts for the baggage, as the channel was deep and the current swift. As they went on up-river, they found increasingly fine woods, though the smaller plants and grass had been beaten to the earth, apparently by hail.

At last they got their first view of the Rocky Mountains. To the north, the magnificent chain of mountains looked like a blue line on the far-off horizon; to the south, the mountains seemed higher and more massive, their summits clad in snow which glittered at intervals like silver crowns. Bourgeau must have rejoiced to see high mountains again; indeed, among the whole party there was great excitement at this sudden and unexpected sight. They had begun to feel that the prairies went on and on for ever. The unending, curved horizon was becoming monotonous. Now, at last, there were the Shining Mountains.

A less attractive sight, which they saw over and over again, was trees destroyed by the ravages of fire (almost invariably due to wanton carelessness and mischief, as a result of signal fires, often used for trivial messages), which brought starvation and misery to the Indian tribes themselves by spoiling their hunting-grounds.

Now the expedition turned south once more to the true prairies. Food was again getting short. The explorers were finding, as the fur brigades had found long ago, that it took a lot of meat to keep a party of travellers going. As the Rocky Mountain Stoneys had been tenting and hunting in the neighbourhood for a long time, there was no game to be had, but Blakiston had not yet arrived and they had to wait for him. They waited for several days, but at last they were so driven for provisions that they had to move on. Hector went to the Forks of the Medicine and Red Deer rivers to bury a letter for Blakiston there, before they struck off towards the Bow River, the main feeder of the South Saskatchewan. One of the Stoneys had killed a moose; poor though he was, he very hospitably gave the visitors half the meat. They now made a cache of all their bulky articles, so that they might travel unencumbered while in the mountains, and left directions for Blakiston to follow their cart-track. At the first noon halt, he and his guide caught up with them; his carts came after him the following morning, when the whole party, again all together (and this for the first time while travelling), moved on in search of food and towards the mountains. Scouts sent out to reconnoitre after two buffalo bulls had been seen brought welcome word back to camp that night that there were buffalo in great quantities about ten miles to the east.

Having started before daylight next day, the party made a long breakfast halt to let the buffalo begin to lie down after feeding. As the day wore on they were not so swift as in the early morning. Palliser described the hunt:

> We were now more than two miles' distance from the buffalo, who were not in sight, as we had taken care to take up such a position as that they could neither see us or get our wind; they were in such numbers that their peculiar grunt sounded like the roar of a distant rapids in a large river, and causing a vibration also something like a trembling in the ground.
>
> We had scouted the animals pretty well, so that all that remained for us was to eat our breakfast and make for the point of attack. Breakfast finished, our 'runners' saddled and mounted, the whole party moved slowly on, the carts following in the rear of the 'runners'. Having ascended the slightly elevated ridge we then beheld our game, four or five thousand buffalo, some lying down, some grazing with the old bulls in the outskirts. At our appearance the wolves, who almost invariably accompany bands of buffalo, sneaked about and around, eagerly watching our movements, and perfectly aware that the events about to come off were to terminate in an abundant meal after the field was left to themselves. A few antelope were gracefully moving near the buffalo, and over the heads of all noisily soared some crows and ravens, and appeared quite aware that something was in the wind. Soon after seeing us the buffalo were in motion at a steady lope,

crowding gradually into a thick black mass, and now the hunters came on at a steady canter increasing with the speed of the buffalo into a hand gallop; the old bulls were soon left in the rear as the pace improved, some stood blown and staring after they had made ineffectual attempts at charging the hunters on their headlong way after the swift cows. The run was magnificent, and there was considerable emulation between my Saskatchewan and my Red River men. We killed 17 cows, generally speaking in good condition, and were now not only sufficiently provided with meat for our present wants, but also enough to dry and preserve for the expeditions contemplated in the mountains. Several of the party got apparently very severe falls owing to the badger holes, but none were seriously hurt. In the evening we had fixed our camp and cut up and drawn in our meat.

They called this camp 'Slaughter Camp'. It was close to the site of modern Calgary. From it they had a magnificent view of the Rocky Mountains, as the sun set behind their snowy peaks. After their long, hard, but fascinating journey they had come at last to the western limit of the plains.

They spent several days there. While the men sliced and dried the meat, Palliser made plans for the expedition's third big job, the search for passes through the formidable wall of mountains, which was now within sight. First, though, he was anxious to have one more try at seeing the south-western extremity of the British prairies before he left them to cross the mountains. This might be his last chance to do so, as he planned, if possible, to go straight on to the Pacific.

The expedition had not been able to carry out the original plan of following a route due west across the plains just north of the boundary. They had had to zigzag north and south over the vast expanse of prairie. They had seen far more of that enormous country than they would have seen had they been able to keep to a straight line of travel, but they had not been able to follow the South Saskatchewan up for more than a few miles above the Elbow, nor had they seen anything of the country along the boundary west of Roche Percée. Between the Qu'Appelle–South Saskatchewan valley and the border there still stretched miles of unexplored, inviting wilderness. Palliser decided that he and Sullivan, with Beads, Baptiste Gabriel, and two more men should make a quick trip south along the edge of the mountains, to see what they could of the south-westernmost corner of the British prairies, at their base. At the border they would make a dash eastward from the Rockies, hoping to close by at least a little the gap between the westernmost point they had reached during their first season in 1857 and the country they were now to traverse on the flank of the mountains this second summer.

Palliser's party set out on August 3, travelling till long after dark and spending the first night without wood or water; next morning they soon struck the Bow River. They made a raft for their saddles, guns, and other equipment and stores, by folding the leather tent into a round shape. They swam the horses across the bitterly cold river (which had its source in glaciers not far away), dragging their tent-leather boat after them. South of the river they came again to rich, partly wooded country. They saw a solitary buffalo cow. Palliser went after her on Pharaoh, his cherished buffalo-runner. The chase took him far to the east, almost out again onto the bare plains, but he came back with a load of useful meat. He found his party camped to the north-west of a high hill. Climbing it, he found a beautiful clear spring at the top, choked with buffalo bones. Probably a large band had perished there, rolling one over the other in a snowdrift.

Next day they came to the Porcupine Hills, crossing a nameless tributary of the Bow. The men approved of Palliser's suggestion that it should be called the Arrow River, as it belonged to the Bow. On the fifth day, they camped about six miles from the border in full view of Chief Mountain, a natural landmark just south of the forty-ninth parallel. Leaving Sullivan in charge of the camp and taking the two best buffalo-runners, which had not been worked on the journey but had run free to be as fresh as possible, Palliser and Gabriel set off to the east to see what they could of the boundary country in the single day they had to spare. They climbed another conical hill fifteen miles north and east of Chief Mountain. From the top they could see far across the plains. They traced the feeders of the South Saskatchewan by their fringes of poplar and willow or by their banks, along the sandy waste, as they rose from reservoirs in the mountains, flowing east at first and then bending away to the north. The Belly River flowed eastward from Gros Ventre Lake (today's Outpost Lake) almost at their feet, finally sweeping away to the north, to pour its waters into the South Saskatchewan. Palliser's view to the south was obstructed by high land, but to the north he could not see any tributary likely to prove a feeder of the Missouri; all the waters he could see seemed to bear away to the north, after running a few miles to the east. (The next season's work was to throw more light on that problem, though Palliser could not then know it.)

Now, just as Palliser would have given anything for one half-hour more of light, the sun set gloriously behind Chief Mountain. They were a long way from the base camp, and finally they gave up trying to find their way back to it through thick woods and among numerous lakes. They made a makeshift camp and waited for daybreak. Next morning they found they had been only three miles away!

Starting back at once for the rendezvous at Old Bow Fort, the abandoned Hudson's Bay Company post, they followed the top of an extraordinary ridge, but they got into difficulties when they took a short cut, on Gabriel's advice, instead of following the regular Kootenay Trail. After getting entangled in thick bush and fallen timber, they had to cut back to the east again, once more running out of food. Chasing an elk across a swamp, they had been uncommonly near losing their horses in it; the poor beasts sank to their bellies and were rescued only with great difficulty. Palliser shot a deer that sprang out of the bushes as he was dismounting. Then Beads shot a deer, which kept them going, but they were very glad to see the large white tent of the men they had left behind, now camped, according to instructions, at Old Bow Fort. The Bow River was too deep and swift to cross at that point, so they had to go some way up it, fording the Kananaskis before they could find a crossing-place. They passed three successive falls of the river; these falls, like the whole surrounding scene, were wild and beautiful. They were now right in the mountains, which towered majestically above them. Above the third fall they crossed the river easily, descended its opposite bank again for about four miles, and reached the hunters' camp before two o'clock, close to the ruins of Old Bow Fort. Palliser wrote:

> . . . the only portion remaining of this building are the stone chimneys; the rest of the fort, which was only of wood, has long since been burnt by the Indians. The scenery around is mild and beautiful. Its site is at the base of the Rocky Mountains, which tower above it to the height of 3,000 or 4,000 feet, the white summits of which, from a sprinkling of snow that had recently fallen, formed a pretty contrast with the dense sombre forests at their feet. The Bow River flows by in all the wildness of mountain character, foaming at intervals over ledges of rock in its valley, and then rushing onwards between high banks, clad with luxuriant vegetation.

They were not yet at the end of their troubles. The men Palliser had left to hunt and make a cache of meat for each of the separate parties on their return from the mountains had had very little luck. They were terrified that Blackfoot and Blood Indians would soon appear, coming in for the winter, like the buffalo, from the open plains to the wooded foothills. Then the wife of one of the hunters was taken ill; Palliser was afraid she was going to die. He must have longed for Doctor Hector! He blistered her severely and gave her a great deal of medicine. He was sure she had smallpox, that dreaded scourge brought by the white men to the Plains Indians, but at last she began to get better, though she was still very weak.

While she was ill, Palliser was busy with arrangements for

stores of food to be left for the returning branch expeditions. It was unlikely that any of them would find much game in the mountains; they would probably all need supplies on their return to the plains—as indeed they did. Preparations had to be made for the second winter as well. Palliser sent two men back to Edmonton to start cutting hay to help the horses through the latter part of the winter and early spring. The other men who were not with the mountain parties were to go home. Then, at last, Palliser was free to look for Sinclair's reputed pass.

CHAPTER TWELVE

New Passes through the Rockies: The Kananaskis

At the very foot of the Rockies the explorers were astonished to find almost as much uncertainty as there had been in London about passes through that heart-breaking barrier of mountains. Travellers without knowledgeable guides were apt to wander indefinitely and hungrily up one likely-looking valley after another, only to find that each ended in sheer precipices that only a mountaineer could scale, or in forbidding glaciers and snowfields that no pack-horse could be expected to negotiate, and there seemed to be few knowledgeable guides. South of the American border there were well-known passes from the head-waters of the Missouri River, freely travelled by the 'mountain men' of the Far West. Three hundred miles north of the border the Athabasca Pass was also well known. Through it ran the main route in British territory across the mountains, an overland link in the transcontinental canoe route established by the Nor'Westers and still, in 1858, used by the brigades of the Hudson's Bay Company. This much-travelled pass led over the crest of the Rockies from a tributary of the Athabasca River. Travellers by it had to make their way from the North Saskatchewan River across country to the Athabasca River, up the Athabasca, past Jasper House, and up a tributary, the Whirlpool River; at the summit they found a little lake called the Committee Punch Bowl, in honour of the men who ruled the Honourable Company. The Punch Bowl drained both ways, 'down north' to the Arctic, by the Athabasca-Mackenzie system, and westward to the Pacific, by the Columbia. The trail from the Athabasca Pass followed the Wood River down to the Canoe River and the Boat Encampment at the most northerly point of the Big Bend of the Columbia. It was said that this pass was not fit for horses, though horses in fact carried passengers and furs and trade goods and mail across it. It was true, though, that it was only a connection in the great water-way, ill suited for large-scale overland travel, as well as inconveniently far to the north.

About possible passes leading from the head-waters of the branches of the Saskatchewan River through the mountains between the Athabasca Pass and the border to the Columbia-Kootenay Valley there was extraordinarily little precise, dependable information to be had.

It was known that the Kootenay Indians crossed regularly to the prairies by such passes to hunt buffalo and that through them the tribes of the Blackfoot Confederacy sometimes pursued both their hereditary enemies, the Kootenay, and the Kootenay's admirable horses. It was not known exactly where these passes lay, nor what they were like, nor whether they were suitable for use as routes for overland travel. Could roads be built through them? Or railroads? And were they, in any case, in British territory, or did they lie to the south of the forty-ninth parallel?

It was true that David Thompson, the great fur-trader explorer, had crossed Howse Pass in 1807 and used it for four years; also that Joseph Howse of the Hudson's Bay Company had been sent in 1810 to see what the Nor'Westers were doing in the mountains and had used the pass too. The Piegans, who frequented the approach to the pass, objected to white men travelling through it to trade with their enemies and had forced both the Nor'Westers and the Hudson's Bay Company to abandon the route. Howse Pass had been forgotten, along with David Thompson's great map on which it was marked.

Of passes farther south, it was known only that Sir George

Simpson had crossed the mountains from east to west by one of them in 1841; that Father de Smet, a Jesuit missionary, had come from the Oregon over the mountains, travelling from west to east in 1845; and that in the same year two British officers, Lieutenants Warre and Vavasour, had also crossed the mountains going the other way and meeting de Smet far to the west.

Sir George Simpson, in his book *A Journey Round the World*, which was published in 1847, had described the pass by which he travelled, but his description was by no means sufficiently explicit to guide a traveller. Even when, in 1845, he was arranging plans with the British War Office for the two young military men to make a quick journey to the Oregon, his letters were vague and not entirely consistent. In one he cited the latitude of the pass to be used as 'about 50° 30′ and in another as 51°.

One of these young officers was Lieutenant H. J. Warre of the 14th Regiment, who had been with Palliser's brother-in-law, William Fairholme, on the hunting expedition to the Grand Prairies of the Missouri, which originally fired Palliser's interest in the Far West. The War Office had decided to send this young officer, ostensibly on a second hunting trip, with Lieutenant M. Vavasour, R.E., but actually on a secret mission to study and report on 'the capabilities' of the Oregon territory 'in a Military point of view'. The Oregon Territory, on the lower Columbia River, was then in dispute between Great Britain and the U.S.A. Sir George arranged for the officers to go, under the escort of the veteran chief factor, Peter Skene Ogden, who knew the mountains well and the Columbia country even better, by what he described as the most direct route and by the pass the farthest to the south in British territory. Actually, with a small party of twelve, they did not feel strong enough to go far south, and in the end probably travelled by the White Man Pass. No mention is made of Palliser's having seen the official military report. He may have read it, but, even if he did so, it too was so vague that it would have been of little help. He may have seen the book of sketches Warre had published on his return, but this, also, gave only the most meagre geographical information. The two military men felt that Sir George had exaggerated the possibilities of the pass as a route for the transport of men and military stores. They described it as a defile unsuited to the passage of troops; the high, steep, and rugged passes of the Rockies were, in their view, sufficiently difficult to make the Oregon country inaccessible from the east. Here again was a contradiction of views that called for a third opinion.

Father de Smet, the Jesuit missionary, travelled from the Oregon to the prairies, meeting Warre and Vavasour with his old friend, Peter Skene Ogden, west of the mountains at Pend'Oreille Lake. He also wrote of defiles and desolate regions, but as well, of enamelled meads, fine forests, and beautiful lakes. His description of the pass was poetic rather than precise and gave little definite evidence as to its practicability for heavy transport.

Besides these travellers, James Sinclair, son of a Scottish father in the service of the Hudson's Bay Company and a partly Cree mother, a graduate of Edinburgh University, and a man of many-sided enterprise, had in 1841 successfully led a train of emigrants through a pass from the Saskatchewan to the lower Columbia. When Palliser met Sinclair in 1848 on his Missouri hunting-trip, he admired and respected him, and discussed with him possible routes through the mountains. Sir George Simpson had written of Sinclair's party of 1841: 'The party of Red River settlers, proceeding to the Columbia, who followed us, were however more fortunate, as they fell in with some Indians who conducted them through a still more Southerly pass than we pursued, not only shorter but better in every respect, so that even with families, and encumbered with baggage as they were, they effected the passage of the Mountains with infinitely less labour, & in a shorter time than we accomplished it.'

Even so, Sinclair himself was apparently not satisfied that it was the best pass; in 1848 he had told Palliser that he planned to try another pass, which he described to the young Irish sportsman. In 1854 Sinclair succeeded in taking a second train of emigrants through the mountains, with some 250 head of cattle. The 100 emigrants and most of the cattle arrived safely, without suffering any serious privation, according to Sir George, nor getting involved in any difficulty with the Indians. Clearly the pass through which he took 250 cattle was worth considering as a regular overland route. But which was it? Sinclair had been shot in 1856 when some Indians attacked the American post at the Cascades on the Columbia where he happened to be. He went out to calm the Indians, to whom he was well known, but was shot before they recognized him. Sinclair was dead, but Palliser meant to find his pass and examine and record it carefully. This task he reserved to himself.

Some of the emigrants Sinclair had led through the mountains decided, after his death, to go back to the Red River; they did not like the Americans' bustling way of life. This group the expedition had met the year before at Fort Ellice, and Palliser had interviewed them about passes through the mountains. They told him they had come back by the North Kootenay Pass, under the guidance of a Red River half-breed named Whitford. It had taken the party of seven men, three women, and several children nine days to get through the mountains; they had run out of food and had been forced to kill one of their horses. Luckily they had not encountered any Blackfoot and when they reached the North Saskatchewan the Indians there had treated them very kindly. The journey from the Columbia to Fort Ellice had taken them, altogether, three and a half months. Palliser says nothing about their comments on the pass they had travelled through on their westward journey with Sinclair in 1854, but the story of their return journey must have confirmed his idea that the pass Sinclair had described to him, presumably his 1854 route, was the most promising route to examine; the difficulty was that none of the local men, not even the so-called guides nor even the knowledgeable Gabriel Dumont whose services Hector had enlisted at Lake St. Ann's during the winter, seemed to have any idea where it lay. Only one of the other men, old Paul Cahen (or Cadien or Cayenne) claimed to know anything about the mountains off the beaten track, and even he knew remarkably little, as it turned out. One of the men, James Richards, had travelled with Sir George's party in 1841; later on, that year, he pointed out to Hector the entrance to Simpson's Pass, but for the most part the information the 'guides' could give was so vague that it was of hardly any use.

Palliser knew that the entrance to the pass he planned to try was up a tributary of the Bow River. Sinclair had described it to him; he hoped to find it in spite of the guides' vagueness. He gave the tributary the name it still bears, the Kananaskis, in memory of an Indian who, according to local legend, made a most wonderful recovery there after a blow of an axe which had stunned but had failed to kill him. That this was the right entrance to the pass was later confirmed by Blakiston, who reported that he had seen on the banks of the Kananaskis the remains of the carts that Sinclair's second emigrant train had abandoned when they could not drag them any farther into the mountains.

Palliser set off from Old Bow Fort on August 18. He forded the Bow River above the Kananaskis and started up its lovely valley. They could see an opening in the mountains and headed for it through woods of white fir and fine poplar, with dense undergrowth. At length they came on an old track, much encumbered by masses of fallen timber lying in all directions, the result of fires in former years. A few skeleton tents—that is to say, poles arranged in the shape of an Indian wigwam—told them that they were following a hunting track made by the Indians, evidently a very long time ago. Of the emigrants' route with their 250 cattle they appear to have seen no sign. They crossed the Kananaskis River, getting a magnificent view of its valley, hemmed in on either side by an unbroken wall of mountains, the sides of which for 1,000 feet were richly clad with pines.

They could have brought the carts to the place where they

camped the first night without great difficulty, if it had not been for the density of the woods and the obstructions caused by the fallen timber, obstructions of which all travellers complained; these were to give them even more serious trouble later on.

> *The obstacle which a burnt forest presents to the traveller is of all others the most arduous; sometimes we were in a network of trees, lying at all angles the one to the other, and requiring no small amount of skill to choose which should be removed first. It was extraordinary to observe the great care taken by our horses in extricating their feet and legs from dangerous places. The poor brutes seemed to be very expert at this kind of work, and even when caught they would evince the utmost patience, and free themselves as gently as possible.*

After working hard with their axes almost all day, clearing the fallen timber, the party was exhausted. They saw mountain trees burnt in places so precipitous that no human hand could ever have reached them, which convinced them that lightning started fires in the mountains.

This was grizzly bear country. They passed several bears' dens, and one bear had taken up lodgings within twenty feet of their camp-fire. Standing on their hind legs, the bears would strip the bark off the trees to a height of nine or ten feet, to get the turpentine that oozed out. Unlike the black bears, they were never known to climb trees.

It was becoming increasingly difficult to feed the horses, so they stopped to let them graze when they came to a patch of prairie which offered good pasture. They must have wondered how Sinclair had managed with the emigrants' cattle. At the western extremity of a second stretch of sward, the wild, beautiful Kananaskis River leapt over a ledge of rock from a height of twenty feet and rushed on its way through a dense forest of pines. Today that falling water generates hydro-electric power for Calgary.

Their Stoney hunter and old Paul had each killed a

black-tailed deer, and now the Indian pointed out two wapiti. Palliser managed to kill them both; as they were not likely to get any more game, they stopped thankfully to cut up and dry the meat.

They were now very near the height of land and their observations showed that they were still well within British territory. Higher up the valley was the glacier that is the source of the Kananaskis River. This glacier sends down the mountain sides hundreds of small streams, which, under the sun's rays, had the appearance of silver threads. They fancied that the mountain goats higher up, which looked like small white spots in slow motion, eyed them as intruders. They caught some splendid trout, one kind with white flesh, and another, of a far superior flavour, with bright salmon-coloured flesh. The river here widened into a lake, the Lower Kananaskis Lake, which they crossed. A little farther on they came on a second magnificent lake, the Upper Kananaskis Lake, hemmed in by mountains and studded with islets, very thickly wooded. Wapiti seemed to prefer these islands to the denser forests of the mainland, and the Kootenay Indians used to come over the height of land to hunt them. This lake was the scene of a maddening contretemps: 'While going round the edge of this sheet of water, where the fallen timber greatly embarrassed us, one of our horses, strangely enough, adopted the other alternative of swimming across the lake. This effort of intelligence caused us serious misfortune and dismay, as his pack contained our only luxuries, our tea, our sugar, and our bedding.'

The broken, rocky country beyond the lake, with great blocks of limestone heaped up in artificial-looking masses, was difficult for horses, but, on the whole, apart from fallen timber, the route had so far been easy; there had been only an inconsiderable rise from Bow River to the foot of the lofty cone-shaped mountain, the more northerly of a pair of conspicuous mountains that flanked the height of land they were to cross.

Next morning they climbed for two and a half hours to the

edge of the pine woods. After taking observations they climbed on, finding the ascent surprisingly easy. They stopped at a spring to rest the horses, and then, in a few more minutes, gained the height of land. Here they camped at the summit of the pass, about half an acre in area, where there was some tolerable grass for the horses and a small lake. From this lake, Palliser wrote, flowed the first waters they had seen which descended to the Pacific Ocean. His statement is a little puzzling, as the summit lake was found by the Alberta–British Columbia Boundary Commission to be on the Saskatchewan River side of the divide. In any case they filled their tea-kettle with waters flowing to the Columbia, while their scanty supper of tough elk meat was boiling in Saskatchewan water. On the divide they were above the tree-line and they passed a chill and uncomfortable night, with glaciers nearby on either side of the pass and misty clouds wrapping the mountain summits—and very little wood for their camp-fire. There were few plants, and the only animal they saw was the *siffleur* (marmot), whose shrill whistle they heard for the first time by their camp that night. It was about the size of the common badger of the plains and lived in crevices in the rock. It was excellent eating when fat and, they were told, its skin served to make robes for the 'Sposshewass' (Shuswap) Indians—the only clothing they had.

From their little tea-kettle lake, they began the descent of the western slope of the Rockies. The first 300 feet was difficult for the horses, a steep slope covered with loose shingle, but soon the river (which the men called Palliser's River—its name to this day) broadened out and the slope became less steep.

They noted a remarkable change in the vegetation. On this western side of the mountains, watered by rains brought by winds from the Pacific Ocean, tree and plant growth was very luxuriant. They found shrubs they had not seen before, including many that bore berries.

The river grew wider and wider, but was still shallow. The valley was of great breadth, but, even so, fallen timber was still a nuisance, forcing them to cross and recross the river, or ride along its bed as the only clear track. Farther on, the mountains closed in on the river, which raced through a gorge. When they made a considerable ascent to cut off a bend, they were almost stopped by fallen trees, piled five or six feet high, and laced together by a dense growth of young pines that crowded themselves above the fallen wood. Bright moonlight helped them in hewing their road through, but it was nearly midnight before they could find water and some scanty herbage for their jaded horses. They sent axe-men ahead next morning to cut a road for the horses through the tangle of wind-felled trees.

As they travelled they made regular observations to determine their position. They noted the character of the rocks and soil. They feasted on berries, especially raspberries and blueberries, which were much bigger on this side of the mountains and, when dried, were an excellent addition to their tough wapiti meat. They came on recently deserted Kootenay tents, formed of flat boughs of 'cyprée and prushe' (cedar and hemlock) and covered with thick bark. At last they reached the main stream of the Kootenay River. The measurements they had made with their aneroid barometers showed that the pass they had come over was 5,800 feet above sea level at the highest point, 1,700 feet above Old Bow Fort, and 2,150 feet above the Kootenay River. The estimate was too low by some 1,600 feet, as the altitude of the pass is 7,439 feet. Palliser realized that the aneroid barometer they had had to use, as a result of the accident to the mountain barometers, was not too reliable, but even so, it is a big discrepancy. It was clear that the pass was not an easy one; it seemed doubtful whether, after all, it was really the pass that Sinclair had meant.

Whether it was Sinclair's pass or not, they had crossed the mountains with their horses. They knew that the Columbia lay a short distance off but had neither enough time nor provisions to hack their way through the fallen timber to get to it. Ravines, rocks, and gullies also gave them trouble. At one point precipitous mountains on both sides of the Kootenay forced them to make a raft to cross the river, with the horses swimming behind. Palliser and the Stoney guide went up a mountain to get a view of the Columbia, while Sullivan and the men made camp very near the first Columbia Lake which is within a mile or two of the Kootenay River. A violent storm came on, and Palliser and the guide were out all night without protection. Even in camp, the rest of the party were soaked to the skin. To complete their bad luck here, another accident deprived them of all further use of even the aneroid barometer.

A Kootenay Indian, the first human being they had seen on the west side of the mountains, now appeared. Though not one of them could speak a word of his extraordinary, chuckling language, he nevertheless succeeded in informing them that he had seen Lieutenant Blakiston's party; that they had passed five days previous; that no traders had come to the Kootenay Fort yet; that the Colvile Indians had plundered them of their goods; and a wonderful amount of news besides, all by means of certain signs intelligible enough to their Indians and half-breeds.

The Indian went back to his camp to tell his people of their arrival. The explorers soon descried in the distance about twenty riders coming at full speed towards them. When they met them they were struck with the miserable appearance of the members of this tribe; most of them were entirely naked, except for a cloth round the middle; they had neither bridles nor saddles, but guided their horses by a long hide fastened round the lower jaw. At the Indians' encampment, their misery was even more conspicuous; they were living on the berries that are so abundant on the Tobacco Plains and were possessed of absolutely no utensils for cooking, though they had numerous plates and dishes of basket-work, which they made from the roots of the pine. In contrast with their great poverty in many things, they were very rich in horses: the owners of the eleven tents had at least 500, including some very fine animals. They also had a few cattle.

Palliser tried to get a guide to take him to Fort Colvile (the Hudson's Bay Company post in the Columbia Valley some distance south of the border), there to leave messages, in accordance with his recent instructions, for Captain (later Colonel) Hawkins, R.E., who was in charge of the British section of the joint United States–British Boundary Commission, which had just started to work its way eastward towards the crest of the Rockies from the Gulf of Georgia, surveying and marking the section of the International Boundary laid down by the Oregon Treaty of 1846. It was only later that Palliser discovered that the Kootenay had sent a war-party against the Indians at Fort Colvile and stolen their horses. They could not be persuaded to make the trip with Palliser, but would not tell him why, because they knew the missionaries would disapprove of their raid.

Palliser traded tired-out horses and trade goods for fresh horses; among these were horses the Kootenay had stolen from the Colvile Indians, though he did not know it. When he did find out he was glad that he had not succeeded in riding into Fort Colvile on horses stolen from the Indians there.

Once it was clear they could not get on to Colvile, they started back across the mountains on September 1, making for an opening they had noticed in the hills that skirted the river. After desperate climbing and two days' very hard work in the burnt woods, they found that the mountains presented one unbroken wall hemming in the Tobacco Plains. They were compelled to retire. Being now in the centre of a vast system of mountains, where not a single animal nor even a track was to be seen, they decided to try the North Kootenay Pass, in approaching which they would again pass by the Kootenay camp. There they hoped to be able to exchange a horse for one of the Kootenay's cattle. For some days they had had very little to eat and that little mostly berries, which made most of them sick. When they got to the Kootenay camp, the old chief, though reluctantly, gave them a two-year-old ox in trade. With this for food they set off again down the Kootenay, but neither the half-breed nor the Indian hunters in the party would eat the beef. A young Indian they had met tried it, but spat it out again in disgust.

They crossed the Elk River and began a steep and bad ascent. Wigwam River, a tributary of Elk River, led them up into the mountains. On the height of land they stopped to contemplate the sea of peaks all round them. Palliser guessed that they were 6,000 feet above sea level; as the barometer was broken, he realized that this could not be an accurate estimate. (It was 750 feet too low.) Starting downhill on the eastern flank of the Rockies, they stopped for dinner at the first spring they reached, once more upon waters that flowed into the Saskatchewan. They had a second, flanking range to cross, where they nearly lost the track in a sudden snow-storm, but at last they got over the difficult mountain heights and, leaving wind and snow behind, came back into shelter and fine, warm weather in the beautiful foothill country.

They were now out of the mountains and also out of provisions. Palliser missed a moose that they started, but he managed to kill a deer; the Indian guide killed a swan, and old Paul made a fine catch of mottled trout. They were no longer hungry when they came in sight of Windigo—Cannibal—Mountain. They killed two grizzlies, but two other bears escaped, after springing at the Indian's horse and tearing some of the hair out of its tail. As they travelled on, food supplies began to get short again; game once more grew scarce, but at last, after they crossed the Bow River, they came on buffalo. They killed three, which gave them meat for the whole way on to Edmonton. Their tea and sugar had gone long before.

Their last adventure was an encounter with some Blackfoot near their old Cache Camp. At sight of two tents, Palliser kept the party under cover, only letting old Paul, who was himself half Blackfoot, go to visit them. Paul found that they were once more at war with the Cree and Stoneys and had killed his brother-in-law. Paul himself had great difficulty in getting away from them. As a precaution they drove the horses in and guarded them closely all night. Four days later, without further excitement, they reached Fort Edmonton, which was to be their base for the second winter.

CHAPTER THIRTEEN

New Passes through the Rockies: The Kicking Horse

The other members of the expedition had meanwhile set off into the mountains ahead of Palliser, while the Captain was still on his side trip to the boundary. With a 300-mile mountain barrier to explore, Palliser had divided up the party so that, among them, its members could cover a wider range of possibilities. Palliser had instructed Hector to follow whatever route seemed to him most interesting from a geological point of view, and Bourgeau, similarly, whatever route seemed to him most interesting from a botanical point of view. They started off together with Blakiston for the mountains, which were now in constant view. The undulations of the prairie became higher and more definite till they formed a broken range of hills. Here they camped to let the hunters make a final onslaught on the buffalo. They stocked up with meat but had to travel for two days before they found poplar trees big enough to make poles for drying-stages on which it could be exposed to the clear, powerful sun.

Hector wrote enthusiastically of the scenery, of a magnificent plateau, glowing with a rich profusion of brightly coloured flowering plants. He found the sight of snow on mountains, with the foreground sharply lined by projecting ledges of rock, exhilarating after the dreary monotony of the arid plains. As the carts travelled slowly on, Hector made side trips into tributary valleys and up mountain sides, mapping and geologizing as he went. It was very difficult to get the carts over the Deadman's River (today's Ghost River) even at the shallow rapid where it joins Bow River. They met some Stoney Indians, who were very well disposed towards them and went along with them, giving them much welcome help on an increasingly bad route. The valley was growing narrow and rocky; the carts, upsetting repeatedly, slowed them up. Already the scenery had assumed quite an alpine character.

When they got to the site of Old Bow Fort, they stopped to reorganize their mode of travelling; from here into the mountains the carts would be useless. Leaving horses and supplies for Palliser with old Paul, Hector and Bourgeau set off together up the valley of the Bow River, both choosing this route because it allowed them to enter the mountains at once, without travelling further in open country that yielded little of interest from either the geological or the botanical point of view. Hector was delighted to find, at last, a profusion of cliffs and gorges whose rocks he could study, after his frustrating experience on the plains with their deep soil. Bourgeau, son of the high Alps, was blissfully happy now that he was back among mountains.

Hector's Stoney Indian friend, who had promised the previous winter to act as his guide in the mountains, turned up just in time to join the party. His name meant 'the one with the thumb like a blunt arrow'. Hector could not pronounce it, so he called him Nimrod, as he was known to be one of the best hunters in the tribe. Peter Erasmus was Hector's special protégé; the son of a Dane and an Indian woman, he had been an interpreter at a Wesleyan mission. Hector trained him to use the instruments. Sutherland and Brown came from Red River. They had eight horses altogether, three to carry the instruments, bedding, ammunition, and tobacco. Hector had been assured that they would find plenty of game, so they carried no provisions except tea and a few pounds of grease.

Up to the point at which they passed the track to the ford over the Bow leading to the Kananaskis Pass, their trail passed through fine, open woods of young pine, over high, level terraces. Then the valley narrowed; the horses with their tender feet had great difficulty in crossing the heaps of loose, rounded stones that had been swept down by the torrents. They plunged into a labyrinth of dense forest, struggling on over fallen timber, till they had to climb a rocky spur of mountain. From the top they looked up a wide valley, full of lakes—the Lacs des Arcs, or Bow Lakes. Where they stood they were hemmed in by precipices several thousand feet in height, but seemed to look right through the range of mountains into comparatively open country.

Hector and Bourgeau went exploring above the timberline, on Grotto Mountain, Bourgeau finding plenty of alpine plants that made him think of home. They followed up the bed of a torrent to where the stream began with a trickling fall several hundred feet in height, splashing into a clear pool with green mossy banks. In this they performed their morning ablutions. They found a huge cave, which made Hector think of Robinson Crusoe. It had a high, arched roof and narrow mouth. It had its old goat, too, but this one had long been dead. The floor was battered quite hard by the hooves of sheep and goats.

Bourgeau decided to linger in this neighbourhood (near modern Banff), but Hector pressed on, getting more and more excited and delighted by his geological finds. There were fossils which helped him to judge the age of the rocks. There were interesting formations, which he could easily study, such was the baldness of the upper part of the mountains. Hector kept detailed notes about each mountain and valley, making sketches and maps as he went along. When they had to stay in camp for a day, to let Nimrod go hunting to restock them with provisions, Hector went off to study a range to the east. Where he could, he measured the height of the mountains: The Mountain-where-the-water-falls (Cascade Mountain) was nearly vertical. He took a base line on a little prairie at its foot, from which the summit could be seen. This proved to be 4,521 sheer feet above the prairie.

Here an old Stoney Indian, a former guide to Mr. Rundle,

the missionary, came to visit them. He had travelled by a route running south of The Devil's Head, a craggy knob in sight of which they had camped before reaching Old Bow Fort, and along Lake Minnewanka. They guessed—rightly—that this was the route Sir George Simpson had used in 1841.

Nimrod went hunting and got two mountain sheep. This wild mutton they came to consider the finest food they could get. Nimrod reported that the trail ahead was so bad that the men would have to go on to clear it out. This gave Hector a chance to climb Cascade Mountain. He had to work round to the north face; while he was resting, a humming-bird (of all unlikely creatures among the alpine plants!), blown by a strong western gale, flew against his face. Soon after, he started a large band of wild sheep from a corrie. As long as they stood still and looked at him, he could not make them out, they matched the grey rocks so well. It was startling when they turned to run away and suddenly became very conspicuous; every part of their bodies, seen from behind, was pure white. Just as suddenly, they seemed to vanish, when their inquisitive habits made them wheel in a mass to have another look.

In the corrie, too, there were mountain marmots whistling to each other in a very loud, shrill note. Hector also heard the squeaking note of the little pika or tailless hare. He thought it one of the most comical animals he had seen: 'It is about the size of a small rat, but made exactly like any other rabbit, excepting that it has round open ears. It sits up on its hind legs and calls its note in the most impudent fashion faster and faster as you approach, but always ready to pop out of sight so quickly that you can hardly shoot them, at least with a flint gun.'

He came down into the valley to the north, sliding over the tops of the trees of a diminutive forest. Though they were only one or two feet high, their long branches spread like a thatch over the slope.

Next day the party started off again. To the south of a mountain that Hector named after Bourgeau lay the pass by which Sir George Simpson, on his journey round the world in

1841, had crossed the main range. By the white water swirling down tributaries from the south they could tell that the mountain streams were all in flood. Their old Stoney friend, who was now travelling with them, told them that to get through Simpson's Pass they would have to travel for half a day in the bed of the stream (Healy Creek) between perpendicular walls of rocks. The floods made this impossible, so, instead of attempting Simpson's Pass, they went on up the Bow River. Here its valley widens again to magnificent proportions, with the vertical walls of the Sawback Range, as Hector named it, along its eastern edge. The mountains to the west are quite different; with precipices like battlements and blocks of rock on top, Hector thought they looked like towers and bastions. Apparently standing in the middle of the valley was a very remarkable mountain, exactly like a gigantic castle. Hector called it Castle Mountain. (It has been renamed Mount Eisenhower, in honour of a presidential visit.) A quagmire in the bottom of the valley taxed their horses' strength, but it was a choice between wading through the bog in the valley and cutting a road through the fallen timber on the mountain side. In spite of the difficulties, they travelled seventeen miles before camping.

The heat was now intense in the middle of the day— greater than it had been on the plains. At night it was correspondingly cold, and each morning the tops of the mountains were wrapped in fog. They now began to use the little leather wigwam that Hector had acquired, by trade, from the Stoneys. Peter Erasmus got lost while out hunting and spent a chilly night in the mountains without even a coat.

Nimrod hurt himself while he was tracking a moose he had wounded. He fell on the knife in his girdle, breaking it and injuring his back. He managed to follow the moose another four miles and signalled to the doctor, who joined him:

> . . . *a wary turn through the woods for half a mile brought us to the game, and advancing against the wind without disturb-*

ing a branch we got within 40 yards of him, standing with his long nose straight out, and his antlers laid back on his flanks. I gave him the benefit of both my rifle barrels, which was the first notice he had of our proximity. After that he only bounded about 70 yards before he fell. When we approached him, however, he showed fight, and got up again, but it would not do, as he was fast going.

He was a fine bull, over six feet tall at the shoulder.

While the others sliced and smoked the moose meat, Hector and Sutherland climbed Castle Mountain to within 2,000 feet of the summit. This cost them twelve hours' hard walking, for they had to make their way round to the north face.

Now they had to cross the Bow River to the entrance of Vermilion Pass. Here the river was only sixty yards wide, but very rapid, taking their horses above the girth even on the oblique ford they had discovered, though the water was not especially high. They did not see the little tributary of the Bow (which the Banff-Windermere highway follows today) as it entered the Bow below the ford. Instead of following its gently sloping valley, they had a tough climb up the face of a 150-foot terrace of loose shingle. When they found the wide valley of Little Vermilion (Altrude) Creek, they found that its bottom was rather soft, so they kept up on the side of the hill; they actually had to come downhill to the height of land, which took Hector by surprise, it was so near the Bow River and so low. Hector checked its altitude by repeated observations with the aneroid barometer and sympiesometer. He reckoned it to be 540 feet above the Bow River and about 5,000 feet above sea level, an estimate not far from its actual altitude of 5,376 feet.

The first water they saw flowing to the Pacific was a muddy stream that turns off to the west about 300 yards from the lake from which the Little Vermilion flows to the east to join the Bow and Saskatchewan. Hector named a large central mass of snow-capped mountains to the south-east Mount Ball, after

John Ball, Palliser's friend, the Under-Secretary of State for the Colonies in 1857, whose influence had been decisive in persuading the government to finance the expedition and who was himself a notable mountaineer.

Now, on a night that ended with a heavy, soaking mist, it was Nimrod's turn to spend a night out. He had killed a moose too far away to get the meat back to camp; he slept beside it and ate all he could of it. When he got back, they went on down the valley of the Vermilion River on the western slope of the mountains, crossing Vermilion Plain, which was completely covered with yellow ochre. This the Kootenay Indians used to make the brilliant war-paint they traded to the Plains Indians.

The going became easier, as there had been several fires which had burnt off even the fallen timber. Fireweed (willow-herb) grew everywhere among the burnt woods, in sheets of brilliant pink flowers and fluffy silver seed-pods. They found plenty of raspberries and other small fruit too, but it was not all smooth going. After a vain search for an easy road, they got involved in a forest of cedar which was almost impassable. Hector wrote gloomily: 'Night overtook us, so that we had to camp in a little swampy "opening", tying up several of our horses, as they might be inclined to start off in the night to seek for food. During the night we had a thunder storm and heavy rain.'

At daybreak they went down to the river again. This seemed a better bet than blind attempts to find an easy trail. As every bush and tree was loaded with moisture, it soon did not matter much whether they went into the river or not, so that they frequently saved a difficult turn by accepting a ducking. The river led them through a gorge with white slate banks. Nimrod advised the men to take away some of this soft white slate; that night they were all busy manufacturing pipes from it.

Nimrod set off early the next morning to hunt. He soon came back so frightened that he was as white as it is possible for a Red Indian to be. Chasing a deer, he had suddenly come on a panther, but, further than saying that he had wounded the animal, he would tell them nothing. Panthers were not very common in the mountains; seeing them so seldom, the Indians were much more afraid of them than they were of grizzly bears, although there was no comparison between the ferocity of the two animals. The Indians generally killed a few every year, on the Red Deer River or along the Bow River, and in spring the Blackfoot Indians sometimes ran them with horses, as they ran buffalo out on the plains. Meeting one alone and unexpectedly in the woods was a different matter. Poor Nimrod had to endure some chaffing about his inglorious encounter with the panther.

The woods had now become so thick that they could see nothing; Hector sent Peter Erasmus and Nimrod off to spy out the land ahead. It was still soaking wet weather, so they stripped to their shirts to travel light and were gone all day. They came back with great accounts of the size of the timber where they had been; they had found a faint trail on the other side of the Kootenay River, leading up the valley. The whole party crossed the river next day and followed its valley up-river, to the north-west, as Hector knew Palliser was exploring to the south. Hector noted sadly that the mountains (Brisco's Range) on the far side of the valley, though not very high, ran in an unbroken wall barring the way to the west.

At camping time Nimrod had another scare about panthers. One was crying near by; it sounded exactly like a baby. Nimrod said it was the call panthers gave when they came on the tracks of men or horses. He was convinced that it might come into the camp at night and slept with his 'dagare', or big Indian knife, close to his hand.

The constant moisture on the western slope of the mountain, they now found, had completely rotted their stock of dried moose meat. This was serious, as there were now scarcely any signs of game, though they saw kingfishers, terns, curlew, and avocets. They began to see new plants, too, plants they did not know, and very fine trees.

They came on two sizeable lakes, one with waves splashing

on a shore of pure white sand. It looked so fresh and appealing that they went in for a swim, only to find that a few yards from the shore there was a muddy bottom that was almost unfathomable.

The Kootenay rises from these lakes; without any break in the continuity of the valley, the waters of the Beaverfoot River flow in the opposite direction, to the north-west. Hector rightly judged that the Beaverfoot was a tributary of the Columbia, in spite of the guides' insistence that it flowed into the Saskatchewan. He was hoping to find some transverse valley by which to reach the Columbia proper and was much disappointed when he found that the Kootenay-Beaverfoot valley ran on continuously. He did not realize that a little farther west, beyond Brisco's Range, the valley of the main stream of the Columbia itself ran on continuously with a lower part of the valley of the Kootenay, in the great Rocky Mountain Trench. It was clear that a passable road could easily be built through the Rockies from the plains to the Kootenay, along the route they had followed; the only real difficulty had been fallen timber, which could be cleared. It looked as if it was going to be much more difficult to find a possible route from the Kootenay on westward to the Pacific.

Travelling grew worse and worse and they grew hungrier and hungrier. They tried to catch some trout and failed; their only tackle was some large wooden hooks and twine. The horses had nothing to eat either, as there was no grass except in soft places where it was too boggy for them to feed. They got involved in fallen timber again, which meant constant leaping and scrambling, which cut the horses' legs badly and which, as Hector mildly put it, tried their patience and tempers a good deal. Finally, after several days of this, one of the pack-horses, like Palliser's intelligent animal, to escape the fallen timber, plunged into the stream, luckily where it formed an eddy. Hector described the historic incident:

> . . . *the banks were so steep that we had great difficulty in getting him out. In attempting to recatch my own horse, which*

had strayed off while we were engaged with the one in the water, he kicked me in the chest, but I had luckily got close to him before he struck out, so that I did not get the full force of the blow. However, it knocked me down and rendered me senseless for some time. This was unfortunate, as we had seen no tracks of game in the neighbourhood, and were now without food; but I was so hurt that we could not proceed further that day at least. My men covered me up under a tree, and I sent them all off to try and raise something to eat. Peter I sent up the mountain in the angle of the valley, to take bearings, and to see what the mountains were like to the west.

Elsewhere it is related that Hector's men, having come to the melancholy conclusion that he was dead, dug a grave for him. He regained consciousness within a minute of being buried alive in it. Before he recovered his speech, he just managed to wink an eye to show that he was alive.

Badly hurt as he was, Hector was still concerned about observations and about a possible route to the west. He did not forget to note the height of the mountain (though Peter Erasmus failed to get to the top) or to describe the rocks and the way in which they were arranged. The men came back empty-handed. Nimrod had seen wapiti tracks, but had found no game. They saw flocks of geese flying south that evening, but they were out of range.

Next day Hector began to feel better. He took a meridian altitude to find the latitude, while the men were off hunting. One of them shot one of a large flock of goats, but it fell over a precipice, so that they got none of the meat. Nimrod went a long way after the deer, but ran a sharp spike through his foot and came back lame after missing a fine wapiti buck. Even Hector admitted that they were now in a bad way. He produced a private cache of about five pounds of pemmican, just enough for one meal for them all. He determined to make it last for three days, which should, he hoped, from the look of the stream he meant to go up, give them time to get back to the east side of the mountains, where they should find game.

On the last day of August they started off. The motion on horseback gave Hector great pain, but they managed to get along slowly till noon. Nimrod had notched trees the day before to mark the best route, some way from the river, which the men had named Kicking Horse River. In spite of the pain, Hector still managed to record the kind of rocks they passed and their formation. They followed up the course of the river along which only twenty-seven years later the Canadian Pacific Railway was to be built. Famished, they camped in a magnificent canyon. They started very early next day, as they had nothing left to eat at all. Nimrod, hampered by fallen timber and his lame foot, got a long shot at a wapiti but missed. The valley ended suddenly in a steep, upward, pine-covered slope; they found large blueberries and loitered a good deal to eat them.

After a considerable climb they had to cross the river, which was boiling and leaping through a narrow channel of pink quartzose rock. They crossed with great difficulty and then had to clamber over moss-covered rocks, their horses often sliding and falling.

> *One, an old grey, that was always more clumsy than the others, lost his balance in passing along a ledge, which overhung a precipitous slope about 150 feet in height, and down he went, luckily catching sometimes on the trees; at last he came to a temporary pause by falling right on his back, the pack acting as a fender; however, in his endeavours to get up he started down hill again, and at last slid on a dead tree that stuck out at right angles to the slope, balancing himself with his legs dangling on either side of the trunk of the tree in a most comical manner. It was only by making a round of a mile that we succeeded in getting him back, all battered and bruised, to the rest of the horses.*

They travelled eight hours before they camped, when at long last they reached a stream flowing to the east; they were back on the Saskatchewan slope of the mountains, leaving behind the Kicking Horse River and the glacier from which it flowed. They camped in a beautiful spot beside a lake, with excellent pasture for the horses—poor starving brutes. Hector killed one grouse. They were glad to boil it up with some ends of candles and odd pieces of grease, to make something like a supper for the five of them after a very hard day's work. They had climbed to a great height and, in their famished state, felt the sharp cold that night severely.

By now Hector had nearly recovered from his accident, so he set off next day at daylight with Nimrod to hunt. They came on a large stream flowing from a great glacier at the head of a valley to the west; they followed it down to a river, which Nimrod recognized at once as their old friend the Bow. They had managed to cross the Rocky Mountains twice, by two different passes, both well within British territory.

Nimrod set off again to hunt and this time he was lucky. They heard most furious firing in a wood and Nimrod returned in a high state of glee; he had shot a moose, thereby saving the poor old grey with the bruised countenance, that had fallen over the cliff: Hector had promised to kill him if they got no game by evening. Hector had not wanted to kill a horse, as experienced travellers had warned him that the flesh of a horse so badly out of condition merely created a craving for more, without giving strength or vigour to the hunters. Soon, too, few horses would be left to carry the necessaries for the party, who would then undergo great sufferings, and might even perish, as had some American expeditions. As it was, they had not realized till they got the meat of the lean moose how depressed and weak they were; desperation had kept them going.

Next morning, Hector wrote:

> . . . *as we were still cooking the tit-bits of the moose, a Stoney Indian suddenly popped on our camp, having smelt our fire a long way off. He said there was a camp of eight tents six miles farther west, so slinging our moose meat on the horses we set off to join them. It was snowing nearly the whole day,*

this being the first of the season ... Immediately on our arrival at the camp, which was in a pretty secluded spot, by the side of a mossy lake, the women took the whole management of our affairs,–unpacked the horses, put up the tent, lined it beautifully with pine foliage, lighted a fire, and cut wood into most conveniently sized billets, and piled them up ready to hand. They then set about cooking all sorts of Indian delicacies,–moose nose and entrails, boiled blood and roast kidneys, etc.

The Indians had themselves arrived, starving, two days earlier, but had killed six moose in two days. It was good moose country, well wooded, with muskegs in which grew a special kind of willow.

The Indians in hunting are very observant of the cropping of the willow tops, and there was something quite exciting in the significant gleam of Nimrod's eye as he pointed out where the willow tops were yet wet with the saliva of the animal, or when, in walking rapidly through the woods, he would stop suddenly and pick up a morsel of half chewed leaf which it had dropped, and when he found that it had stopped to take several bites from one bush, then he pulled off his gun cover and looked to his priming.

The next day Hector had another adventure to record:

During the night the great pine tree by which our tent was pitched caught, from a roaring fire we had lighted against its root, and neglected to put out when we turned into our blankets, trusting to its being green. But the fire caught the dry grey lichens which drooped in festoons from the branches, and which, being highly charged with turpentine, gave out a magnificent blaze, the roar of which luckily wakened me up, and, without waiting to see how much was burning of the forest, I caught our powder and my trowsers and bolted right into the swamp. It did not communicate with the other trees,

*however, but after brilliantly illuminating the forest for half
an hour, and having consumed the foliage and resinous bark,
it died out, leaving the charred trunk and branches as sturdy
as ever. The glare of light which this fire threw on the dark
forest and swarthy faces of the Indians, who gathered round
to watch its progress, was very striking.*

The following morning, a Sunday, they were awakened at
an early hour by the hymns of their Stoney friends, who, every
morning and evening, joined in worship, and on Sunday did
so several times. None of them would go hunting on the holy
day.

When Monday came the Indian women sliced and dried
the meat for Hector's party. It was very lean, and no fat or
grease was to be had in trade from the Indians; this was a bad
look-out, as it was nearly as hard to live on the dried meat of
a lean animal alone, without grease, as it was to starve
altogether. Hector gave the women some presents for their
pains—principally needles and thread, a few buttons, fire
steel, and flints.

He got rid of their old friend, the bruised grey horse, and
by giving the Indians a little 'to boot' got a very good animal
in exchange. Another addition to the party was an orphan boy
who wished to join some friends at a camp on the North
Saskatchewan.

Hector had determined to try to make his way to the
North Saskatchewan by travelling up the Bow River to its
source, where, he was told, they would see great valleys filled
with ice and would then come on the North Saskatchewan.
The Indians warned them that they would find no game
except white goats, which at that season were not fit to eat.
Hector, nothing daunted by the party's recent near-starva-
tion, trusted that his store of dried meat would last until they
reached the North Saskatchewan, where there should be
plenty of mountain sheep; he decided to risk it.

They struck through the woods to the Bow River, but were
held up for some hours by a violent snow-storm. The Bow,

where they came upon it, was a very small but rapid stream. They passed Goat Mountain (Waputik) and Hector Lake (so called later by Dawson), with a glacier reaching nearly to the water. All afternoon it was bitterly cold; the night was clear, with a sharp frost. They made a regular winter encampment with pine foliage under them.

Next day they travelled fast, as they were so high up that the timber was small and open. The Stoney boy shot several trout with his arrows and taught Hector how to catch the tree-grouse with a snare. 'He took a small piece of sinew twine and made a nooze, which he fastened on a slender pole, and advancing slowly to the bird gently passed the nooze over its head, and pulled it off the tree. The grouse did not seem frightened in the least, but sat gravely looking at him all the time, and actually when the nooze was close dodged its head in it.'

They passed Bow Lake, fed from the Wapta Icefield, and reached the height of land between the Bow River and the North Saskatchewan. Its summit was much higher than the summit of either the Vermilion or the Kicking Horse Pass. They had a splendid view down the Mistaya Valley, the mountains on each side forming a vista at least twenty-five miles long. They kept to the top of the valley for a mile or so and then took a breakneck trail through the woods to the bottom. They followed the river down to a beautiful lake, Mistaya Lake, with its shores clothed with deep-green pines, and a spout-like glacier reaching down to its west shore, a perfect ice cascade. Here they camped.

Every now and then they saw a huge mountain to the east; Hector called it Mount Murchison after his patron, the great geologist and president of the Royal Geographical Society. The Indians said it was the highest peak they knew of, and Hector's measurements indicated that it was thirteen or fourteen thousand feet high, though he realized that this was a rather rough estimate. The mountain is actually 11,300 feet high. Hector thought that the mountains were mostly not more than eleven or twelve thousand feet high, but it was difficult to measure them, especially as his aneroid barometer stopped working at a height considerably lower than the mountains they were examining.

For some distance farther they followed the left bank of the Mistaya River—which Hector called the Little Fork of the North Saskatchewan—but at last struck off through dense woods to the North Saskatchewan itself. Even so near its source, this was a large river, deep and swift, 150 yards wide, flowing through a spacious valley. Its densely wooded sides sloped gently back to the base of the precipitous sides of the high mountains that walled it in. There they got their first view of Donati's comet, which was causing so much stir in scientific circles. That night, too, they heard, at intervals, a great noise like distant thunder, which Nimrod said was caused by ice falling in the mountains.

A clearly marked trail led them up the river, but it disappeared where the bank along which it ran had been washed away by the river; then they had to take to the shingle flats which were carpeted with alpine flowers, growing from seeds that had been washed down from the mountains. They crossed the river where its course bends from the south and a tributary joins it from the west, climbed a glistening white, chalky slope and plunged into one of the densest forests they had encountered. Luckily the many fallen trees were so rotten that they did not hold them up as badly as did those where there had been recent forest fires. The woods brought them to a large lake, Glacier Lake, which filled the whole valley, except for a narrow margin along its north shore; even that was much encumbered with fallen timber. As they were chopping their laborious way along, the same horse that had played that frolic once before again plunged into the water and swam off into the lake. They had to leave him alone, lest their endeavours to get hold of him should only start him for the other shore of the mile-wide lake. After a time he turned to land again, but his pack was so soaked that they had to halt for the night where they were. Hector sent two men on to cut out a track in the remaining hours of day-light, while he tried to dry and save the few skins and plants he had collected, and which had unfortunately been packed on this enterprising animal.

Their camp was a curious one: the fallen trees on the slope of the hill were so large and so interlocked that the party had difficulty in finding places to stretch themselves here and there among them. They tried unsuccessfully to catch some fish, hungrily regretting that they had not been quick enough to shoot the big-horn sheep they had met earlier in the day, a rare species in those parts. They tried to shoot some bats, the noise of the shots echoing back and forth across the lake six or eight times.

The men hewed out a track westward, and next day they worked their way up to the top of the lake where there was a stretch of open grass fringed with woods below the glacier. Hector took observations for latitude and explored the valley. At sunrise next morning, while the other men hunted, he and Sutherland set off to climb the great glacier between Mount Lyell and Mount Forbes, which feeds the river. Nimrod refused to venture on the ice. He told all sorts of stories of disasters that had befallen those Indians that had done so: if they did not get lost in a crevasse, they were at least sure to be unlucky ever afterwards in their hunting.

They found that most of the water in the river issued from ice caves that were hollowed beneath the great glacier of the main valley. There were so many crevasses that they found, try as they might, that they could not climb it. At last they found a smooth, continuous slope of ice, which they ascended. It was cold work for their feet, as they wore only moccasins, without socks of any kind, but at least the moccasins gave them a sure foothold. They toiled on and at last reached a point from which they had a splendid view up the valley. They saw that the glacier they had climbed was a mere extension of a great mass of ice that enveloped the higher mountains to the west. They had to work their way round an enormous crevasse and finally had to jump it where it was still four feet wide and, as Hector found by timing the fall of stones, 160 feet deep. The ice coming down from the higher glaciers cascaded over the edge of a huge precipice. Hector found the blue pinnacles of ice, tottering over the edge of the cliff, very striking. It was the noise they made in falling that they had mistaken for thunder a few days before.

They tried to climb a peak on the north side of the valley that looked more accessible than the others. After some difficulty in getting off the glacier, they began to climb the rocky precipice. They started an old goat and got quite close to him, trying vainly to make him jump onto the ice by rolling stones down on him. They reached the summit, a narrow ridge, at three o'clock. At some points they got along only by crawling, and some abrupt nicks in the knife-like edge had to be passed by dangerous climbing—and that without benefit of boots, ropes, ice-axes, or any of the other paraphernalia of modern mountaineers. They came down in a snow-storm, after carefully studying the glaciers and peaks and valleys stretching away into the distance on every side. At one point they nearly had to turn back, as they came to a precipice that was closely hemmed in between a wall of ice and a wall of rock. However, by knotting their leather shirts together and taking off their moccasins, which were now frozen, they managed to get past the difficulty. Pushing on rapidly, they reached camp at eight o'clock, for a cheerless supper of dry, lean moose meat, which had not much more nourishment in it than chips of parchment. It was all they had; the hunters had been unsuccessful.

During the night they saw a great glare of flame down the valley at the lower end of the lake; the fire they had left at their halting-place among the fallen woods had set the forest alight. Next day, on their way back, the fire they had so carelessly started gave them trouble. When they reached the lower end of the lake, Hector wrote:

> . . . *the fire had already destroyed a large area of the forest. The wind was luckily from the west, so that by keeping close to the stream, and going in the water whenever practicable,*

we got along; but, as sometimes we were forced to pass over the smouldering ground, our horses' legs suffered a good deal. When a forest of green and rotten timber, such as this was, burns, the fire progresses in a different manner from among dry woods. The layer of dried foliage, often a foot deep, smoulders away slowly, and when a dry tree is met with, or one braided with the turpentine lichen, then a sudden blaze takes place. The first passage of the fire is rapid, but it often remains smouldering for months in spots.

Now, after a short trip up Howse River (Hector's Middle Fork), they headed back north-eastward down the main valley of the North Saskatchewan. The Indians had told them that once this country had been rich in game, but eleven years earlier there had been great fires all through the mountains and in the woods along their eastern base; after that a disease had broken out among all the animals, so that they used to find wapiti, moose, and other deer, as well as buffalo, lying dead.

Despite the lack of game, Nimrod and the boy killed two goats, but when they tried to eat the fat and exceedingly good-looking meat of a fine young kid they found that the rank, musky flavour gave rise to intense nausea. Once more they were reduced to the unrewarding, lean moose meat.

Another day's travel brought them out on the Kootenay Plain. Here, before there was any European communication from the Pacific Coast, there had been 'an annual mart', where Kootenay Indians from across the mountains met traders from Rocky Mountain House lower down the North Saskatchewan. The trail was still well beaten.

Hector spent a day exploring, botanizing, and geologizing. The men went hunting again and this time succeeded in killing four sheep. Next day they collected the meat, while Hector climbed yet another mountain. A large tributary joins the North Saskatchewan here—Cline's River, by which a Hudson's Bay trader called Cline had made a yearly journey from Jasper House to the Kootenay Plain to trade.

That afternoon they passed out of the mountains at four

o'clock, just thirty-eight days after they had entered them at Old Bow Fort. The country quite suddenly became comparatively level, though there were still low hills a little back from the river. Passing the last rocky point, they started a band of ewes and killed two of them.

Hector had remained behind to examine the high banks of the river, when a great storm of thunder and hail obliterated the horses' tracks. He pushed on in some doubt as to whether he had passed the main party. Suddenly his horse shied at a bush, and immediately out sprang a splendid panther. Hector wrestled with the soaked leather gun-cover but could not get it off his rifle. The panther stood for a few seconds within twelve feet of him, lashing his tail as if in doubt whether to spring, while Hector's horse danced about in a state of great disquietude and Hector studied the great width of the panther's face and the length of his tail. At last the panther made off into the brushwood again. Later, Hector, led by the men's signal shots, found the camp.

There was still a long journey ahead to Fort Edmonton. They could see that there had been heavy snow on the mountains, though on the plains they were drenched with rain. Hector went on ahead to find a good camping-place, where he planned to rest the horses before they started on the last lap of the trip. Dismounted, he did not notice three bears digging for roots, but Nimrod, arriving on horseback, saw them. They both fired, but missed and failed to catch them in a long chase.

They spent seven days in camp at Big Horn Creek. The country here was very beautiful, in spite of fires, with timber bluffs, rich pasture, and poplar and willow bushes. A party of Stoney Indians joined them. Together they organized a large-scale sheep hunt. They shot ten sheep in all. Nimrod claimed five, Peter Erasmus two, and Hector one; the nine Stoneys accounted for only three among them. Nimrod was the great man among the Indians; he spent his time in camp idling and smoking and lording it over the rest—the prerogative of a good hunter.

With rest and good pasture the horses improved quickly. One that had been severely burnt in the forest fire, Hector exchanged with the Stoneys for a sound though less fine animal. They left the invaluable boy with the friendly Stoneys and gave them everything they could spare before they set off again for Fort Edmonton. Four days' travel brought them to Rocky Mountain House, but the place was deserted; the traders had not yet arrived back from Edmonton to take up their winter quarters there. They camped in the kitchen, but did not feel as comfortable as in their usual camp out of doors in the woods. They had now used up their sheep-pemmican and found that they had lost a bag of dried meat that the Stoneys had prepared for them; so once again they were without provisions, with 180 miles still to go.

During the night there was thunder, and they woke up to find the ground white with snow. It was now October 1; the same kind of weather had ushered in the winter the year before at Carlton. The poplar trees had long since turned yellow. Clearly the winter was upon them. The Big Horn Stoneys' horse strayed off in the night, leading several of the others astray too, and the men spent the whole of the following day searching for them. The snow had disappeared the next morning, but there was still a hard frost. They crossed first the Saskatchewan and then a second river, travelling east-south-east to Last Hill Creek, where they came to a familiar track. They stopped an hour earlier than usual to shoot rabbits for supper. Next day they travelled twenty-three miles, and, hearing a dog bark when they were about to camp, turned off to the north in the direction of the sound and found a camp of Stoneys and Thickwood Cree. Hector traded his leather tent for some wapiti meat. Snow fell again that night, but next day, despite the drifts, they covered twenty-eight miles. By evening the storm had become so violent that they had to stop and make a regular winter camp. In the morning they were quite covered over by a heavy drift of snow. On the open plain it was two feet deep. They drove the horses to a swamp where they let them feed till midday.

Hector tore up his blanket to make wrappers for the men's feet, as it was now very cold. In the afternoon the snow stopped and they crossed Battle River and Pigeon Creek. They had to swim Pigeon Creek, which was deep, though it was only twenty feet wide. They plunged through it, making a rapid dash on horseback, without taking off their clothes. The effect of the plunge on the worn-out horses was that, a few miles farther on, they began to give out, so that the men could hardly get them along. Next day they travelled slowly, all on foot, driving the jaded horses through the deep snow. By nightfall they were still twenty-five miles from Edmonton. Things were a little better next day, as a sharp frost set the snow and it was not quite so deep. Exhausted and hungry as they were, they stopped at noon to wash their faces at White Mud Creek before arriving at the fort. When they reached the river-bank opposite the fort, Hector had the satisfaction of distinguishing Captain Palliser and the rest of the party awaiting them on the other side. The last entry in his journal is a typical understatement: 'The swimming of the horses was a troublesome work, as some of them were very weak.'

CHAPTER FOURTEEN

New Passes through the Rockies: The Kootenays

M eanwhile Lieutenant Blakiston had been examining the North Kootenay Pass, which Palliser, before he left on his side trip to the boundary, had asked him to survey in order to ascertain exactly where it lay.

Blakiston was still feeling edgy; the tension and disagreement between him and the other members of the expedition had not been resolved with Palliser's return and the coming of summer. They had in fact grown more bitter, and now, after Palliser's departure to the border with Sullivan, they came to a head: Blakiston set off with Hector and Bourgeau to the Old Bow Fort, but by the time he got there his grievances had got the better of him. He left a letter for Palliser, 'wherein', as he wrote, 'I threw off his command', though this did not prevent him from taking expedition men, stores, and mounts with him for a personal journey through the mountains, carrying out the instructions Palliser had given him, but refusing at the end of the summer to hand over his observations and maps for the expedition's report. Instead, he sent a report to General Sabine, who had drawn up the instructions for the magnetical observations. In it he took a number of digs at the other members of the expedition, though he explained to Sabine in a personal letter that his disagreement with Palliser was only official and that they were still as good friends as ever. In his letter of resignation he accused Palliser of allowing private matters to influence him in his public duties. Accustomed to the precise ranks and gradations of authority in the army, he had been pressing Palliser to let him know his, Blakiston's, exact position in the expedition. Later Palliser explained to the Secretary of State that he had not wanted to appoint one of the party to command the expedition in the event of his own absence or death, but when Blakiston 'thought proper to adopt a course of conduct' which left him no option, he decided that Hector, with his longer field experience, his steady judgment, and his ability to get on with the other members of the expedition and with the men, should have the responsibility. It appeared to Palliser 'quite impossible that the objects of the expedition could be carried out' under Blakiston's command. He remembered the earlier trouble at Carlton and had himself observed 'evidence of want of Judgement and Temper' in the able and ambitious young artillery officer. On his arrival at Fort Carlton in June 1858, he had found that relations between Blakiston and the other members of the expedition, as also between him and the officers and servants of the Hudson's Bay Company at the fort, were the reverse of friendly. He tried to prevent any collision between Blakiston and the other members of the expedition.

Blakiston was upset at finding that he was to consider himself under the orders of another member of the party—a civilian and a younger man at that. He was also disappointed that Palliser had refused to sanction a pet scheme of his: he wanted to leave some men to build a canoe in which, when he came back from the mountains in the fall, he proposed to voyage down the whole length of the South Saskatchewan. Palliser thought this project over the night before he left. Just before he rode off on his trip south to the border he refused Blakiston permission to make the canoe voyage, because he thought it was too dangerous for one member of the party to go alone down this unknown river. Blakiston reported bitterly on October 21, 1859: 'I need only further say that it is still equally unknown.' He went off in 1859 on an expedition of his own, to explore another unknown river, the Yangtze Kiang in China.

When word reached London of Blakiston's separation from the expedition, the civil servants at the Colonial Office were at a loss to know what to do in such an unconventional situation. Could the government publish his report, when it had not been authenticated by the commander of the expedition? Indeed, should Blakiston's expenses since his separation be paid? His conduct had been most irregular. It was eventually settled that he should be asked to explain his insubordinate action, but by then he was in China. In the end, the civil servants decided sadly, after a long exchange of minutes, that the whole expedition had been a very peculiar one and that at its outset the documents had been prepared in a 'loose way'. Blakiston had never really been told officially that he was under Palliser's command. Ultimately everything that the War Office asked for in the way of pay for Blakiston, and that he asked for in the way of expenses, was charged to the expedition; his report was included as a separate document among those published in the blue-book of 1860.

But all this happened later on, when Blakiston had returned, alone, from British North America. On August 11, 1858, he wrote his letter announcing to Palliser that he no longer considered himself connected in any way with the expedition; he left it at Old Bow Fort; then he set off to survey the Kootenay Pass, to determine whether or not it was wholly within British territory. He had with him three Red River half-breed *voyageurs* and a Thickwood Cree Indian hunter; ten horses, five to carry the packs (containing ball and powder, tobacco, a few knives and other Indian trade goods, dried meat and pemmican, tea, sugar, and salt) and two boxes containing instruments and books.

The party crossed the Kananaskis, where they saw the remains of carts they thought had been left in 1854 by James Sinclair's party of emigrants from Red River. Blakiston was convinced that Sir George Simpson had used this same

Kananaskis Pass in 1841 and also Sinclair, on an earlier trip. This was one of the things about which he disagreed with Palliser, who was equally convinced that they had not used this pass, both from what Sinclair had told him when they met in 1848 and because James Richards, the man who had been with Sir George on his famous trip, later pointed out to Hector a different route as the one Sir George had taken. Sir George himself had written that Sinclair had crossed the mountains in 1841 by a pass some way farther to the south than the one through which his own party had travelled. We know now that there are a great many passes through the mountains and that Simpson's pass was considerably farther north than the Kananaskis Pass, which Palliser explored, while the pass by which Sinclair had crossed in 1841 was probably the White Man Pass, lying between the Simpson and Kananaskis passes.

Like his disowned colleagues and other travellers, Blakiston found that the greatest obstruction was not so much soaring mountain precipices as fallen timber. On the way south to find the entrance to the Kootenay Pass, Blakiston's party kept as far as possible to the east, to be clear of the mountains. They could see right across the foothills to the mountains; one snow peak, which he dubbed 'the Pyramid'— the modern Mount Assiniboine—impressed Blakiston especially. It wore a plume of cloud which looked like steam from a volcano.

After three days' travelling Blakiston camped in a valley which offered a fine piece of prairie pasture for the horses. He took an observation of the sun, which he hoped to be able to compare with another observation next day, to check his chronometer. This important instrument was carried, turn about, for one day each, by one of the men, who, for that day, did nothing else but carry it as carefully as possible. Blakiston was afraid that if the same man carried the chronometer two days running he might become careless.

The next day being Sunday, they stayed in camp. Blakiston found that rest one day in seven was required by man and horse, the former taking advantage of it to wash and mend clothes. He noted that in clear weather there was always a cool breeze from the mountains in the middle of the day and in the afternoon.

Next day they encountered some Thickwood Stoney Indians and a few Cree, who were about to camp. Blakiston reported that, 'as usual, when with or near any Indians, my flag, a St. George's Jack, was hoisted on a pole in front of the tent. I gave them a present of some tobacco and fresh meat ... During the afternoon I held a talk with these Indians. I told them plainly for what reason we had been sent to the country; that Her Majesty was always glad to hear of their welfare, and that any message which they might have for Her, I would take down in writing.'

The Indians were well disposed towards the party. Education had made some progress with them, thanks to the Wesleyan missionaries, the Reverend Mr. Rundle and his successor, the Reverend Thomas Woolsey. They complained of their treatment both by the traders and by the Plains Indians. They asked for white men to come to teach them how to farm, so that their children might live; wild animals were getting scarcer every year. Blakiston obtained from the Indians a pair of saddle-bags and traded a lame horse, with some ammunition and tobacco 'in boot', for a strong Indian pony.

Near the Highwood River he made a cache, for use on the return journey, of ammunition and pemmican rolled up in a buffalo robe and hung fifteen feet above the ground in a spruce tree. Next morning they were delayed by the horses' straying but reached a river that Blakiston called the Belly (today's Oldman) in time to camp in its wide prairie valley. There the Indian hunter killed a buffalo while Blakiston took observations and measured the height of the river levels, those characteristic steps from the bed of the river to the plain above.

They crossed the Oldman River to the south bank quite easily, as, though swift, it was not more than three feet deep. Through the gap in the mountains through which the river flows, they could see a high, dome-shaped peak; Blakiston called it 'Gould's Dome' after a celebrated naturalist. Apart from this one gap, the near-by range of mountains seemed to stretch for twenty-five miles without a break, and with no distinct peaks. Blakiston named the entire range Livingstone Range, after the African explorer. This must have pleased Palliser, who was a great admirer of Livingstone and had sat next to him at the first meeting of the Royal Geographical Society that he had attended.

Whenever he could, Blakiston took careful bearings on all the main mountain peaks. The evening before he turned into the pass, he noted two outstanding mountains about thirty miles south, one of which he called Castle Mountain. Still farther south, jutting out from the main chain of mountains, standing by itself, he saw Chief Mountain, the peak that marks the border. Disappointingly, on the crucial morning when the party gained the entrance of the Kootenay Pass, the weather was thick and hazy with occasional showers of rain, which prevented him from getting a good view of the country.

At the mouth of the pass another of the branches of Oldman River issues from the mountains. Blakiston called it Railway River, from the striking advantages he felt it offered for the entry of a railway into the mountains. This must have been one of the northern tributaries of today's Carbondale River, which does not, in fact, lead to any recognized pass.

Here they struck the tolerably well-beaten Kootenay Trail, which they followed up the narrow valley (of the Carbondale River) between high, wooded hills. They were now fairly in the mountains and had already passed the point where their Indian guide knew anything of the road except by report. He thought that it would take them three or four days to cross the mountains. The guide Palliser had allotted to Blakiston was not with the party. His wife had fallen ill and the lieutenant had started without him. Though the guide had promised to overtake the party, he failed to do so; his wife was still ill when Palliser got back to Old Bow Fort. Blakiston felt that the guide's absence turned out to be all to the good. He had come to have no great faith in the so-called guides; in his opinion they were seldom worth their pay.

Blakiston calculated that the entrance to the pass was forty miles north of the boundary. The pass turned off along a little creek, which grew smaller and smaller until it dwindled into a tiny stream falling in a cascade. They climbed rapidly and soon came out, above the tree-line, into the region of rock and alpine plants, where there were large patches of snow. Scudding clouds kept them from getting a good look at the scenery, but Blakiston knew they were 'now on the watershed of the mountains, the great axis of America; . . . in that portion of the Rocky Mountains comprised between the parallels of 45° and 54° north latitude, rise the four great rivers of the continent, namely, the Mackenzie, running north to the Arctic Ocean, the Saskatchewan east to Hudson's Bay, the Columbia west to the Pacific, and the Missouri south to the Gulf of Mexico; thus we may say, that in a certain sense that portion of the mountains is the culminating point of North America, and I now, on the Kootanie Pass, stood as nearly as possible in the centre of it.'

The proper and punctilious officer gave way to excitement: ' . . . a few steps further and I gave a wild shout as I caught the first glimpse in a deep valley, as it were at my feet, of a feeder of the Pacific Ocean. It was the Flathead River, a tributary of the Columbia. At the same moment the shots of my men's guns echoing among the rocks announced the passage of the first white man over the Kootanie Pass.' Other white men had probably crossed the pass before, men like the Canadians Hugh Munroe and Picard; some half-breeds had certainly done so, including the group of returning emigrants led by Whitford, whom Palliser had met at Fort Ellice, but Blakiston was equally certainly the first white man whose crossing was put on public record.

He halted to read the barometer, which showed an altitude of 5,960 feet. It is actually 6,749 feet, but he had only an undependable aneroid barometer.

A rapid descent of two hours took the party down to the

Flathead. They spent Sunday in a pleasant camp in its beautiful valley, with mountains all round; here there was wood, good water, and good pasture—everything to be desired by the traveller. Blakiston took observations, wrote up his notes, and sketched the mountains over which they had come the day before. They saw two or three humming-birds in the camp, and the men shot ducks and grouse and caught trout, to make an agreeable change in their diet.

The track led them on next day through thick woods, where fallen timber, the inevitable obstacle, slowed up the horses, in spite of some cutting the Kootenay had done to clear the trail. This now led up the valley of the Flathead to near its head-waters, which were mere mountain torrents. A steep ascent, up which the path zigzagged, brought them to the summit of a 'knife-like ridge, from which an extensive view of the mountains was obtained ... All appeared, however, utter confusion, such slight differences were there between the different mountains and ridges. One peak alone showed itself above the general surface.' This was his old friend, Gould's Dome (now Tornado Mountain, not to be confused with the contemporary Gould Dome, a lower mountain farther to the south-east). Once more he took bearings and read the barometer to measure the altitude.

They were now on a height of land between two branches of the Columbia. They had hardly started down the western slope of the Rockies when a violent storm broke. They were wet to the skin in a few moments. Blakiston commented ruefully, 'my own habiliments were far from waterproof, being simply a flannel shirt and pair of leather trowsers with a striped cotton shirt over all.' He was clearly not the stickler in sartorial matters that he was in scientific affairs. Indeed, the Reverend Thomas Woolsey had written in his journal, after meeting him at Fort Carlton the previous winter, that if he were to offer an opinion of the *chapeau* of the precise artillery officer he would pronounce it 'a shocking bad hat'. After a very steep descent, the horses in some places having difficulty in keeping their feet, they camped for the first time in a

Columbian forest. Blakiston was vastly impressed with its splendid trees and described several species that were new to him.

Before noon next day, they reached the Wigwam River, where it had cut its way down between tremendous cliffs two or three hundred feet high, worn into fantastic pinnacles and blocks. The track left the river and swung off, over a very rocky piece of country, to the broad Kootenay, where another river ran into it. Blakiston thought this river was still the Wigwam. It was, in fact, the Elk, which they had missed by following the trail overland. Later he had misgivings about this. For the most part in his report he emphasized and re-emphasized its unimpeachable accuracy, but at this point he admitted 'that there is one point on which I may have been mistaken, namely, that the river at its [the pass's] western extremity, into which the Wigwam River falls, is perhaps not the main Kootenay River . . . but may be the Stag or Elk River, a branch of it'.

He was not quite sure which river he had hit on, but he was certain that this was the most southerly pass in British territory. There are, in fact, three others farther south, though accessible on the west only through United States territory, which were recorded years later. Though he recognized that there might be other, more advantageous places at which a railroad could cross from the Saskatchewan Plains to the Pacific, he was confident that the North Kootenay Pass was the shortest route through which a railway could be constructed. He described a detailed plan for one:

> . . . *it would follow the course of my track marked on the map. A cutting of about 3 1/2 miles would lead to a tunnel of nearly 5 miles in length, which would pierce the Watershed mountain, and come out in the valley of Flathead River, the whole having a grade of 1 in 130, or 47 feet per geographical mile. On emerging into the valley, the line would skirt the base of the mountains to the north of the track, thereby avoiding a steep descent, then following up the river with a grade of 40*

feet per geographical mile, it would reach the rise of the western ridge at a height of 5,100 feet above the sea. This would be the culminating point of the line, from which in a distance of 10 geographical miles it has to fall 1,900 feet to the North and South Bluff, and after that, by a slope of 54 feet per geographical mile for five miles, to reach the Tobacco Plains, crossing the Kootanie Fork by a bridge. This I propose to accomplish in the following manner:—From the culminating point, to pierce the ridge by a tunnel of three geographical miles, and continue the line along the side of the hills to the north of the track until reaching the North Bluff, the whole with a grade of 190 feet per geographical mile. This portion of the line of ten geographical miles would have to be worked by a wire rope and one or more stationary engines.

The obstacles to the passage of a railroad were thus 'two mountains and one steep slope'. Of the remaining 300 miles from the west end of Kootenay Pass to the mouth of the Fraser River, on the Gulf of Georgia, he reported that no mountains were visible to the distance he could see. Though he wrote that he could say nothing of this region, he did not class it as mountainous in his summing-up of the possibilities of a railroad from Lake Superior to the Pacific: 'out of the whole distance one-half is over level prairies, and but 40 miles through mountains.' This somewhat over-optimistic report arrived in London when a new Secretary of State for the Colonies was in office—Sir Edward Bulwer Lytton, well-known novelist, who was accused by his political enemies of having too vivid an imagination when he contemplated a coast-to-coast railroad through British North America.

In the meantime, still slogging on with their horses, they lost the trail and had to camp for the night, as there would not be daylight for long enough to allow them to cross the Kootenay, as the Indian thought they must. Looking for a good crossing-place, Blakiston found the trail again, farther down, on the same side of the river.

Travelling on down-river through magnificent open forests and stretches of prairie, he reckoned that towards evening they crossed the boundary line, camping two miles within United States territory.

In a few minutes a Kootenay Indian arrived on horseback. The Thickwood Cree, James, who had started out as a hunter but had become a 'guide' on the defection of the original guide, knew only a word or two of Kootenay. The language struck Blakiston as being most guttural, and unpronounceable for a European, every word appearing to be brought up with the utmost difficulty from the Kootenay's extremities. The Kootenay could not speak one word of Cree, so they had some difficulty in comprehending him, but a small present of tobacco and something to eat were eloquent of goodwill. He took his leave and, shortly after, several more arrived from the same camp, a chief among them. They were mounted on fine horses and raced up to the camp as hard as they could gallop, no doubt with the idea of creating an impression. The language of presents had been clearly intelligible! One of the new-comers understood Blackfoot, so the evening was spent in talk with them.

Next morning, in a thick fog, they found, within a few hundred yards of the river, three diminutive log houses. Two of them were not over ten feet square, and to enter them it was necessary to crawl through a hole—an apology for a door. The other, a little bigger, was the Kootenay chapel, which had been built when a missionary had been there the year before. This was the celebrated Fort Kootenay, marked in large letters on Arrowsmith's map. Hudson's Bay traders came there only for the winter, returning to Fort Colvile each spring. Blakiston's observations indicated that the post lay a little over five English miles south of the boundary.

In the afternoon he went with a chief to visit the Kootenay's camp, four miles to the east, where he was under the necessity of shaking hands with every man, woman, and child. The people had a rather dirty and wretched appearance, but their herds of horses and some few horned cattle showed that they were not poor. Indeed, as soon as Blakiston had pitched his tent, at a short distance from the Indian lodges, he was inundated with presents of dried and fresh berries, dried and pounded meat, and cow's milk. Nothing was asked in return, but of course he paid for this food in tobacco, ammunition, and the like. The Kootenay at this season appeared to subsist almost entirely on berries: saskatoons, which Blakiston found a delicious fruit, and a small species of cherry, presumably choke-cherry, and also a sweet root, which they obtained to the south.

They grew some little wheat and a few peas; a patch of the former, about forty yards square, which he saw near their camp, although rather small-headed, looked good, a proof that this grain throve in latitude 49° at an altitude of 2,500 feet.

The Kootenay possessed more horses than any Indians the lieutenant had seen or heard of on the east side, a camp of only six tents having about 150 of them, old and young. They showed some knowledge of the animals and treated them kindly. They were adept in throwing the lasso, being brought up from their youth to its use. They also had some domestic cattle, six tents having twelve or sixteen head, and it was said that some individuals at a distant camp owned as many as twenty or thirty each. Blakiston was most favourably impressed by these Indians:

> *They are perfectly honest and do not beg, qualities which I have never yet met with in any Indians . . . On now taking leave of the Kootanies, with whom I have been camped for nearly a week, it is but justice to say, that they have behaved in a very civil and hospitable manner; and although our clothes and other articles have been lying about in all directions, we have (with the exception of some hide lines, moccasins, and other articles of leather, which the half-starved dogs have eaten) not lost a single article . . . Whether this honesty is to be attributed to the knowledge of Christianity spread among them by the ministers of the Roman Catholic church, or whether it is innate in them, I can only say that it*

is a great contrast to the effect produced by the missions in the Indian territory on the east side . . .

They are nearly all baptised Roman Catholics, and are most particular in their attendance at morning and evening prayers, to which they are summoned by a small hand-bell. They always pray before eating. On the Sunday that I spent with them their service, in which is a good deal of singing, lasted a considerable time. One of their number preached, and seemed to be well attended to.

Since there was clearly no danger of starving here, they remained several days, trading horses, buying provisions, and finding out as much as possible about the country by actual observation and by Indian report. Blakiston made an excursion to the north of the boundary with his sextant to obtain as nearly as possible the precise position of the line. He found no remarkable feature to mark it, but noted the place where it crossed the hills. He sketched the mountains to the north, one of which stood out very distinctly. This he thought marked the point at which Palliser, following the old emigrant pass, had emerged from the mountains after a journey of six or eight days. It was probably Mount Joffre.

The Kootenay crossed the mountains every summer to hunt buffalo, trading the meat for tobacco, knives, and blankets at the Kootenay Post. Sometimes they crossed on snowshoes, too, late in the winter when there was a crust on the snow. They told him about another, less steep pass farther south, which Blakiston thought should be explored, even though he knew that it must lie, at least in part, south of the border. He prevailed upon a Kootenay to accompany the party across as a guide.

They set off on the return journey on September 2, on a clear, sharp morning. Blakiston felt satisfied that he had done all that came under the spirit of his instructions, and was happy to be able to recross the mountains by another unexplored route. He was disappointed that this time it was not his fate to see the Pacific, but it apparently did not occur to him that he might have explored the Crow's Nest Pass, of which he had been told, in British territory, farther north. Perhaps the report of the natives that it was a very bad road, and seldom used, deterred him, though later it was the one chosen for the second railway route through the mountains.

As he travelled up the Flathead back into British territory and through the more southerly pass, which he called the Boundary Pass (and which is now called the South Kootenay Pass), Blakiston made careful notes and sketches that he thought might be useful to the Boundary Commission, which was then working its way east from the Gulf of Georgia to the crest of the Rockies, marking the new boundary accepted by both the United States and Great Britain under the Oregon Treaty of 1846.

Heavy rain next morning changed to snow, giving the mountains a good white coat. The Kootenay with the party, four men and two women, had gone on ahead. Blakiston followed their clear tracks in the snow up a steep ascent and along the edge of a very steep hill, where both they and the horses had difficulty keeping their footing. It was cold work trudging through the two-foot-deep snow in thin leather moccasins without socks; to make matters worse, it was blowing and snowing all the time. None the less, Blakiston, with the assistance of the Indian, James, who was always most willing, unpacked the horse with the instrument box at the watershed, to measure its altitude. He made it 6,030 feet above sea level; later surveys made under easier conditions and with more accurate and elaborate instruments make it 6,903 feet. The zigzag descent was easier, and soon they came on a small mountain torrent flowing eastward, thus regaining waters flowing to the Atlantic after an absence of sixteen days.

Travelling down Blakiston Brook, they reached Waterton Lakes, which Blakiston named after a celebrated British naturalist. The beauty of the scenery greatly impressed him— as it now impresses the many visitors who stay at the Waterton-Glacier International Peace Park. Blakiston camped there for two whole days for the sake of the horses. Game was abundant, including grizzly bears, and they obtained both fresh meat and large trout and pike.

His observations convinced Blakiston that the boundary line passed just over Chief Mountain, which stands out in the plains, a tremendous landmark; in fact, it is a little to the south of the boundary. Blakiston concluded, rightly, from information that the Indians gave him, that a tributary of the south branch of the Saskatchewan, now called St. Mary's River, rises to the south of Chief Mountain. Chief Mountain, he realized, is not part of the watershed between the South Saskatchewan and the Missouri, but simply the end of a spur jutting out from the main range. Blakiston noted, as later travellers have noted, that his corner of the mountains was a very windy spot, with gales of wind first from one and then from the opposite direction. He was also impressed with the greenness of the prairies on the eastern flanks of the mountains as contrasted with the dry Tobacco Plains on the west.

On September 10 the party started off on the more than 300-mile trip back to Fort Edmonton. On the way they visited a camp of forty-five tents of Blackfoot Indians. Blakiston reported:

> *I was received with the usual hospitality, and having expressed a desire to change a horse or two, I had no trouble the following morning in exchanging one and buying another for ammunition, tobacco, blankets, old coat, etc. This tribe has the credit of being dangerous, but from what I have seen of them, I consider them far better behaved than their more civilized neighbours, the Crees. I made it a rule never to hide from Indians, and, although I had but a small party, to go to them as soon as I knew of their proximity. I also always told them for what reason the British Government had sent the expedition to the country; and I never failed to receive manifestations of good will, neither was there one attempt made to steal my horses, a practice only too prevalent among the Indians of these plains.*

Steady travelling somewhat to the east of his outward

track, interrupted only by a digression to the west for the purpose of retrieving the cache of food that he had left on the outgoing journey, and a day's rest at Bow River on a Sunday, brought them to Fort Edmonton on September 29.

After a couple of weeks there, Blakiston set off again, down-river, in the boats with the Red River men, having refused to reconsider his decision to separate from the expedition. He arrived at Carlton at the end of October 1858, and left again on December 27 on his way to Red River via Cumberland, walking on snow-shoes and driving a train of dogs a distance of 800 miles. He got to Red River Settlement on March 1, 1859. Here he remained, hoping to receive a favourable reply from the Secretary of State to a letter he had written offering to prosecute further explorations or magnetic surveys. He was eager to go on exploring. Ironically enough, Palliser had earlier recommended that he should be attached to the Boundary Commission, but of course when he left the expedition he lost his chance. When Bulwer Lytton's refusal arrived, he took the earliest opportunity, on the break-up of the winter, to proceed by the overland route to Saint Paul on the upper Mississippi, 530 miles away from Red River Settlement. He visited Washington, still collecting material for his report, and finally got back to London in time to put it together before he went off with his regiment to China, there to satisfy, on his own account, the taste for exploring that he had acquired in British North America with another historic expedition up the Yangtze Kiang.

His report was well received by General Sabine at the Royal Society, and at the Colonial Office where a minute was written describing it as the 'chiefly useful result of the exploration'. Blakiston also wrote a number of scientific articles about his magnetic surveys and the birds of the interior of North America; he left sketches and maps and zoological specimens at Woolwich Institute. His papers were later burned and his sketches and collection of birds seem to have disappeared, but that shout as he crossed the pass still rings out from the stiff pages of the blue-book.

CHAPTER FIFTEEN

Blackfoot, Balls, and Buffalo

Blakiston had gone home, but the rest of the party settled down for their second winter on the great plains, this time with Fort Edmonton as their base. The largest fort in the Saskatchewan country, Edmonton was built altogether of wood. There was one good-sized house two stories high where the officer in charge of the post lived and where the explorers and other visitors also stayed. Adjoining the house were the storehouses for trade goods and furs and the log houses inhabited by the men engaged by the company, together with their wives and families; the whole was surrounded by twenty-foot wooden pickets or piles firmly driven into the ground close together.

The forty men, thirty women, and eighty children who lived there were almost entirely supported on buffalo meat. They needed 700 pounds a day, a quantity difficult to supply, as some of it had to be hauled in from as much as 250 miles away, an expensive and precarious business. The excellent whitefish from Lake St. Ann's were therefore very useful. Food also had to be provided for the brigades of boats that carried the furs out, down the Saskatchewan in the spring. Little agriculture was carried on, partly from lack of knowledge of even the leading principles of agriculture, but principally from the disinclination of both the men and the women to work steadily at any agricultural occupation.

A great friend of Palliser's, Captain Arthur Brisco, now joined the party. Formerly in the 11th Hussars, he had distin-

guished himself in the Charge of the Light Brigade at
Balaclava, in the Crimean War. With him was a Mr. Mitchell,
another English gentleman, who had come out to the Far
West in search of adventure and big game.

Mr. Christie of the Hudson's Bay Company had arrived
on the same day as Dr. Hector, to take over the post from Mr.
Brazeau, who had been in charge during the summer, but
who was now to return to Rocky Mountain House. Mr.
Christie's hearty welcome made the explorers feel quite at
home in their winter quarters.

Their first care, as usual, was the horses, which were now
very much the worse for all the fatigue they had undergone
during the exploring season. They were put out to pasture
with the horses of the fort, with three men to look after them.
Two men had been sent back in advance of the rest of the
party to cut hay; before Palliser got to Edmonton they had cut
seventeen stacks, which they hoped would be plenty of fodder
for the winter months.

Most of the men would not be needed during the winter.
They had to be paid off and sent home. This was a complicated business, as Palliser explained:

> *All payments in this country being made in kind, adds
> considerably to the trouble of paying wages, which are first
> calculated in skins, and then paid in kind. The value of the
> skin differs in different parts of the country, thus, a skin in
> Swan River district is about 2s., and in the Upper Saskatch-
> ewan it is about 2s. 3d. . . . . Mr. Christie, who understood the
> pricing and value of the articles, very kindly undertook the
> payment of the men, which is thus conducted:–Mr. Sullivan
> made out account of wages due to them, deducting advances,
> etc. I then signed this, and each man presented it to Mr.
> Christie, who sat in my shop in the fort, surrounded by
> ready-made clothes, blankets, beds, axes, knives, files, kettles,
> tea, sugar, tobacco, etc., and the man kept taking what he
> wanted till Mr. Christie called out 'assez', upon which the
> account closed. Frequently Mr. Christie would say, 'Now you*

*have but half a skin left,' when his customer would im-
mediately turn to the ribbons or beads for an equivalent of the
difference. I did not pay any men of my Red River brigade
until all the St. Ann's men were settled with, because they were
returning to Red River, where they could get what they
wanted on better terms there. The freight up the Saskatchewan was necessarily heavy, all which was taken into wages
account at the time of their agreement. Nevertheless, like
children at the sight of toys, it was difficult to deter them from
purchasing, and I had considerable trouble in laughing them
out of the idea of buying an expensive article, in order to carry
it back to the place it came from at considerable trouble and
inconvenience.*

There was now a chance for the members of the expedition to enjoy a considerable period of repose and good food,
which they badly needed. They settled down to prepare maps
and reports; they worked up observations and rode over from
time to time to make sure the horses were all right. Hector
arranged for regular meteorological observations to be taken
throughout the winter, and then took advantage of the Indian
summer to go off for nine days on a geological trip to Fort
Pitt. He was much impressed by the agricultural and stock-
raising possibilities of the country south of the river between
that post and Edmonton.

After Hector's return, Palliser went off for four weeks
with an Indian to hunt in the country to the south of Fort
Edmonton. Before the snow fell he was able to see a good deal
of the country and found the soil rich and fairly wooded,
chiefly with clumps of poplar and birch. The whole country
afforded fine feed for horses, even the swamps, which were
now hard with frost. Hunting was good. They killed deer,
wapiti, moose, and black bears.

Palliser was back at Edmonton in early December. Meanwhile Hector had been off, when the rivers were frozen, on
another, longer trip, travelling with dogs and three sleds. He
took with him Peter Erasmus, James Richards, and a Cree

Indian called 'the Fox'. He wanted to study the whole sweep
of country along the base of the mountains near the Devil's
Head, north-east of Banff; he took the middle Blackfoot track
from Edmonton to the south. For a week the air had been
'filled with crystals of ice, causing a dazzling haze, and which
fall steadily, the air being dead calm, and cover the ground
and the branches of the trees with a beautiful efflorescence.
The haze gives rise to well-developed parahelia, or sun-dogs
as they are called, almost every day towards noon.' Where the
Blackfoot trail swung off to the south-south-east they turned
to the south-south-west and soon reached the Battle River,
which they followed for some distance, and then crossed to
pick up another track, the Wolf's Trail.

It was now the end of November, but for one day rain
made it very heavy work for the dogs to drag the sleds over
the moist snow. It soon turned cold again, with heavy snow
next day, a temperature of 23° below zero a few nights later
and 37° below the night after that. Hector described that
exceedingly cold night:

> We had a splendid camp around dry pine woods, and kept
> up a roaring fire all night, generally having six logs on at a
> time, each about one foot in diameter and eight feet long. The
> stars were wonderfully clear, and, when Jupiter was near the
> meridian, we distinctly saw, as it were, two irregularities on
> its margin with the naked eye, and which, with a common
> field glass were clearly defined as two of the satellites. For
> several days at this time, even with the small sextant telescope,
> two large spots were observed on the sun's disk. This phenom-
> enon may have had something to do with the production of
> the sudden extreme of cold which occurred at this time, and
> which I have since learned was felt all over the central portion
> of the continent.

Even with the snow covering it, they observed clear traces
of the cart-track, always used by travellers who crossed the
mountains, that led to the Old Bow Fort. They travelled up

the Red Deer River on the ice for three days. Just above the point at which the trail crossed the river, they came to the fork where the Little Red Deer River and the Medicine River join the main stream of the Red Deer. The Indians were anxious that the company should establish a post here, which Hector thought would be an excellent idea.

A porcupine provided a fine supper. The Indian saved the quills for embroidering moccasins and leather shirts. He extracted them by a very ingenious process, taking advantage of their barbed points. He flapped his leather gun-cover against the porcupine, then withdrew it with a jerk, which pulled most of the quills out, and left them standing in the leather; then there was no difficulty in grasping them by their blunt, soft roots and pulling them out in handfuls. Next day they stole a hearty supper of fresh meat for their dogs from some wolves, which had chased and killed a buck on the ice of the river. In the chase the buck had swum an open place in the river; his hair was completely covered with a coat of ice, which had slowed him up so much that the wolves had caught him. Hector's party drove them off before they had finished their meal.

Next morning they all fell through the ice themselves, but got out safely. However, as Hector commented, wet clothes are not to be trifled with when the thermometer is at -20°; so they got quickly to land, made a big fire, and dried themselves.

They came in sight of the Rocky Mountains that afternoon. The next day, finding the ice on the river too open for travel, they turned off on the track of an Indian party, which led them to the camp of Hector's old friends, the Indians who had been so good to him that autumn when he had come starving out of the mountains. The group had been pitching camp along the base of the mountains since then and were now bound for the edge of the woods, as they had heard that the buffalo were close and the Blackfoot far off. One of their hunters came in the same evening, having shot a splendid buck. He had stalked it, and got so close that he had driven his arrow fourteen inches into the deer. Although nearly all

the Indians used guns, they had not yet forgotten the use of
their ancient weapon.

Hector took on as guide an Indian from this camp. Next
afternoon it was bitterly cold, and the Indian, who wore only
a thin deerskin shirt and leggings, and a small worn-out
blanket coat, began to freeze. Hector unlashed his sled and
gave him one of his blankets, but the Indian did not recover
at once, so they made camp and started a large fire. Ordinar-
ily, in severe weather, the Indians did not leave their tents, let
alone travel all day as the doctor's party was doing. Hector,
who had a large buffalo robe, let the Indian make the blanket
into a coat with a hood and gave him his second blanket for
sleeping.

Next morning they were awakened by the northern lights,
a beautiful display of green and red streamers, so bright that
they thought it was dawn. They came that morning to Prairie
la Graisse, through which Sir George Simpson had passed on
his journey in 1841. Hector was surprised that, even on the
spot, it was so difficult to learn by which route the Governor
had crossed the mountains. He concluded—correctly—that
Simpson must have used a pass known to exist close by the
Devil's Head. This was the gap running from Ghost River by
Lake Minnewanka to the Bow River at Cascade Mountain.
The previous summer they had had the route to Simpson
Pass, up Healy Creek, pointed out to them by Rundle's old
Indian guide.

The party had to go down an exceedingly steep 400-foot
bank that night, to camp beside Waiparous Creek. They
untackled the dogs, and each held on by the tail line of his sled
and, sitting in the snow, dragged behind to prevent its acquir-
ing an impetus. Hector had an accident:

> *I was going down in fine style after this fashion, when a young*
> *pine tree got between my legs and pulled me up short, the jerk*
> *broke the line; and the sled with the instruments and kettles,*
> *slid off like a shot. As the slope terminated by a perpendicular*
> *cliff of 90 feet, over which I could just see the tops of the tall*

> *pines growing up from below, I thought there was no hope,*
> *but when just on the brink it struck a rock that whirled it*
> *round, so that it buried itself in the snow without further*
> *damage.*

When they woke next morning they found that they had been quite snowed up by a heavy storm during the night. Hector was up first. He saw a curious sight: there was not the slightest trace of the camp—men, dogs, sleds, and fire all were covered by unbroken snow. He noticed that when this occurred the additional warmth, and perhaps the knowledge of the extra work on rising, made them always much later in starting. The dogs also made the most of it; no whistling or calling would make them reveal themselves, and the knowing ones were only to be found when the traveller, walking round the camp in every direction, tramped on them.

Deadman's River (Ghost River) was not yet frozen, so they could not travel up it with the dog trains. It was the only possible route into the mountains, as the country everywhere was covered with dense forest. They had to turn back, but first Hector made a trip to the north-west, along the base of the mountains. Virginia (white-tailed) deer were so numerous that they got one nearly every day to keep them going; indeed, after they had turned back for Edmonton, in one valley they started band after band, just as if they were passing through a deer park. Later they came upon a small band of buffalo and killed two and camped to enjoy the marrow-bones, for which they had keen relish after faring so long on lean venison. The Stoneys, whose camp they came to again next day, were delighted to hear that there were buffalo near by, as they had not found any and were starving.

They were now at the edge of the woods and could look out across the plain below, which with its snowy surface and the dark, well-defined margin of wooded country looked like a great frozen sea. To the west they had a fine view of the mountains.

Following along the edge of the woods, they came on the

ruins of an old Indian stockade, which had at one time been thrown up by some war-party that was being pursued. It consisted of conical lodges of heavy trees piled in such numbers as to resist shot, and was surrounded by a breastwork of logs that communicated with a large enclosed space where the horses had been concealed. It was well adapted for defence and yet was in so secluded a spot that a large party might lie there in concealment.

They had been following the Little Red Deer River, but now swung away over high ground. Once more they got a splendid view of the mountains; Hector took bearings of all the points he recognized. At dark they struck the river again and followed it till water that had flowed over the ice forced them to camp. In the pitch dark something stirred in a thicket. Richards took a quick shot in the direction of the sound and killed a young bull.

Both Indians with the party were by now getting tired out. The Stoney, especially, seemed to be a soft walker, who had been but little used to snow-shoe work. Although the Indians could perform great feats and go long distances when hunting, they did not stand up to the daily travelling as well as the half-breeds.

Next day Hector had the best view he had ever had of buffalo quietly feeding. He had gone ahead with the Indian, and saw a large band. They got quite close by crawling in the snow, which was twelve inches deep on the open ground. The buffalo in feeding used their noses to plough the snow like pigs; they did not scrape like horses with their forefeet. Hector and the Indian easily got within fifty yards before they fired, but the frost had so weakened the lock of the Indian's flint gun that it would not go off; so they only killed one buffalo, and a very lean one it was. Away in the distance, towards their Cache Camp of the summer before, they saw the plains quite covered with buffalo and turned north to the river, as they did not wish to disturb them.

The Fox and Erasmus spent next day stocking up with choice meat while Hector geologized. His dog, a notorious thief, actually poked its nose into the kettle as it was boiling on the fire, and took out a piece of meat.

The snow was deep and two of the party always had to go ahead to beat down the track for the dogs, but they made a very long journey each day until, after again striking the Blackfoot Trail, they were forced to stop, so strongly did the wind from the north blow in their faces, with the temperature at -9°. When the wind dropped at three a.m. they set off again, their way lighted by a magnificent display of northern lights, streamers of all colours, so bright that they remained visible until it was quite light and the sun had almost risen.

They pressed on, though the cold wind sprang up again. The poor Stoney, as before, was the first to freeze. In the afternoon, after having walked 536 miles (exclusive of side trips) in twenty-nine days, they reached Fort Edmonton, just in time to join in the fun of Christmas Eve.

In a letter to Sir George Simpson, Palliser described the celebrations:

> *We have spent a very pleasant Xmas, here and was very agreably [sic] surprised by not seeing a drunken man during the whole of Xmas week–Mrs. Christie and I gave two balls in the large room opposite the dining room. The room was splendidly decorated, with swords bayonets flags etc., Bourgeau and Sullivan were the decorators, they made a splendid wooden Lustre to hang from the ceiling, and lighted the whole place up with candles and reflectors it was a brilliant sight and they all enjoyed themselves very much–a great many came from St. Annes, we had about 200 people, I counted 170 after several had gone. They began at 8 and kept it up till 3 in the morning–I intend giving another as soon as the mail starts, but we are all very busy till then.*

Besides the secular celebrations, services were held by both missionaries in the principal room of the fort. The French priests of the Roman Catholic mission at Lake St. Ann's frequently visited the fort. Father Lacombe, the head of the order, was, Palliser reported, a most excellent, benevolent gentleman, possessing many estimable qualities most valuable in a missionary. He spoke Cree as well, and had gained a good deal of influence—not so much, however, among the Indians as among the half-breeds. Later on he was to use his influence to keep the Blackfoot from joining in the second Riel rising in 1885.

Palliser also reported on the other missionaries:

> *The merit of introducing a Christian influence among the Indian tribes in this part of the country is principally due to the efforts of the Wesleyan missionaries. Mr. Rundle, who must have been a very able and influential man, is spoken of among them with reverence and enthusiasm to this day. Mr. Woolsey also, the present missionary, is a most excellent benevolent person. The Indians which I consider to have thus benefited by the Christian precept and example, are the Thick-wood Crees and Rocky Mountain Stoneys, who, being remote from civilisation, are not so liable to be corrupted by the baneful proximity of the white population.*

Occupied since his return to the Fort early in December in writing his reports to go off with the winter mail, Palliser had been too busy to hunt, but after the mails had gone he was free to go hunting at last; he had, in addition, a good reason for going up-river on a trip.

He was determined to explore the Blackfoot country, and when on several occasions Blackfoot visited the fort he told them that he intended next year to travel right through the heart of their country. He decided to go up to Rocky Mountain House to make friends with their chiefs, with a view to facilitating the progress of the expedition through their country in the following season. Captain Brisco and Mr. Mitchell were also anxious to hunt and to see the country; having a fair lot of horses, they determined to try the trip, although it was rather a bad time of year for travelling on horse-back. Palliser accompanied them with Sam Ballenden and two dog sleds. It was a pleasant trip. They fell in with plenty of buffalo. Travelling very slowly, on account of the horses, which often had very deep snow to struggle through, they reached Rocky Mountain House early in the month of February.

Mr. Brazeau, an American in charge of the Hudson's Bay Company post—which was small and in a very shaky condition—gave them a hearty welcome. He found the post lonely, being by nature a very sociable man. Palliser added that he was also most entertaining. Brazeau, who came of an old Spanish family and had been educated in the United States, had been for many years in the American Indian fur trade and spoke six Indian languages—Stoney, Sioux, Ojibwa, Cree, Blackfoot, and Crow—as well as Spanish, English, and French. Trade was brisk, but he was most wretchedly supplied with goods for the trade and had had to turn away bands of Blackfoot, eighty and a hundred strong, well laden with buffalo robes, bear skins, wolf skins, and other less valuable furs.

Palliser made frequent hunting excursions from Rocky Mountain House. These gave him opportunities to get acquainted with the Blackfoot and their chiefs. He was visited by all the chiefs to whom Dr. Hector had given papers the previous winter. These were considered by them valuable documents. After reading them and granting more, Palliser made them some presents, such as ammunition, tobacco, and cloth, which he had brought from Edmonton for the purpose. One particularly influential chief, Old Swan, adopted Palliser as his grandson, a relationship that was to be helpful later on.

When spring arrived, Palliser and his two friends, with their men, set off down the river in a small skiff that Mr. Brazeau had had made for them. They hunted as they went, in a manner reminiscent of Palliser's earlier trip down the Missouri. When the brigade of boats from Rocky Mountain House caught up with them, they joined it, returning to Fort Edmonton in Mr. Brazeau's boat with his family.

Chapter Sixteen

Rivers Flowing to the Frozen Ocean

C hristmas and New Year festivities over and reports and letters sent off to England by the winter express, Hector, too, set off again, this time on a trip to Jasper House, on the Athabasca River, which flows 'down north' to the Arctic Ocean. He took with him once again Erasmus, Richards, and a *voyageur* in the company's service, one Louison. Each of them had a dog train. Each sled carried about 350 pounds—their bedding, instruments and other gear, and pemmican for twenty-eight days. It was beautiful weather, though cold, and Mr. Christie brought a party along to camp with Hector the first night, out at the horseguard, about twenty-five miles from the fort. He brought two horse carioles and several dog sleds with provisions for the picnic. As the track was hard, they covered the twenty-five miles in four and a half hours and spent the afternoon visiting the horses, which had fine feeding and shelter in the tracts of prairie along the Sturgeon River. The horse-keeper gave up his log hut for their use and they passed a very merry evening.

Hector described an incident that took place that night, which showed what a good train of dogs could do, provided they had a hardy and expert driver:

> *Mr. Christie found on arriving at the 'guard' that he had forgotten a letter he wished me to take to Jasper House. He at once sent back his clerk, Mr. Sinclair, to the fort with his dogs, although that gentleman had just driven them the 25 miles*

out to this place. Sinclair got to the fort before midnight, and sent back a man with the same dogs, who arrived with the letter for us before we were up in the morning, the dogs having thus run 75 miles in a good deal under the 24 hours.

However, M. Lecombe [sic], the Roman Catholic priest, has been frequently driven from the mission at Lac St. Ann's to the fort in his dog cariole, a distance of 50 miles; after which his man Alexis, one of the best runners in the country, has loaded the sled with 400lbs. of meat, and returned to the mission before next morning.

Next day the picnic party went back to the fort and Hector's little party headed north to the great river that would lead them westward. They had to use snow-shoes and kept on the lakes as much as possible; the trail, cut through the woods to Fort Assiniboine on the Athabasca River (a tributary of the Mackenzie system), was much obstructed by their old enemy, fallen timber. They crossed the Pembina River, the most southerly stream of the prairies that flows to the Arctic Ocean, and two days later they came to the valley of the Athabasca itself. They made a long and steep descent to the river and travelled up it on the ice to Fort Assiniboine, a deserted post of the Hudson's Bay Company, on a beautiful level prairie. Then it consisted only of a few ruined log huts, though once, as the end of the overland link between the Saskatchewan and the Athabasca, it had been much frequented by brigades crossing the mountains by the Athabasca Portage. The party took possession of the kitchen and by cutting down some of the old palisades soon got plenty of firewood. Before they left they pulled up the floor of a room in the hut and cached a bag of pemmican to take them back to the fort on their return from the mountains.

When they went on up the Athabasca the snow was deep on the ice, so that two of them had to go ahead to break trail, and the ice where the river current was rapid was full of open holes. It suddenly grew warmer and a great storm of wind from the south-west came in fierce gusts, bringing down the trees all around their camp. At ten o'clock at night the storm ceased, the sky cleared, and the thermometer at once fell thirty-nine degrees, from 40° at seven p.m. to 1° at ten p.m. Once again Hector was recording the effects of the chinook.

Snow fell heavily for a day and a night, making it weary work with the snow-shoes. Even three of the travellers going ahead to break the trail did not make it firm enough to bear the dogs up until the first sled had passed. None the less, by going steadily, they managed generally to make eighteen miles a day, despite some mishaps. Louison, coming down a steep bank, stupidly smashed his sled. They had to put the load on the other sleds and leave the broken one behind. Two of the dogs, which Hector had bought just before starting, and which were quite wild, made their escape within a few days after they started, but still continued to follow them, skulking behind like wolves, and joining their companions only at night. They tried every plan to capture them, but in vain. They once caught one of them in a snare, but he cut it through with his teeth before they could secure him.

Next day they halted at noon to cache another bag of pemmican, by building logs over it, carefully fitting them together by notches. The great danger to a cache was the wolverine, a small, rough-haired animal, like a miniature bear, much stronger in proportion to his size than any other animal in the country, and possessed of great cunning. It was very difficult to defeat his marauding propensities, about which many wonderful yarns were told round the camp-fire.

At last they fell in with some Thickwood Stoneys who had been starving most of the winter and looked very miserable. They were anxious to trade ammunition for furs, and Hector got them to exchange two pairs of rather worn-out snow-shoes, which were the cause of one man's beginning to suffer from *mal du raquette,* an agonizing inflammation of the tendons of the foot.

Two days later as they were preparing to camp they observed smoke rising out of the woods; they climbed the riverbank to find four tents of Iroquois half-breeds, a long way from their ancestors' traditional hunting-grounds east of the Great Lakes. These were freemen—that is, men not in the service of the Hudson's Bay Company—who had been trappers for the North West Company before its merger in 1821 with the Honourable Company. They too were badly off for provisions, and were living altogether on the little hare. Even that was very scarce that year.

From the high banks of the river they got a splendid view of the mountains, after travelling for some time in such dense forests that they could see nothing of the country. The mountains stood out in bold outline, especially Roche Miette, a landmark south of the Athabasca. They had to cover the last forty miles to Jasper House in one day. The ice was clear of snow at last, so they did not need to use snow-shoes, a great relief after walking on them constantly for seventeen days. But their difficulties were not over. One lake seven miles long was swept by such a violent wind that they could hardly make headway against it over the smooth ice. The ice of the upper lake was so covered with sand, blown from the dunes on the eastern shore, that the dogs could scarcely pull the sleds along. Above the lake the river was so open that they could not travel on the ice; they swung off on a track through dense woods. It was quite dark when a spur of mountain forced them back to the river, here a rapid stream with a mere fringe of ice about its margins. They had to cross it—a memorable episode! This is Hector's description:

> *After searching about for a crossing place in the dark without success, we took the most shallow place we could find, where the river was very rapid, and without taking the harness off the dogs, unfastened them from the sleds, and pitching them into the water, pelted them with pieces of ice, so that they swam for the other side of the river. We then got off the edge of the ice ourselves, and found the water took us above the waist, and getting the sleds, loads and all, on our shoulders, waded through the rapid, which was about 100 yards wide, and so reached the left bank. The wind, which had changed at sunset*

to N.E., was bitterly cold, so that the plunge into the water felt rather warm at first, but on re-emerging we at once stiffened into a mass of ice, for, as I found half an hour afterwards, the thermometer stood at -15°. In this state we again tackled the dogs, that were all frozen into a lump with their harness, and after a run of two miles through the woods, we reached Jasper House at 10 p.m.

Mr. Moberly, the Hudson's Bay officer in charge, received them most kindly.

Frozen as he was, Hector, immediately on arriving, set up the thermometer in a good position facing the north, for the purpose of taking a series of observations. He was just in time, as the next day was February 1, the day on which he had arranged that Sullivan should take hourly observations at Edmonton, to make a comparison. The doctor started at midnight to do the same at Jasper House, continuing, with Moberly's help, for twenty-four hours.

He still had time and energy to notice that 'Jasper House is beautifully situated on an open plain, about six miles in extent, within the first range of mountains. As the valley makes a bend above and below, it appears to be completely encircled by mountains, which rise from 4,000 to 5,000 feet, with bold craggy outlines; the little group of buildings which form the "fort" have been constructed, in keeping with their picturesque situation, after the Swiss style, with overhanging roofs and trellised porticos.'

Jasper House, like Fort Assiniboine, was on what had been the much-travelled main route across the mountains, with a regular system of communication to the west twice a year as lately as 1853:

In March, when the snow had acquired a crust, the express, with letters and accounts, started from Edmonton by the route I had just followed, and continued on to the boat encampment, to which place, by the time they arrived, owing to the earlier spring on the west side of the mountain, the brigade of

> boats had ascended from Vancouver.* The mail from the
> western department was then exchanged, and taken back to
> Edmonton, and thence to Norway House, along with the
> Jasper House furs.
>
> The second time of communication was in autumn, after
> the Saskatchewan brigade returned to Edmonton in the
> beginning of September, upon which the officers and men
> bound for the western department, taking with them the
> subsidy of otter skins that the Company annually paid the
> Russian Government for the rent of the N.W. coast, crossed
> the portage to Fort Assineboine, then ascended the Athabasca
> in boats to Jasper House with pack-horses, reached the boat
> encampment, and then descended the Columbia to Vancou-
> ver, where they arrived generally about the 1st of November.
> The journey from York Factory on Hudson's Bay to the
> Pacific coast by this route generally occupied three and a half
> months, and involved an amount of hardship and toil that
> cannot be appreciated by those who have not seen boat
> travelling in these territories.

The men at the post had almost nothing to eat except the
big-horn sheep. The three Iroquois hunters of the fort set off
every day before daybreak to intercept the sheep on their way
back from an early morning visit to salt-licks in the valley.
They used dogs that were superbly trained to turn the sheep
as they rushed up the mountain to reach the most inaccessible
precipices. Then came the hardest work—carrying the meat
down the mountain. A second man would go up next day to
bring the carcass down, using a tump-line, the forehead-strap
that their ancestors had used on portages on the ancient
canoe routes through the eastern forests.

Lynx meat, excellent eating when fat, supplemented the
wild mutton. Eighty-three lynx had been shot that winter,
Moberly himself bagging half of them, as he had a splendid
dog that hunted them till they climbed a tree, then watched
them till his master came with his gun. The mutton was lean,

---

*Fort Vancouver on the lower Columbia, not the modern Vancouver, B.C.

the lynx were fat; so they stuffed the lynx meat with minced mutton, roasting it whole. This made a very savoury dish.

Hector was busy for a few days making observations and checking his instruments, but he still fitted in some geologizing trips. He lost one of his best dogs, which had scraped up out of the frozen snow an old head of a fox that had been poisoned. Poison was freely used against the wolves and foxes. Hector recounts one instance:

> *A pack of thick-wood wolves have been killing a number of the horses belonging to the Company during the winter, and the hunter having found a fine young mare just freshly killed the other day, salted the carcass well with strychnine, and this morning we set off to observe the effect. Crossing the lake we walked about two miles through the woods, when we fell on the track of the poor mare and her pursuers. She had been hard pressed by three of them, one on each side, cutting off the bends she made, while the others followed close behind, and at last had seized her haunch and thrown himself down, so that he left a broad track where he had dragged through the snow. On reaching the carcass we found that the strychnine had done its work, for there lay four enormous wolves, besides five or six of a smaller species, while about a score of large ravens were lying about, either dead or in different states of paralysis, some lying on their backs with only power to croak, and others wading about in the snow in a most solemn manner, with their wings trailing behind them. The large wolves, who were the real offenders, were splendid brutes. The two youngest were nearly black, while the old ones were grizzled grey, like Scotch stag-hounds. The largest measured two and a half feet at the shoulder, and was five feet eight inches in length. The hunters say there is yet another of the family, and that the survivor is well known by his track, as he has only three feet, for having once been caught in a steel trap, he freed himself by gnawing off the foot he was held by.*

Hector told another tale of assassination:

> *There was once a little tribe of Indians known as the Snakes,*
> *that lived in the country to the north of Jasper House, but*
> *which, during the time of the North West Fur Company, was*
> *treacherously exterminated by the Assineboines. They were*
> *invited to a peace feast by the latter Indians, when they were*
> *to settle all their disputes, and neither party was to bring any*
> *weapons. It was held about three miles below the present site*
> *of Jasper House, but the Assineboines being all secretly armed,*
> *fell on the poor Snakes in the midst of the revelry, and killed*
> *them all.*

He wrote rather wistfully of a trail to 'Smoking River', a branch of the Peace River, a two-day journey to the northwest. He could not spare the time to travel its rugged length to what the hunters described as the finest land in the country. The vast herds of buffalo and wapiti that Sir Alexander Mackenzie had reported in 1793 on the prairies of the Peace River were no longer there. Even twenty years before Hector's visit there had been plenty of buffalo and wapiti, but by 1859 the northern limit of such herds was at least three degrees farther south. Wild horses, too, which had once provided ample food supplies, had by then dwindled away, as large bands had been driven down to Edmonton.

The weather was very variable—the chinook again. Hector had much to say of the vagaries of this wind and of the warmth of this mountain region as compared to the plains to the east. Though one man, sent to bring in wild mutton, froze his feet, as it had been so warm at the fort that he had worn no socks under his moccasins, another man swam cheerfully into the river for a duck that had been shot in front of the fort.

Hector tried to climb Roche Miette, the mountain block that dominated the valley. With Moberly he got up 3,500 feet, after a long and steep climb, to a sharp peak far above any vegetation, but the great cubical block that forms the top of the mountain still towered 2,000 feet above them. It was quite inaccessible, at least from the side they were on, though one man, the hunter Miette, had once climbed it from the south side. From their vantage-point they could follow the course of the Athabasca River winding through pine forests to the north-north-east for forty or fifty miles and breaking through the outer range of mountains. Hector could see the ugly-looking place where they had crossed the river in the dark on their way to Jasper House; if they had only seen where they were going they might have hesitated to attempt it. Moberly sat smoking on the peak, enjoying a balmy breeze, while Hector searched for fossils at the bottom of the 150-foot-deep gully between this and the massive summit block, in a wind so cold that it numbed him.

Hector had made sure that he had kept enough pemmican in reserve to take them back to their first cache, as he did not want to draw on Moberly's slender stock of provisions for more than what his party needed while staying at the fort. He now discovered that his three men, not liking the lean mutton that everyone else was eating, had taken the bag of pemmican out of the store and eaten it all. As such a misdemeanour was not to be passed over, he sent them back at once to Edmonton, leaving them to get down to the first cache as best they could. He did not feel he could leave them hanging about at Jasper House while he was away on a trip still farther into the mountains. Hector kept three of the dogs, but the men took his sled with them, since he could not use it on his mountain journey.

A party of freemen had arrived at Jasper House, and Moberly was afraid they might disturb the scanty local game, on which the post depended for food—an anxious business, as there was no one there during the summer and autumn to lay in supplies of meat and fish. Moberly and Hector therefore went to visit their camp. It was a cold ride, the temperature ranging between seven and fourteen degrees below zero. The Iroquois freemen were living in huts built of pine branches. With them was an old Canadian named François, who was famous for his well-trained hunting dogs, which by their wonderful abilities kept him supplied with food when much better hunters were starving. They engaged one of the

Iroquois hunters, Tekarra, to make the trip towards the source of the Athabasca and afterwards to guide Hector through the woods back to Lake St. Ann's.

As they were returning from the freemen's camp to Jasper House, the new guide fell with his horse while crossing a creek, and bruised his foot, a bad beginning to the snow-shoe trip ahead. In spite of this accident, they started off next morning—Hector, Tekarra, Moberly, and a Canadian named Arkand. Moberly drove the dogs along the ice of the river and successive lakes into which it widened out; the rest travelled with the horses along the edge of the valley. It was twenty degrees below zero, so they felt that Moberly, sheltered in the bottom of the valley, had decidedly the best of it.

Two days out, they came to the point at which the track divided, one branch going to New Caledonia, the Hudson's Bay Company's Fraser River district, and the other to the Boat Encampment on the Columbia. This is the point at which the Canadian National Railway today swings off up the Miette River to the Yellowhead Pass, while the highway still follows the Athabasca to the south-east, and on to Banff. Crossing a high ridge to cut off a great bend in the river, Hector had a fine view up the valley, which, he reported, ran without interruption for thirty or forty miles. Years before, when the trail was kept clear, to reach the Fraser at a point at which boats could be used took six days, but the route had been abandoned for so many years that it would have taken much longer at the time of Hector's visit. The valley also connected, by way of the Bad (Maligne) River, with the Kootenay Plain on the North Saskatchewan, which Hector had visited the summer before.

Meanwhile Tekarra had been hunting with some success, in spite of his sore foot, but his exertions had so much inflamed it that he could not guide them up the valley to the Committee Punch Bowl at the summit of the Athabasca Pass. Instead, they followed the main stream of the Athabasca, passing the mouth of the Whirlpool River, which flows from the Punch Bowl. Climbing a mountain opposite the valley of

the Whirlpool, Hector could see up the river to two mountains. From Tekarra's description he easily recognized these
as Mount Hooker and Mount Brown, between which the pass
ran, and which the expedition's instructions had set as the
northern limit of the territory to be explored. These mountains have been one of the mysteries of Canadian geography,
as early travellers so exaggerated their height that no one has
been able to identify them.

Tekarra and Arkand now turned back, but Hector and
Moberly went on, on snow-shoes. As they halted for a rest they
had an encounter with that toughest of all animals, the
wolverine. Hector wrote that the animal came

> . . . *wabolling down the river on ice. We remained still till
> he got quite close without seeing us, when Moberly fired and
> put the ball right through him, so that his blood spouted out
> on the snow. He at first rolled over, but on our approaching
> him he started up and ran off, staining the snow with blood.
> We followed on our snow shoes, and pressed him hard, so that
> he ran up the bank and made for the mountain, where,
> getting into a clift of the rock, he escaped us. The distance he
> ran while losing so much blood, surprised us very much, as at
> first we thought he was killed outright.*

The river was now becoming quite a mountain torrent,
hemmed in by lofty and rugged mountains, one of which
Hector named after his companion, Moberly, and one after
Mr. Christie of Edmonton. They turned down-stream again.
Coming on the tracks of nine reindeer, as Hector called them
(presumably caribou), that had crossed the river, the men
followed them till darkness forced them to give up. They
reached the camp, where Tekarra and Arkand awaited them,
after a walk that day of thirty-six miles, and had to lie down to
sleep without supper as none of them had killed anything.
Next day Moberly went back to look for the 'reindeer', again
without getting a shot, though he saw them. Meanwhile
Hector followed the bend in the river that they had missed

coming up. There was smooth, sound ice for six or eight miles, but the river then became so rapid that it was not frozen. It was so hemmed in by rocky precipices that Hector had difficulty in getting along at all, but at last he managed to get off the river into the woods. There the snow was so deep that he had to walk on and beat a track for a few hundred yards at a time, then return and drive the dogs on to the point he had reached. This process was so slow that he did not get to camp till nightfall, covering a mere sixteen miles that day.

Next day they got back to Jasper House, where poor Moberly found that his fine, lynx-hunting dog had eaten poisoned bait and died, the second valuable victim of strychnine since Hector's arrival. That evening one of the hunters brought in a splendid ram, which he had caught by setting a snare in a path leading to a salt-lick.

Next day Hector packed up his instruments, which Moberly had promised to take down by boat in the spring. He also ruled a register on which Moberly was to enter the thermometer and barometer readings, which he had undertaken to record regularly until May. As Moberly wished Tekarra to return at once from Edmonton to bring back a supply of ammunition, he sent with Hector a young lad named Louis Cardinal to accompany him back. It was a rule in the company's service never to let a man take a long journey alone.

Tekarra reckoned that the journey to Edmonton would take twelve days, but expected to get plenty of rabbits and perhaps larger game, so they carried only a few days' provisions: eighteen pounds of pemmican, two pounds of flour, and a little tea and sugar. As soon as they left the river to strike through the woods, they had to carry everything on their backs, apart from what little they tied on the backs of two of the strongest dogs. Besides the provisions, they each had a blanket and a few extra pairs of moccasins and blanket socks, as well as Hector's papers, books, and sextants, two kettles, an axe, and a gun.

After a little searching they found the blazings on the trees that marked the track, and followed them steadily south by east. The snow was deep enough to let them walk smoothly over the fallen logs, but it was so soft that it was hard work for the leader, and the loaded dogs could not keep up, so the men had to carry everything themselves. Farther on they followed McLeod River. The ice was covered with deep snow, which had turned to slush in places where the water had overflowed the ice.

The first day they saw and shot only one rabbit; this was worrying, as their pemmican was only sufficient for three days. They put themselves on short rations at once, but killed all five of a covey of wood grouse next evening. In two more days their pemmican was all gone, as they had shot nothing more. Next day they saw moose tracks, but a sudden change in the wind gave the animals the alarm and they escaped. Much disheartened, the men walked moodily on till evening, passing through fine tracts of country, contrary to the reports Hector had heard.

An open patch of burnt timber gave them a distant, exciting glimpse of mountain peaks, but the fallen timber caught their snow-shoes and made the men fall, too, which was very trying to their tempers, already much soured by starvation.

Then their luck turned. Hector wrote:

> . . . *at noon we arrived at a little swampy valley, where the snow was trodden down as if by the tracks of a large band of buffalo. However, Tekarra after looking around said, it was only the place where three moose-deers had been feeding all winter, and with wonderful quickness he picked out their most recent tracks, and told us to go on steadily and only to halt if he fired three shots, which was to be a sign he had killed one of them. We had only gone a mile when we heard a shot, and immediately after two others. This at once banished our fatigue, and regardless of the deep snow and fallen timber, we made off in the direction of the firing. Here we found Tekarra busy cutting up a fine three-year-old moose, which was the*

youngest of two he had seen. We at once made a fire by the carcase, which lay among fallen timber where the snow was about four feet deep. Our appetite was tremendous, so that, although the flesh of the animal was so lean that at other times we would not have eaten it, we continued cooking, eating, and sleeping the remainder of that day, and the whole of the next, by which time there was little left of the moose but the coarser parts of the meat. Our three dogs also, who had eaten nothing but the bones of the grouse and our cast-off mocassins since leaving Jasper House, enjoyed themselves to the full; indeed both the dogs and masters conducted themselves more like wolves than was altogether seemly, excepting under such circumstances.

Next morning, March 1, they started off, quite refreshed, each carrying a load of cooked meat sufficient to last them several days.

The sun was very powerful during the day, which made the snow wet and heavy for snow-shoes. Three days later they recrossed the watershed dividing the Athabasca drainage basin from the Saskatchewan system. Here they left the rivers flowing to the frozen ocean for waters draining to Hudson Bay. Firm ice on the lakes and rivers now made it possible to travel fast. They covered thirty-five miles one day, which brought them to the north-west corner of Lake St. Ann's. Next day they reached the mission station. They found the priests very worried and on the point of sending out, at Mr. Christie's desire, a search-party to relieve them, as they had heard from Hector's men, who got back safely, that the doctor was to return through the woods, and from the half-breeds that game was scarce, so they had great fears for his safety.

Erasmus was waiting for them, according to instructions, with a fresh train of dogs, so Hector went off again with him at ten o'clock the same night, and having a good track and fresh dogs they ran the remaining fifty miles to Edmonton in ten hours, arriving there for breakfast in the morning.

Two weeks later, hearing that a clerk at Fort Pitt was

seriously ill, Mr. Christie and the doctor set off to see him. They travelled at night, when the snow was firm, but when they came to the edge of the plains the weather began to change for the worse. The quantity of snow increased and there was no beaten track. Having to use snow-shoes slowed them up. About half-way to Fort Pitt they met some trappers who advised them to strike to the south where they would find a track to Fort Pitt, on which they had been hauling meat from a buffalo pound.

They had left the woods only a few miles, striking out onto the bare, rolling plains, when a great snow-storm set in, so violent that they could not distinguish objects a hundred yards ahead. By mere chance they hit on the pound, but it was quite deserted. They found only one old Indian and his wife in the neighbourhood, both suffering from snow-blindness and so, also, starvation. Thinking that the next day would bring them to Fort Pitt, they gave the Indian couple nearly all their provisions. The snow-storm was as bad as ever and the wind had so swept and drifted the snow on the plains that they could not find a trace of the track. To make matters worse, Hector found that, by an incredible oversight, he had left his compass behind. There was no sun and no landmarks to steer by. Occasional low hills helped a little, since Hector knew by experience that the side on which a few stunted poplars and willows grew usually faced somewhere between north and east. All the same, by the middle of the day the five members of the party had five different ideas as to where the north lay, which Hector took as sure proof that they were lost. They travelled on rapidly for two days in this state of uncertainty and at last fell on a fresh trail, which led them to an Indian camp.

On hearing where we were bound for, the Indians would hardly believe us, for we had turned completely round, crossed the ordinary winter road, and were now within a few miles of the Saskatchewan, at the Snake Portage, and were travelling on the trail leading from that place to Edmonton; or, in other

*words, we were already half way back to our starting place.
We at once turned right about, and, as the weather cleared
up, we reached Fort Pitt in two days, arriving at 6 o'clock on
the morning of the 28th, well starved, and some of us quite
snow-blind. We had thus taken eight days and a night to
make the trip; but all the while had travelled at a rate that,
without losing ourselves, would have brought us to Fort Pitt
in four days and a half, having, instead of 195 miles, travelled
more than 300. This unfortunate expedition, which luckily
was attended with no serious consequences, only shows how
even the best equipped parties must run a risk in winter when
travelling in this country. Chief factor Christie, himself an
experienced traveller, being the bourgeois of the whole district,
of course had two of the best men he could get. I had in
addition Erasmus, whose qualities as a traveller I had well
ascertained in several hard trips, and who moreover had
travelled by this very route to Fort Pitt in the beginning of the
winter; and yet, in spite of all this, and of my own knowledge
of the country, which I had already mapped, without doubt
we fairly lost ourselves, wore out our dogs with hunger and
fatigue, and only escaped great privation and risk by mere
accident.*

At Fort Pitt not only Mr. Chastellan, the clerk, but many
others were labouring under a kind of low fever, so that
Hector had at once quite a large practice. For another reason,
too, it was lucky that they had arrived. A party of eleven
Americans had left St. Paul in the spring of 1858, to attempt to
reach the gold mines on the Fraser River. They had only got
as far as the Moose Woods on the South Saskatchewan when
winter set in. They managed to travel over the snow as far as
Fort Pitt, where they spent the winter working for the
Hudson's Bay Company, making nets, harness, and the like in
return for their food and provisions for their journey onward
in the spring. There had been some jealousy and discord in
this party of independent men, who had neither a leader nor
discipline on their long journey, during which they suffered

many privations. A quarrel about some trifling matter between two of the men had come to a head a few days earlier. They drew their revolvers and fired six shots at each other, at a distance of only a few yards. The one that first drew his weapon was mortally wounded and so rendered unsteady by the first shot fired at him, which accounts for the escape of his antagonist from this murderous style of encounter, with only one ball lodged in his hand. Three balls lodged in the body of the aggressor, so that he survived only a few hours.

As the occurrence had taken place within a company fort, Mr. Christie thought it his duty to exercise his authority as a magistrate. He investigated the whole case and, examining the witnesses on oath, drew up a full statement in triplicate. One copy was for the Hudson's Bay Company Council at Norway House and another for the Americans to take with them. The dead man had clearly been the aggressor, so Mr. Christie did not feel warranted in detaining the other man for further trial in a country where there was neither law nor government, but he advised that he should give himself up and stand trial when he reached the Coast so that he might be freed from future imputation.

Hector stayed on to look after his patients. He needed some things, including his instruments and other working-gear, from Edmonton. It took Mr. Christie four days to get back to Edmonton and, without resting, the two men who went with him returned, with their dog sleds heavily loaded, in three days. They had run forty-eight miles a day when going and sixty-two miles a day returning, making the round trip of 380 miles in seven days. Such was the zest for travelling with dogs in the Saskatchewan country that no one considered this at all a wonderful feat. The snow was still deep at Fort Pitt, though at Edmonton they had had genial weather and a mild south-west wind.

The time passed pleasantly. The Hudson's Bay Company officer in charge was James Simpson, Hector's travelling companion of the previous winter. Some of the Americans were very superior men, and there was in addition an English amateur hunter, a Mr. Louch, who had been out after buffalo with Indians on the plains.

Spring was in the air. Immense flocks of little snow-buntings appeared. On the night of April 17 the three-foot-deep snow began to melt very suddenly. Next day the first geese and ring-necked plovers arrived, and three days later the ice began to break up on the river from the weight of melted snow on it.

Hector was anxious to see what the district between Fort Pitt and Edmonton was like in early spring. Mr. Simpson provided horses for the light cart that had been made for him. To this he attached an odometer he had obtained from one of the Americans. The party included Hector's man, Peter Erasmus, and some Hudson's Bay Company men who were going up to help with the fur brigades.

On April 26 they crossed the ice on the river and started for Edmonton. Not many hours afterwards, the river suddenly rose nine feet and, bursting the ice, it cleared the stream by the next day. Spring had come with a vengeance, though it was nearly a month later than the year before. They had trouble crossing many of the streams as these were much flooded. Repeatedly they had to go through the arduous business of swimming in and rafting on the icy waters of creeks not more than fifteen or twenty yards across—creeks that in summer were only dry gullies. Hector was astonished at how quickly the grass sprang up when the snow cleared away, always first and fastest where fire had consumed the grass the previous autumn. They reached Edmonton in six days, after much warm rain and, at night, vivid lightning. This was fast travelling for early spring, as the odometer showed they had covered 195 miles by the track.

Farming operations were well advanced when they reached the fort. Mr. Christie had plans for establishing agriculture on such a scale as to make the company more independent of their half-breed employees.

The brigade of five boats from Rocky Mountain House arrived on May 9. Each was thirty-five feet long and capable of carrying seventy-five 'pieces' weighing ninety pounds each. Building them was one of the most important responsibilities of Rocky Mountain House in the late winter. Palliser came down with the boats. After being separated since Christmas, the members of the expedition were now all together again— except, of course, for Blakiston.

Besides the Rocky Mountain House brigade there now arrived Mr. Moberly's brigade, from Jasper House, and Mr. Colin Fraser's brigade, from Lesser Slave Lake and the Athabasca. Colin Fraser had been Sir George Simpson's ceremonial piper on his great transcontinental journeys. Fraser's daughters, who had probably met Palliser at the Christmas Ball, sent him some beautiful needlework after his return to London. His letter of thanks is in a little Fraser family museum near Edmonton. With the letter he sent Colin Fraser some new pipes, 'by the best makers'. These are still owned by one of Colin Fraser's grandsons at Fort Chipewyan on Lake Athabasca.

Traditionally the boat brigades had been manned by the old Canadian *voyageurs*—hardy, jovial, respectful, and well-conducted men. They were now becoming rare, as were the old hands from the Orkney Islands. Their place was being taken, Palliser noted, by lazy French half-breeds from Lake St. Ann's, who, if ordered to do anything they disliked, went off as soon as they had received their advances to join the Indians on the plains. This added greatly to the difficulties of the chief factor, whose heavy work and responsibility much impressed Hector.

The fort was now very lively, as all were busy preparing for the great annual voyage to the coast of Hudson's Bay, which occupies the whole summer . . . the repacking of their furs, the launching and loading of the boats, and all the necessary preparation, gave the inside of the fort an air of business and mercantile activity that looked more civilized than anything we had before seen in the Saskatchewan. Outside the fort, however, the large motley encampments of Indians, voya-

geurs, and Lac St. Ann half breeds, with their women and children, dogs, and horses, at once destroyed the illusion, the crowds of loiterers showing that the lazy population still maintained that proportion usual in this country to the number of those that work.

The chief factor's work at this juncture is no sinecure. He has all the surrounding population condensed on his hands, and just at the time when every scrap of food acquires tenfold value. Those that start down the stream have not only to carry food for themselves, but also for the brigades to many other parts of the country, while in the fort are to be left the women and children with perhaps only two or three men, and if the buffalo are distant they will certainly suffer a summer of great privation. But the crews of the boats bring their families to loiter round the fort and to see them off, and great trouble and anxiety arises from endeavouring to escape feeding these, and yet without offending the hot-tempered half-breed voyageurs, who have generally received advances, or are in debt to the Company, and would gladly seize any excuse for deserting.

The explorers, too, had preparations to make. Letters and reports had to be written, maps drawn, and specimens prepared and packed to be sent off with the boats when they left.

With them, too, went M. Bourgeau to fulfil an engagement in the Caucasus made prior to the formation of the expedition, when Her Majesty's Government did not contemplate its extension beyond 1858. He was also to complete the botanical work of the expedition at Kew under Hooker's direction. His going was lamented by them all. The expedition would feel quite incomplete out on the plains without his methodical habits and quaint drollery. Palliser wrote:

We were very sorry indeed to lose our friend, who was a great favourite with us all. In addition to his acquirements as a botanist, he united the most sociable jovial disposition, ever ready not only to do his own work, but assist anyone else who asked him. He also possesses the most untiring energy in camp, and no fatigue ever deterred him from immediate attention to the securing and preservation of his specimens, as his collections sent home abundantly prove.

He travelled in the last detachment of boats to set off. This left on May 25, carrying not only M. Bourgeau but the chief factor, Mr. Christie, to whose help and kindness the expedition owed so much. With them, too, went Mrs. Christie and the family, including, no doubt, the remarkably pretty baby whose birth during the winter had given them all such pleasure. The sadly diminished party of explorers saw the boats off. Next day they set out themselves on their final season's work.

CHAPTER SEVENTEEN

Through the Blackfoot Country

When the boat brigades went off down the Saskatchewan, Palliser was still anxiously awaiting instructions from the Colonial Office. He had written by the winter mail to ask for permission to spend a third season in further exploration and to return to England by the Pacific Coast. He had allowed the trusty and active servant of the expedition, James Beads, to go down with the Red River men the previous October so that he could bring back the reply from the Colonial Office as soon as this should arrive at the settlement. Beads had been anxious to go to Red River, as news had reached him that his brother had been killed by Sioux on his way from St. Paul to Red River.

While they waited for word from England, the explorers worked hard to have everything in readiness for a prompt departure when and if the hoped-for authority to continue their work came. As always, the horses were of paramount concern. Almost all of them had survived the winter, and any time that could be spared from writing reports and drawing maps had been devoted to getting them into condition by shifting them about to get the benefit of the best feeding-grounds, exercising the buffalo-runners, and physicking the sick, of which there were several in the band. More men, too, had to be taken on to make up the complement needed for the new season's work, bills had to be settled, and the instruments checked and packed.

When the boats had left, Palliser and the main party

moved off, out onto the plains. There were no buffalo in the neighbourhood of Fort Edmonton. The scarcity of provisions had become acute; the expedition could no longer be supported at the fort. There was nothing for it but to make a start, going in search of food. Hector was left behind to wait for Beads, who was now expected daily with the eagerly awaited dispatches from Her Majesty's Government, which would decide whether they might go on exploring or whether they would have to go home at once.

While he waited, Palliser summed up the work the expedition had already done in its two years, in summer with horses and in winter with dog trains:

> *We had now carried on the explorations from the valley of Red River westward along the boundary line, examined all the country drained by the Assineboine and Qu'appelle River, explored and laid down the whole valley of the North Saskatchewan to its glaciers in the Rocky Mountains, and also the lower portion of the South Saskatchewan, to beyond the elbow, up to 109 ˚ of longitude. Traversed in several directions that region of country between Fort Ellice and Fort Carlton, and containing the Touchwood Hills, Swan River, Fort Pelley, and the lake districts.*
>
> *We had also travelled the piece of country between the two Saskatchewans, examining and laying down Battle River.*
>
> *Again from Fort Assineboine, in lat. 54 1/2 ˚, long. 114 1/2 ˚, through the belt of woods at the base of the Rocky Mountains to Jasper House, in long. 118 ˚, and altogether extending to the southward, by various journeys, our examination of that rich belt of country, along the base of the Rocky Mountains, to the boundary line at the Chief Mountain. And notwithstanding that, in addition to all this exploration of territory, the Rocky Mountains had been crossed and recrossed, and several passes discovered available for horses, yet a glance at our chart showed us that a great block of country in the neighbourhood of the boundary line, viz., from long. 109 ˚ to long. 113 ˚, still remained unexamined, as well as the*

greater part of the South Saskatchewan (commonly called Bow River), which still remained unexplored.

They were to have their chance to examine that great unexplored block of country. Beads arrived at last on June 7. He had made a most wonderfully rapid journey, having accomplished a distance of about a thousand miles on horseback in thirty-four days, travelling alone most of the way after a companion from Red River turned back, until, at Fort Pitt, he secured another companion, Vital, a half-breed, who was on his way to visit some relatives in the Columbia Valley. He had been obliged to abandon one horse on his arduous journey and had made an exchange for a fresh horse at each trading-post he passed through. He had had to swim across the Saskatchewan, losing his clothes in the process; so Hector was forced to wait till he got replacements. With him he brought letters from the Colonial Office authorizing the expedition to go on with its exploration of the still unknown country southwards to the border as well as to return by the Pacific Coast. Their reports of the passes they had examined the summer before had arrived in London just in time to persuade the Colonial Secretary to ask the House of Commons for an additional appropriation for the expedition. The way was cleared for the last great adventure, the attempt to travel right through the heart of the Blackfoot country south of the Forks of the Red Deer and South Saskatchewan to the Cypress Hills beyond, and so along the boundary line once more to the Rocky Mountains.

It was a formidable undertaking. Palliser had had considerable difficulty in getting a party together at all to penetrate country so little known and, by popular repute, so dangerous. Even the Hudson's Bay Company had not traded in these southern plains since the Bow River Expedition of 1822-4 to the Forks of the Red Deer and South Saskatchewan, 100 strong and costing £10,000, had convinced the company that it was not worth while trying to occupy the area. The former posts on the Bow and South Saskatchewan had long stood empty and unused, and though the Fall Indians, who had given the company the greatest trouble, had disappeared, the reputation of the South Saskatchewan country as highly dangerous still lingered on. Only a large and strong party could hope to pass in safety through the country Palliser was determined to explore; and a large and motley cavalcade it was that set off on May 26 towards the Forks of the Red Deer and South Saskatchewan rivers. Besides the explorers and Palliser's friends (the two English gentlemen who had spent the winter with them), there were Americans, a Canadian, a Negro (the famous Dan Williams), a Dutchman, Scotch and French half-breeds, two Blackfoot, and the Stoney hunter, Nimrod, with their women and children. Brisco and Mitchell, with their men, added to the strength of the party without expense to the government, but Brisco insisted on taking along Nimrod (Hector's hunter of the previous summer) as his hunter, to Palliser's consternation. As the Stoneys were mortal enemies of the tribes of the Blackfoot Confederacy, he foresaw trouble. The Americans were the would-be miners whom Hector had met at Fort Pitt the winter before. One at least, Burnham, who came from California, he knew to be very handy and thoroughly trustworthy. They were all anxious to get across the mountains to the gold-diggings on the Fraser and attached themselves to Palliser's expedition, without worrying about high wages, in the hope that this would help them on their way. Although these men were not as effective *voyageurs* as the half-breeds, yet Palliser could perfectly depend on them in case of a panic and desire to return on the part of some of the local men, who all more or less feared the country they were now attempting. Indeed, Palliser felt that without this preponderant Anglo-Saxon strain in the party he would never have succeeded in getting through the country he was resolved to explore. The other Indians were two Blackfoot guides: Petope (Hector's old friend the Perched Eagle) and Amoxapeta, with their wives and children.

The main cavalcade started out with five carts and forty-seven horses. They ran into difficulties in getting the horses and carts up the steep, 200-foot bank of the Saskatchewan opposite the fort; fastening the leaders by their tails to the shafts, they at last succeeded in surmounting the difficulty. They lost two horses next day when crossing White Mud Creek, but Hector, who had come this far with the party, undertook to look for them while he was waiting for James Beads and the dispatches; he found them all right.

The main party pressed on. They had a very small supply of provisions, but hoped, with care and the assistance of some chance ducks that they might shoot on the way, to be able to reach the herds of buffalo out on the plains. They managed to kill a few ducks, but these were very scarce. They dug up some beaver dams on a tributary of the Battle, but had no luck hunting. After a week's travel, food supplies were getting uncomfortably low. Nimrod suggested that they should send off to a camp of his tribe about forty miles to the west, to trade for meat. Their stores included a supply of ammunition, tobacco, blankets, calico, knives (listed in the accounts as 'scalping knives'), cloth, and the like, for Indian presents or for barter, so Palliser sent Sullivan off with one of the men and a little tobacco and ammunition to trade for meat. The next day was the first of June. They finished the last of their provisions, but Palliser managed to shoot a few ducks. The day after, Felix Munroe shot a young wapiti, but it was very lean and tough. The main party camped at Bull Lake for a day while the rest hunted on Eagle Creek, where they got four beaver and a few more ducks. The following day Old Paul Cayenne, who had been Palliser's hunter the summer before, and Felix Munroe, a Scotch-Blackfoot half-breed, being persuaded it was Sunday, did not want to hunt. (It was actually a Saturday.) Oddly enough, they did not mind digging up beaver dams, a far more laborious expedient, which forced them to remain for hours working up to their middles in very cold water with no result. Palliser was obliged, with great regret, to serve out flour, a luxury kept for Sundays only and for cases of sickness.

Next day—really Sunday—they again had their Sunday

ration of flour at midday after leaving Bull Lake. In the evening Felix Munroe brought in the meat of a very lean buffalo cow. While he was after a bull, which he espied a long way off, two Indians appeared to spring from the earth, ran the bull, and killed him with arrows. That night the expedition guarded their horses very carefully.

Now they came to the edge of the woods, where, once more, they had to cut and carry small loads of wood in each of the carts for use on the prairie course south. At long last they came in sight of buffalo. Felix Munroe, Petope, Brisco, and Palliser killed four, but not one of them was good, although Petope 'hardshipped' Palliser's best horse terribly, searching the band before firing.

The ground was so hard that Palliser was afraid Hector might lose their track if it rained, so he sent back to the edge of the woods to bury a letter and some dried meat for him.

Two young Sarcees, allies of the Blackfoot, came into camp. They said that the Indians that had killed the bull a few days before were from their camp, not very far off. The party travelled on rather fast next day and Petope found a stray horse, which, according to prairie law, he claimed, having seen him first. Palliser, knowing it must belong to the Sarcees, would not let anyone have it, and Petope left in a rage. Palliser let him go, but later sent after him, when he had cooled down, and speechified him into acquiescence, 'explaining to him the difference between prairie law, which was to seize all you could, and the Queen's law, which was to endeavour to do your best always to restore property to its rightful owner'.

They were at last lucky in getting plenty of meat. A group, sent on to hunt, killed five cows, though Felix Munroe had a bad fall and broke a gun. They moved camp to the water nearest the scene of the hunt, where the hunters were guarding the meat. Next day they loaded the carts very heavily and pushed on to the Hand Hills, where they made a permanent camp. From these hills, Palliser reported:

We commanded an extensive view of the country, on account

of their considerable elevation over the mountain plain,
which enabled us to see any buffaloes which might traverse the
plains: we were also enabled to recruit the horses, and get them
into condition for the long journey before them, and bled some
of them, which made them feed better afterwards. We also
killed a good many buffalo, and lived on fresh meat every day,
slicing and drying provisions with the overplus, to take along
with us through the country, where we had not so good a
chance of finding game. Lat. 51° 33'; long. 111° 30'.

The entry in his journal for the next day reads: 'June 12th,
Sunday.–Read the prayers of the Church of England,
Ballenden translating the most important ones into Cree, also
first and second lessons. A wet day.'

Rain spoilt some of the meat, most of which the women
had to dry again. It also obliterated their tracks. Palliser was
still worrying about Hector's finding them and sent Olivier
Munroe and Todd back to Bull Lake to bury more meat and
directions for the doctor.

Nimrod's wife had been wanting to get back to her own
people, and Nimrod proposed to take her to them and then
return. Palliser was afraid they might get into trouble with
Blackfoot on the way, but they would not listen to his warn-
ings. He was not sorry to see them go, especially as a war-party
of Blackfoot, about forty-two in number, arrived soon afterwards. He reported succinctly:

I knew them, having seen two of them when hunting last
winter. Invited them to sit down; made them a feast; gave
them a smoke. Made them a speech, in which I told them they
would be sure to have tribulation if they went to war against
the Crees. They replied that they were maddened by the
manner in which the Crees had stolen their horses; and I
replied, that I would use my influence in persuading the Crees
to restore the horses; upon which I made them a few presents
of ammunition and tobacco, and they turned back. Two of
their allies, the Sircees, joined them. One of them I recognized

to be my old friend, the little chief, who took my view of the war question, and spoke against an attack on the Crees. In the evening Nimrod, the Stoney hunter, and his wife came running into camp, carrying their little child. They had been pursued by Blackfeet, who had shot their dogs, robbed them of all they possessed, i.e., the payments received from me in ammunition, cotton and blankets: they were fired at, and had a very narrow escape with their lives.

Palliser at once proposed a diversion:

. . . a race for a flannel shirt. Fifteen champions stripped ready to start. Although among my half-breeds were several splendid runners, I could not persuade any of them to enter the lists. Felix, however, whom I pressed very hard to contend for the prize, remonstrated, saying that he was an old married man, with 5 children, and that it was unreasonable of me to ask him to run; finally he exclaimed, 'I will not run unless you order me, in which case, of course, I cannot help myself.' I replied, 'I order you to run.' With a shrug of his shoulders, and a glance of satisfaction he could hardly conceal, he walked to the starting post. The distance was 200 yards down a gentle slope, and thence up a more rapidly rising ground. Felix and the 15 youths made an excellent start. The race was well contested for the first 120 yards, but as they ascended the rising ground, Felix, who was slightly in the rear when in the valley, began to gain at every stride, passed the three foremost, and came in the winner by three yards, and carried off the red flannel shirt. I then handed a white one to the young Indian who came in second. Late at night the war party returned, broken up, back to their camp.

This was the lighter side of the expedition's encounters with the Blackfoot. Next day things again took a less friendly turn. The Blackfoot chiefs paid them a visit, accompanied by their soldiers. They alarmed the expedition's men very considerably, telling the interpreters that their time was come to die and making other threats of a similar nature. Palliser had taken the precaution, previous to their arrival, so to arrange the fire-arms that, at a given signal from him, each man could arm himself at once. He did not intend to leave the party defenceless, but did not wish to receive his visitors armed. He always wished to convey the idea that an attack on them would be an act of folly, for besides the fearful consequence of a present resistance, a terrible vengeance would remain in store for them from the swords and cannons of the soldiers who would surely be sent out to exact revenge. He found that Petope, his disgruntled Blackfoot interpreter, had been the author of the mischief. He had told his tribesmen that Palliser had sent tobacco and ammunition by his secretary, Sullivan, to the Thickwood Stoneys (Nimrod's people) and that he was now denying the Blackfoot the tobacco they begged for. They offered to trade horses, made a few overtures, and then backed down. This led Palliser to believe that their object was merely to ascertain the extent of the expedition's stock of goods, which he always kept covered. He exchanged one horse with a sore back for a sound one and then firmly refused to do any more trading. By the exercise of patience, firmness, and speech-making he managed to pacify his troublesome customers.

Then Nimrod got into trouble again. Some of the young men made overtures to him, telling him they regretted extremely that some of their people had stolen his horses, but that if he and his wife would accompany them to their camp they would not only restore all his lost property but make him a present of a horse into the bargain. Contrary to Felix's advice, the foolish fellow and his wife were induced to go along with four or five young Blackfoot 'soldiers'. The result of that evening's journey was very nearly the death of the Stoney and the abduction of his wife. Fortunately Mitchell and Sullivan, who were out hunting, were attracted by the gleam of a gun-barrel. When they saw the party disappear into a coulee without reappearing again on the other side, their suspicions were aroused and they galloped up on the height.

Seeing how matters stood, they rode to the assistance of the Stoneys, and the Blackfoot ran away. After this, for two days, the Blackfoot left them alone, though the expedition still kept strict guard on its horses night and day.

The men who had been sent to make the cache for Hector now arrived back; next day Hector himself appeared with Beads. He described the great hardship the few people left at Edmonton during the summer were suffering for want of provisions. They were making up the deficiency by eating eggs and rats. Mr. Brazeau had at last been forced to kill one of the domestic cows: this was, Hector said, the first he had tasted since he left Fort Garry in June 1857; the coarse taste of the fat, after the lighter and more digestible flavour of the buffalo, made him feel quite uncomfortable.

On his way from Edmonton, Hector had encountered nine more American miners. He sent his men on by the Blackfoot trail, with Peter Erasmus in charge, and went with the miners to put them on the trail for the Old Bow Fort. Thence they intended, without a guide, to cross the Rocky Mountains by the pass Palliser had laid down. Hector gave them a map before he left them to rejoin his men—the expedition's explorations were already proving useful. The rain, which had worried Palliser, was so heavy that night that they could not keep up their fire.

The doctor had had a hungry journey, in spite of one good meal, when he and Amoxapeta killed four ducks and collected fifty-five eggs, mostly water-hen eggs. When they came to the edge of the woods, Hector, like Palliser before him, had been obliged reluctantly to broach one of his two flour bags. Then his luck changed. He found Palliser's letters buried in the track—and, presumably, the dried meat—and later that day he and Vital ran a band of buffalo bulls and killed two. Hector's main party, too, had come upon a band of cows, and Beads had killed two of them. They had meat at last, but had to eat it nearly raw as their only fuel, the buffalo dung, was so wet that they could not make a fire worth speaking of. Erasmus, who had been sent ahead to look for Palliser, turned back when he came to some high hills (the Squirrel Hills) out on the open prairie; he, also, was hard up for food and his horse was too tired to face the plains. The grass everywhere was parched and stunted, and except for the rain pools all the water was nauseous. Large bands of buffalo passed them in the night. They crossed the Squirrel Hills and travelled over a wide, level, arid plain interspersed with salt lakes. Arriving at the Hand Hills, they followed along the captain's trail to the western brink, where they came suddenly in sight of his camp in a valley facing west.

These hills were a perfect place for the camp, with pasture that was almost rich, lakes of pure, fresh water, and gullies with a small growth of poplar, while the plain all round the base of the hills was bare and arid.

The troublesome encounter with the Blackfoot had not changed Palliser's plans. He read over the Colonial Office dispatches carefully and then sent for Old Paul Cayenne, Felix Munroe, and the most trustworthy men—Beads, Ballenden, Erasmus, and Daniel—as well as all the Americans. He told them that he proposed to travel south-east to the Forks of the Red Deer and Bow (South Saskatchewan) rivers and from there to pursue a western course through the Piegan and Blood Indian territory to the Rocky Mountains. The Americans' response was that they would stand fast by him no matter where the country or what the danger. Beads, Ballenden, Erasmus, and Daniel likewise declared their determination to go on. Old Paul replied:

> *It is all very well for those who do not know the country to be brave about it, but speak to any of the old ones who know, and who have experience of the country; take me, for instance, who have had my clothes pierced with bullets, and had my relations killed; ask if there is one of us who have not had some of their brothers, or brothers-in-law killed by these Indians. The country is too dangerous, and I have spoken.*

Felix Munroe agreed, saying that the country was dangerous, and even as far as they had yet gone the Blackfoot were sulky and had threatened him and his brothers, as Palliser himself must know. He, for his part, would go on, but the party was too small, and the women and children should return.

Palliser did not want to lose Old Paul. He feared the alarm that would be caused by the retreat of such an experienced veteran as his old hunter, who had been with him the whole of the previous season and the greater part of the winter of 1858-9. He thought that a little additional force would give Felix and the other men more confidence. Finally he persuaded Old Paul to promise to go on if they increased the party by four more half-breeds. He sent Felix back to Edmonton, with letters to Mr. Brazeau, to engage not more than six nor fewer than four good hands, at the wages of the expedition. Besides, he realized that the Blackfoot were very much disappointed at their small presents of tobacco. He had not reckoned on a sufficient quantity for the exigencies of the country. Mr. Christie had begged Palliser to let him have back a bale of tobacco, as the company was very short. Palliser now realized how badly he would need it; he felt sure that Mr. Brazeau would waive his claims in favour of this far greater emergency. Ballenden went with Felix; they took with them plenty of meat for the journey, with instructions to make a cache of half the meat north of the Battle River for the return journey. Petope left them, too, to go back to his camp with his wives. Though he carried off one of their trade guns with him, they were not sorry to get rid of a guide who had proved such a troublesome nuisance.

The party now numbered five gentlemen and fifteen men. Palliser formed the party into five watches to guard the horses day and night. While they waited for reinforcements they took lunar observations and calculated their position; they hunted buffalo, slicing and drying the meat; and they killed three grizzly bears.

Again some Blackfoot chiefs arrived. This time, perhaps because the trouble-maker Petope had gone, they behaved very well. Palliser gave them tea and made bread for them; they had a good smoke and he gave them some tobacco before they left.

Meanwhile Hector had been off up the Red Deer River on one of his geological excursions, accompanied by Brisco and two of their men. They were away two days and brought back interesting accounts of what they had found in the strata along the banks of the river, including a variety of fossils and 'salicified' trees, as well as some round-bodied carp and gold-eyes like the ones they had caught in the Saskatchewan at Carlton.

Burnham, intent on the search for gold, wanted to see if there was any to be found in the Red Deer River. Palliser told him that he feared the geology of the country would not admit of there being any, but went along with him and Paul. They washed and panned for a considerable time; they found no gold, but they did get a couple of gold-eyes, as well as a beaver for dinner.

Sunday passed quietly. Palliser read prayers and served out tea, tobacco, and flour as usual. Next day Felix and Ballenden got back, bringing Piscan Munroe (another brother of Felix) and three French half-breeds—Amos, Wapishoo, and La Douceur.

> *They arrived in a sad plight, not having eaten anything for four days. Their eyes were wild with hunger; they described a sad state of things at Edmonton; Brazeau obliged to kill the working cattle. Such was the fearful state to which the inhabitants of the fort were reduced for want of food, that they persuaded the men to tell them where they had cached the meat provided by me for their return journey from Edmonton to my camp. One of them went back, brought it in, and distributed it among the women and children in the fort.*

These extra men had not arrived too soon. The following day another war-party, this time of about twenty-four young Cree on a horse-stealing expedition, visited them. Palliser sent his hunters out after buffalo but stayed in camp himself to look after the Cree. He did more speech-making and, by telling them how strong the Blackfoot were, turned them back. As they went, they picked up a tired horse that Felix had left the day before at a swamp about five miles off—as Palliser discovered when he sent back to fetch it.

Next day it was the turn of the Blackfoot. A troublesome party visited them. They begged a great deal, but on the whole they were not ill-behaved; they had plenty of provisions and robes, neither of which the explorers wanted. Palliser made them a present of tobacco and gave the chiefs some tea and bread. He also handed them some additional tobacco, saying that it was a present to them from Brazeau, and begged them to go and trade their surplus provisions at the fort.

Now that they had their reinforcements, they were prepared to set off again; and yet, in spite of the extra men, the French half-breeds still showed great unwillingness to move. Old Paul, going back on his promise, came to Palliser and declared off, saying that he was exceedingly sorry to leave him but pleading the commands of his 'mother-in-law' as an excuse. He was, in fact, terrified at the prospect of travelling through the heart of the Blackfoot country. Palliser remonstrated in vain and at last gave him leave to go, and take his nephew as well, because he could not very well go alone. No sooner had he done this than other French half-breeds also began to signify their intentions of turning back. Palliser said he had let Old Paul go on account of his family and his long previous service, but that he would not allow anyone else to leave the camp; a slight murmur of disapprobation arose over this decision. Before the men had time to get together, Palliser asked: 'Who is the first man who will say that he will turn back?' Upon this, one man, bolder than the rest, stood up and exclaimed, 'I will go back.' Palliser took direct action: he rushed at him, seized him by the throat, and shook him, and then, catching him by the collar, kicked him out of the camp. Then he called out to know if any others wished to go back, but fortunately the retrograde movement extended no further. They started at once for Bull Pond Creek.

Two days' march brought them to within ten or twelve miles of a large Blackfoot camp. An aged chief, the Old Swan, who had called Palliser his grandson when they had met at Edmonton and at Rocky Mountain House, came to invite Palliser to visit his camp on the south side of the Red Deer River. He went, with the doctor, Peter Erasmus, and Olivier Munroe, taking for trade and as gifts a little ammunition, tobacco, and calico. Palliser found the camp in many ways a novel sight, even though they had seen so many Indian camps by then. There were about 400 tents. Another hundred Blackfoot had pitched their tents further up the river. Palliser reported:

> *The Blackfeet tents are not only much larger than those of the Crees, but much better provided with internal accommodation, such as leather curtains to protect them from draughts, bedding, kettles, tin plates, and porringers, and in a great many cases with forks and spoons; the tents of the chiefs are about 20 or 22 feet in diameter; but there are some medium [medicine?] tents, or tents where the chiefs assemble in council, that are nearly 30 feet in diameter; some of their ceremonial dresses are peculiar, and the manner in which they perform their singular dances is very energetic and wild. As we entered the camp, men and children of all sizes flocked around us, but the chiefs kept back the crowd every now and then by one word, or even by only a very slight gesture. They came forward, and took all our baggage in charge, and also our horses. There were several cases of sickness in the camp, not of a very severe kind. The Doctor had brought his medicines with him, and relieved several, especially one or two children, and his success with these rendered him very popular. We were in great want of leather to repair harness, renew hobbles, and various lashings; our trade went on briskly, but we did not do much in the horse trading, and, as usual, found these (like all other Indians east of the mountains), very unwilling to part with their horses; they are also very keen judges in horseflesh.*

They spent the night at the camp and got back next evening to their own camp, escorted by the Old Swan and two or three other chiefs and their 'soldiers'.

While they had been away Sullivan had moved the expedition camp to a spot about twenty miles from the Blackfoot camp, beside a creek where there was good grass and fine water.

Petope now returned, bringing back the horse but not the gun he had made off with. On being told that the price of the missing gun would be deducted from his pay, he turned sulky once more. Amoxapeta was being difficult too. He had had a Piegan wife and had shot her dead in a fit of jealousy; he now feared to meet her relatives, in the direction of whose camp the expedition was travelling. It began to look as if they might have to travel without any Blackfoot guides, which Palliser did not think was of much consequence, except that they might have trouble finding water, which would become very scarce by and by.

Again the Blackfoot became very troublesome. Some exercise of caution and sternness was needed to repress their inclination to be too familiar. Again Palliser saw to it that the arms were ranged along the carts—which were so disposed as to make a parapet shelter—but concealed under a curtain of tent-leather, ostensibly placed there for the protection of the goods and pemmican.

Water was indeed getting short. Even a large tributary of the Red Deer River was nothing more than a chain of disconnected pools, and the poor horses were miserably off for grass. The explorers came on another wide valley, which was full of buffalo. Six of them set off to run them, killing ten in all. The buffalo ran right for the camp, some making their way between the carts, where several were shot. The party crossed the Red Deer where they found a good firm bottom and water up to the axle-trees. Brisco got a wapiti in some woods along the river. Next day they climbed out of the valley on to a high plain covered with boulders. They saw buffalo, antelope, and five grizzlies, of which, despite much firing, they only killed one. Lack of water forced them down into the valley again.

Petope and Amoxapeta told them that the best place to cross the South Saskatchewan was above the Forks, so Palliser decided not to take the whole party, carts and all, to the junction of the Red Deer and South Saskatchewan, where the Hudson's Bay Company's old Chesterfield House had once stood, but to ride over to the place himself. Neither guide wanted to go, but Amoxapeta was at last shamed into it. Beads and Boucher went too. A sixteen-mile ride brought them to the Forks. Palliser contemplated the view with some satisfaction, having now, he thought, in July 1859, penetrated from the west to the region they had reached from the east in September 1857. He was actually still about 130 miles west of the westernmost point reached by the expedition in 1857, but he thought the distance was much less, something between thirty and sixty miles. In any case, the long prairie views from each turning-point gave him reasonable confidence that the country in between was much like the country the expedition had actually traversed. From the tongue of high land between the two rivers he studied a huge, beautiful sweep of country. He noted that the Red Deer River was a serpentine stream with broad alluvial promontories crowded with willows and rough-bark poplars, while the South Saskatchewan ran between high, precipitous banks.

It was near sunset and Amoxapeta was getting very jumpy. Suddenly they saw a party of five mounted men who stood a short time to contemplate them and then fled away, although they were on the opposite side of the South Saskatchewan, which would have presented a very serious obstacle even if they had been inclined to give chase. Amoxapeta became very much alarmed and wanted to go back to the main camp. Palliser refused to return: they had ridden their horses too far for that. He saw that he could not persuade Amoxapeta to remain, so he said he might go, a permission he was not slow to avail himself of.

The rest of Palliser's little party went down to camp in the valley of the Red Deer, where they had seen some good grass.

At daylight they found the hobbled horses all safe. They started back, hunting along the river-banks and killing one small deer. They came up with the main party at three o'clock in the afternoon.

They had hardly arrived when a number of Indians from the Blood Indian camp, south of the South Saskatchewan, rode in. The Blackfoot, their allies, had told them which way the expedition was travelling, and one Blackfoot came with them. Wapishoo, one of the half-breeds, who had been left to look after a cart with a broken wheel until help could be sent, saw the Indians coming, took his horse out of the cart, and galloped away. It turned out that the Bloods were friendly. They rode up, coming unarmed as a compliment, and shook hands with Palliser, who pitched camp, invited the chiefs to smoke, and prepared something to eat. Meanwhile the single Blackfoot was happily employed rifling the cart abandoned by Wapishoo. He took three guns and a blanket. Palliser protested to the chiefs, who replied that he was not of their tribe and they were not accountable for him. Palliser contended that as he was their guest they were indeed accountable. They remained silent a little while, then sent two young men after him. They retrieved the guns, which he had cached, but he had taken the blanket away over the river. Palliser thought it better to be satisfied with the partial recovery of the property than to fail in an attempt to get the blanket back, especially as the chiefs promised to make restitution whenever Palliser should visit them in their camp.

The party now had to halt by a salt lake, the only water they could find. The doctor had had a grilling journey with the carts in the sand-hills. The heat had been intense as they travelled through the miles of burning sand; both men and horses were in great need of water. They got a little by digging a pit, and drinking through a silk handkerchief. In the evening they found a valley running north and south where travelling was easier, as it was clear of the sand-hills—the route Amoxapeta should have shown them. Again next day, the travelling was very hard on the horses. They found a human skull on the plain. Two Blood Indian chiefs provided a diversion, which Palliser described:

> ... *very fine young men, with noble carriage and intelligent countenances, rode up, followed by other Indians; they promised to give me a horse each if I would dress them. I gave them coats, and desired Amoxapeta's wife to make the cloth into leggings, and in short we dressed them completely. They thought themselves very fine, but anyone observing their awkward constrained appearance now, contrasted with the easy dignity with which they made up to greet us clothed in their own apparel a short while previous, would indeed have considered the change one for the worse.*

That night they camped in a swamp, where they killed several rattlesnakes. The next day they reached the South Saskatchewan, which was here far wider than it was lower down below the Forks of the Red Deer River. The banks were lofty and there was only one bluff of woods to be seen, where they camped.

CHAPTER EIGHTEEN

South of the South Saskatchewan

W here the expedition camped, the South Saskatchewan was, according to Hector's measurements,
250 feet wide. To transport the baggage across
they had to make a raft—not an easy task where
there was so little wood. More than half the timber they had
was drift-wood; even so there was only enough wood to build
one raft, and that a very clumsy one.

While they were occupied with its construction they discovered that the place seemed, as Palliser mildly remarked,
quite a favourite haunt of grizzly bears.

On arriving at the camp-site they had started three of the
great beasts and poured a volley into the hindmost. Meanwhile
Vital, on horseback, had unexpectedly come upon an old female
bear; she turned on him and frightened him off. Next day, while
Hector was measuring the breadth of the river, McLaurin (one
of the hopeful miners), sitting on the bank holding the staff,
suddenly saw a grizzly coming in his direction. He flung the staff
down and rushed to the bank of the river ready to jump in if the
bear charged him. The poor creature did not have a chance to
charge. All hands were after him at once, and he soon fell,
riddled with wounds. The hunters got another next day, when
some of the men on horseback headed him to where Hector,
Brisco, Nimrod, and Palliser awaited him on foot. Still another
charged a group of the men who were chopping timber for the
raft; in their haste to escape through the bushes they jumped
over one another and broke a gun.

But other problems pressed. Since their one unwieldy raft was not big enough to take all the baggage, they made a kind of boat with the leather tent and so managed to send across not only a considerable quantity of luggage but also the four women—the Stoney's wife, Amoxapeta's wife, and both of Petope's wives. The last thing was to make the horses swim over: the explorers and men

> . . . *all undressed, each jumped on a horse, and swam with the animal, twisting a lock of his mane in the forefinger of the left hand, and striking out with the feet and right hand, thus obtaining full assistance without in the least distressing the animal, who merely partially drew his man through the water without having to support any of his weight; the raft and the leather tent boat were also drawn by the men, holding with one hand on to the horses' tails and hauling a rope attached with the other. The horses who had no riders were driven into the stream, and urged forward by shouts and stones thrown at them till they were forced out of their depth, when they continued to swim steadily across; some of them, however, got into a bad eddy very far below down stream, and were nearly lost. The work was very hard on the men, some of whom swam nine times across the river.*

Once across, they met several Blood Indians, who invited them to visit their camp. On the way they met a number of young men riding at full speed up the river to a point where a fearful accident had just happened. Some women, gathering berries, had come upon a bear—still another grizzly. He had seized one of them and dragged her into the bushes. One of the women jumped on a horse and fled back to the camp with the news. The young men succeeded in killing the bear, but reported the woman not only dead, but frightfully mangled.

Even that was not the end of the day's adventures. They went on to the camp and sat with the chiefs for some time. While they were in one of the tents a sick child was brought in to the doctor, who made some mixture for it out of medicines he had taken with him. Before he had time to give the child anything, one of the medicine-men of the tribe, accompanied by his satellites with their drums, rushed into the tent, snatched the child out of the doctor's hands, and commenced drumming and howling. The doctor told them, through Felix, that he would not answer for the child, who died soon afterwards.

When they went back to their camp that evening, fourteen or fifteen of the Blood Indians went with them, with horses to trade.

The party moved to a camp-site with better grass and water, nearer to the Indians, who told them that they had a great deal of sickness among them. They asked Palliser to come into camp and pray for them, that the sickness might be removed. He complied and read the General Confession and the Lord's Prayer, which Felix translated into Blackfoot after him. Meanwhile the doctor was busy with more concrete cures. Another woman brought him a child that was in a fit; while he was occupied in making up some medicine for it, the medicine-man who had interfered the day before came in again and attempted to take the child away. The child's mother, however, aware of the result of the medicine-man's exertions in the case of the child that had died, sprang like a tigress on the medicine-man and effectually prevented all interference with Hector. The child recovered.

Once again, the Indians became very troublesome. The horses were strictly guarded, but, all the same, 'young scamps' were continually prowling about them. The expedition started off early, but the Indians followed and caught up with them.

Meanwhile Amoxapeta and Petope were getting uneasy and talked of leaving, since the expedition was nearing the country of their enemies, the Plains Assiniboine. Amoxapeta, however, was having domestic troubles. He would have left the expedition long before, but his wife was soon to have a baby and she would not go back with him; she said he might go back if he chose, but that she was far too comfortable and well treated. She called him a coward on one occasion, and when he struck her she told him to beat away, but that he was a coward still. She gained her point, which was to stay with the expedition until the birth of her child; when it was born they stayed behind and let the explorers go on. Petope simply went off without telling anyone, taking one of the horses. Palliser was rather glad to be rid of them; they had proved expensive and useless.

The Blood Indians were still with them, but they too were uneasy. They asked Palliser to a feast. He went, accompanied by Sullivan and some of the men. At the feast the old chief advised Palliser not to go farther into the country; his party would certainly get into trouble. He said that only two white men had ever crossed the country between the Forks of the Red Deer and the South Saskatchewan rivers and the Cypress 'Mountains', as Palliser always called them. These were probably some of Peter Fidler's party who in 1801 and 1802 had travelled from Chesterfield House to the Cypress Hills to get pitch for boat-making. The chief gave such an account of the Assiniboine of the plains that the men were very much frightened. The paleness of Vital's countenance, while he listened, attracted Sullivan's amused attention. Palliser was more worried when one of the young men in the Indian camp became ill and died. He was afraid that the Bloods might imagine that the sickness was associated with their presence. He stayed up all night after he got back to camp, noting more young fellows prowling about the horses.

Hoping to shake off their troublesome neighbours, they started off again at daylight; the Indians hurried to follow them. It was most amusing to see the haste and confusion in the camp, as the Indians endeavoured to get away as rapidly as possible, rushing down their 300 tents, and packing up their traps, while the expedition was defiling past their camp. In spite of the explorers' good start, the Indians caught up with them just as they started on again after a two-hour halt at noon, in sight of the Cypress Hills. The Indians tried to persuade them they could not reach water by nightfall, but they pushed on. They did find middling water after a long trip, camping on a dry watercourse in the outskirts of the hills, where there was water in a few detached pools. A young Indian and his wife, who had been two or three days on an unsuccessful hunt, followed their track and arrived, half-starved, very late in the evening.

Palliser thought that the main body of Indians would hardly travel farther to the south in this longitude. The Cypress Hills, now visible as a blue line in the south-east, were in Assiniboine country. Despite the men's reluctance they started early next day, making straight for the hills through desolate-looking country without either grass or water. Felix, who did not really know the way, took them too far to the west, but the doctor instead of having dinner rode up a very high peak to the south-east, flanking the gully where they had halted, to obtain a view; he caught up with the main party late in the afternoon, to confirm Palliser's opinion that they were actually shirking the Cypress Hills. Being now several miles out of their course, they camped in a gully and started due east next morning, much to the distress of the men.

On the way they met another old Indian chief, named Father-of-All. He had come to take back to Fort Benton, in United States territory, the body of his son, buried nearly seven months before. Palliser dissuaded him, telling him that this would bring more sickness to his camp and would only be fatal to more of his children. He must think of all the young men of his people. After a long pause the chief said: 'You have irons for digging: desire your men to dig me a place; I will bury him: you are wise, and I will do as you bid me.' The men took spade and shovel and dug the son's grave. The father and his soldiers buried him. Duty to his people meant more to the old chief than his personal wishes.

They now realized that their troublesome friends the Indians had followed them after all. Camping early at a small lake at the foot of the Cypress Hills, they found that the Indians were camped three miles to the east. Sullivan, Brisco, and Mitchell remained in camp with the men, to guard the horses and look after the stores. Hector went up a detached hill 1,600 feet above the camp. Palliser and Boucher went to hunt. On their return they saw Hector telegraphing to them; he had seen a bear, but it eluded them.

The Cypress Hills were a veritable oasis in the tract of arid country they had come through. There was timber, rich soil, and an abundant water supply. Palliser could not see the Rockies from any height he climbed, but he saw the three flat-topped volcanic hills, the Trois Buttes (now called the Sweet Grass Hills, or Gold Butte, East Butte, and West Butte), south of the boundary line—landmarks he had seen ten years before from the other side, on the prairies of the Missouri. Palliser recorded that many miles of arid country separated the Cypress Hills from the Rockies, but he said they were part of the Coteau connecting with the hills near the elbow of the South Saskatchewan, and, indeed, the Cypress Hills are part of the height of land defining on the south and east the drainage basin of the South Saskatchewan.

When he got back to camp, the Indians were threatening serious trouble. Felix told Palliser that they were planning to murder Nimrod, the Stoney, who seemed fully aware of their intentions and was very much alarmed. Palliser described how they saved him:

> . . . *we desired him to creep into our little tent, where he lay between two of the men that had got in there; once or twice the Indians wanted to peer into the tent, but Hector, Mitchell, and Sullivan prevented them. We were all now armed, on the plea of guarding the horses; most of the Indians were also armed, one of them who was previously unarmed I now saw cocking and uncocking one of our own guns. I desired Daniel, who was in the tent along with the Stoney, to tell him quietly in Cree not to attempt to run, that we would protect him, and shoot the first man dead who pointed a gun at the tent. I sat on the ground at the tent door with my rifle across my knees, and Brisco kept a sharp lookout on the Indian beside me; I then desired Hector to give up his gun to one of the men, and*

to pretend afterwards as if he were looking for his own gun, and finally to take our gun from the Indian who had armed himself with it. Doctor Hector after taking successively one or two guns from the men, and returning them, at last came to the Indian, took his gun, looked at it, and went away with it towards the horses for a few minutes, and returned to us. Olivier Munroe, brother to Felix, whom we had all looked on previous to this period as a fool, now began to talk to them in tneir own language, much to their astonishment, saying, 'You do not know these men; they think as much of that Stoney as they think of me; they think as much of the smallest man of the whole party as if he was one of themselves. You want to kill the Stoney: well, kill him; but think well! for you will have to kill every one of us; and as to "him" (meaning me), he will be the first to fire.' Felix translated his brother's words to me in French, and I appeared not to be interested, called for tobacco, and passed the pipe round. All this time the horses were saddled, and fastened close at hand, which meant mischief. At a little after midnight, however, they all rose with one accord, jumped on their horses, and galloped off.

Now the explorers were free to enjoy the lovely hills. They encamped in a magnificent valley where water from the height of land shed off into the Missouri and into the Saskatchewan. They were now well supplied with wood, water, and grass, a rare combination of happy circumstances in their experience of this season's explorations. Palliser sent Sullivan, Beads, and Olivier south to the border, while the rest hunted and made provisions for their final journey westward through the mountains. At daylight the hunters were off; Mitchell and Nimrod set off later to hunt in another direction. Ten or twelve shots were heard, and shortly afterwards some Indians galloped into the camp to tell Palliser that the hunters had been surprised and killed by the Plains Assiniboine. This Palliser did not believe, but Brisco suggested that these Indians might themselves have shot the Stoney, and have come to give a false account of the matter in order to deceive

Palliser. Meanwhile he saw the Indians striking their tents and packing off to the northward as fast as they could. Palliser was puzzled. Was there, after all, real trouble?

It turned out to be not a tragedy but a ludicrous mistake. About two hours later Felix came into camp to fetch pack-horses; he told Palliser that he and the other two hunters had come upon a band of wapiti, fired a good many shots, and killed four. The Blood Indians, on hearing the firing, did not stop to discover the cause, but jumped to the most dire conclusion. Very considerately some of the young men rode down to give Palliser the alarm and the rest of the camp got under way for the north again as fast as ever they could, imagining that their dreaded enemies were upon them. Palliser added: 'I rejoice to say we saw no more of our friends the Blood Indians.'

Next day, a Sunday, they quietly read prayers and sliced and dried their wapiti meat. Buffalo appeared, so they spent a couple of days running them and making pemmican.

The party was now about to break up. They celebrated their last night together on the plains by the addition of the luxuries of tea and bread for supper at the doctor's expense—taken out of the scanty little store he had been allotted for his trip in the mountains. Then, having converted the wapiti and buffalo they had killed into pemmican, they broke up camp. Brisco and Mitchell headed south for Fort Benton, in United States territory. Palliser and Sullivan started westward to the Kootenay Pass, intending to meet the Boundary Commission beyond the Rockies. Hector set off for Old Bow Fort on his way to cross the mountains by the pass he had discovered the year before, in the hope of finding a route practicable for horses to the westward, and to try, as far as ever it lay in his power, to proceed by the valleys of Fraser's and Thompson's rivers, avoiding the valley of the Columbia.

Hector left the Cypress Hills with much regret, as he felt it promised to be one of the most interesting spots in the country for studying certain geological problems. He took four of the men and Nimrod.

Peter Erasmus, always considered heretofore the Doctor's own man, having been instructed by the latter in the use of those instruments which rendered him very useful as a surveyor's assistant, now, at the last moment, backed out, he, Peter, declaring the journey too desperate to undertake considering the condition of the horses, the rivers that would have to be crossed, and the prospects of food on such a journey.

Years afterwards, in 1900, Peter Erasmus wrote to Hector, by then Sir James Hector, 'When I think of the past there is one thing I am ashamed of and which I cannot forgive myself, that is when I left you at the foot of the mountains.' Instead of going with Hector he went gold-mining and made a snug little sum of money.

James Beads, at Palliser's suggestion (not by his orders), in the most praiseworthy manner volunteered to go in place of Erasmus.

Besides Beads, Hector's party consisted of two of the Americans—McLaurin and Burnham—, Oliver Vanesse, and his old hunter Nimrod, who had stuck with them through thick and thin to go on this trip and who brought his wife and child. They had with them eighteen horses, nine of them carrying packs with 240 pounds of pemmican, eighty pounds of flour, fifty pounds of sugar, and a good supply of ammunition.

The trip started badly. The first day they saw some buffalo cows; Hector sent Beads after them on his best horse. Beads foolishly took it among stones at full speed and got a bad fall, breaking his gun to pieces. They did better next morning. Hector and Beads, starting ahead of the rest, came on two buffalo and killed them both. While they were waiting for the others, they saw a large band of cows. The day was hot and the buffalo lazy, so Hector managed to kill a fine cow, using one of the spare horses, saving the better runners that had already done duty that morning. The horses were still the first consideration.

The buffalo provided plenty of food, but there was trouble

over water, as there was little or none to be had, even in a deep ravine they crossed. Just as they were about to camp without water, they came on a little swampy pool with good grass round its edge. A thunderstorm that night startled the horses and set them off on the run. The men had to turn out and follow them for a long distance, and at last found them only by the light of the vivid flashes.

After a late start, as the men were still unused to the troublesome work of packing, they came to a large river which Hector thought from Felix Munroe's directions should have been the Belly River;* he decided that it was actually the South Saskatchewan. The banks were high and steep, and in all the miles they could see, up and down the river, they could make out only one small clump of poplars along its margin. They camped on one of the flats in the valley, tying up and guarding the horses all night as Nimrod was uneasy about some tracks he had found.

Cutting across country to avoid the bends of the river, they came at last to the place where the Oldman joins the Bow and found to their surprise that they could easily ford it. (Palliser, crossing it two days later, forty miles farther up, had to swim the horses and make rafts!) To gain time, Hector struck off directly to the north-west instead of following the river, taking a chance on finding water. They hit on a little shallow pool just at camping-time, so for that night at least they had water, but their camp-fire was, as always on this part of the trip, very miserable. They had never had any wood to burn since leaving the Cypress Hills, and the nightly thunder-storms brought just enough rain to wet the buffalo dung.

They found, too, that in spite of all the buffalo they had killed they had not carried enough meat along with them. They were out of it already, and their pemmican had to be saved for the mountains. They set off without breakfast, but by great luck they saw a young bull, and soon had his marrow-bones on the fire. That morning, in the clear air, they

*The name Moo-coo-mans or Belly was apparently used then for today's Oldman River.

got their first glimpse of the peaks of the Rockies rising clear and sharp above the horizon line about ninety miles away. At the same time they could still see the Trois Buttes, the outstanding landmark south of the border, more than seventy miles away.

Suddenly they came upon an Indian cutting up a buffalo he had just killed. He could not speak Cree or Stoney, but by signs and a few Blackfoot words they discovered that he was a Piegan who belonged to a very large camp that was somewhere near. Hector tried to get him to stay with them all night, as he knew that if he got to his camp there would be a whole troop of them bothering them the next day. But the Piegan's desire to tell the news was too great to be restrained, and just as they were going to encamp he rode off in a great hurry. Hector let him get out of sight, then started again; they went as hard as they could till it was quite dark, then they camped, making no fire and keeping the horses close, beside the only water they could find—a small puddle of rain-water.

Anxious to avoid the Indians, they started at dawn. They had not gone more than two miles when they saw a long line of black objects, which at first they took for buffalo. Soon Hector made out, through the telescope, that they were Indians travelling to the north-west. Hector tried to dodge them by turning to the south-west before they could see his party, but he had no sooner done so than forty of them came up from behind with their friend of the night before. Judging from their foaming horses, he had led them all the way back to where he had supposed they had camped.

Some of the new-comers could speak Cree, so, with Beads to interpret, Hector soon found out all about them. They were a camp of 300 lodges, belonging to the American territories. They had heard from the Blackfoot who had been with the expedition of the presents distributed to that tribe. They thought that they had struck the 'lode' and hoped to get their share of the good things also. Luckily, Hector had put a few pounds of tobacco in his holsters (more effective armament than pistols) and now was able, without halting, to carry on the palaver and give the customary little pieces of Pas-tah-lan (tobacco) to all the principal men. More Indians soon began to troop from the camp towards them and shortly they had a cavalcade of several hundred around them, luckily including several of their big chiefs. The Indians tried hard to persuade Hector to stop, to trade horses and give them tobacco, but as Hector's horses were all picked animals he knew he was not likely to get better ones. His principal reason for refusing to stay, however, was the evident wish of some of the young men to do Nimrod some mischief. They tried all they could to edge him away from the party, but Hector made him stick close by him while they kept steadily on at a jog-trot, driving the pack-horses in a band before them. At last, after the party had gone a couple of miles with this rabble at their heels, the Piegans became convinced they would get no more tobacco and began to drop off. The only ones Hector was sorry to see disappear were the chiefs, as there still remained behind a horrid, rascally-looking set. Beads had struck up an acquaintance with one that had been a great deal among the Cree. Hector got him to hold on with them by promising that when all the rest had gone he would get a large piece of tobacco. This Indian's anxiety was now all to get rid of the tail that continued to follow them. His harangues had no effect on the twenty or thirty scamps among them. There was nearly bad trouble. This, in Hector's words, is what happened:

> He [the friendly Indian] then advised me to stop and have a smoke, so after talking to my men I said I would, if they would all stop with me. I only kept Beads, however, and when we had got off our horses and sat down in a ring, as is usual, according to arrangement, Burnham, McLaurn [sic], Oliver, and the Stoney began slowly to drive on the horses again, without attracting attention. I explained this to the Indian by saying that the horses were tired, and would go slowly till I came up with them, and then told them all about the Captain being behind me with lots of tobacco and presents for them, if they would only wait till they saw him, but that I was only

sent on ahead, and had nothing for them. While talking 8 or 10 of the scamps jumped on their horses and followed my men. I heard afterwards that on coming up they tried by signs to make Burnham understand that I wished them to turn back, but he was far too wide-awake to do that. One of them then seized McLaurn's knife from his belt, and was rather surprised by having a revolver clapped to his head, so he returned it. They then caught hold of the pack-horses, and one of them jumped off his horse, and commenced to undo the pack cords; but Nimrod pulled off his gun cover, and cocked the gun, and, as the scamps are generally cowards among the Indians, this made him change his mind. After riding for about 10 minutes, trying all they could to provoke the three men, who, with Nimrod and his wife, were coolly driving along the loaded horses before them, they turned back and rejoined the party where I still remained with Beads, and commenced talking in a loud and excited manner. Our Cree [-speaking] friend at once told us that they were not pleased, and that we should be off. After a little time I prepared to go, and told Beads to tighten our girths, when the scamps now began to press round us, wanting to look at every thing we had, and tried to fire off our guns. However, I had put the caps in my mouth, and made Beads do the same, so that was no go. One of them then plunged his hand into my shot pouch, and took all my ball out, but laughing all the while I made him give them back, for although I felt as ill at ease as ever I did in my life I knew that the only chance was to look unconcerned. At last we got free from them, and being well mounted told our Cree-speaking friend to make a turn and join us beyond some hills that we were just going to enter, and then set off at such a sharp pace that the Indians only followed us a little way, when seeing they were getting far from their own people, who all this time had been moving in the opposite direction, they began to drop off and turn back. When the last of them had gone, we drew rein, and waited for the Indian that had done us such good service, and made him a very handsome present. He told us not to go straight, nor to stop till late, as he heard that some of the young men were going to try and steal our horses in the night. We soon rejoined the horses, and found Nimrod and his wife still of a kind of ashy-grey colour from fear; but like the rest of us in a high flow of spirits from the sense of relief. We went 24 miles without stopping, and then halted to rest the horses, but without water. As night came on we made seven miles more, and then having got among hills where there was short grass that did not show the horse tracks so well as the dry dusty plains, we finished by making a great turn and camping beside some excellent water, but without daring to make a fire. Of course we kept the horses close, and watched them all night, but they were so tired with their long march without rest or water, that they gave no trouble. Our Piegan friends, if they did come after us, must have lost our track, for we saw nothing more of them.

That was the last of their troubles with Indians. The Piegans, as Hector wrote, alone of all the tribes they had met, showed a disposition to be more than importunate. It had been touch-and-go. The clash between the miner and the Piegan scamp—both from south of the border, where violence between Indians and white men was common—had nearly, but not quite, ended in disaster. The party of white men had travelled in safety through the perilous country; more, they had brought with them unscathed a mortal enemy of the Blackfoot; no blood had been shed. It was a triumph.

Not even the adventure with the Piegans had prevented Hector from noting that all the rain they had was quite lost on the hard-baked clay soil, as it at once evaporated when the shower passed. On Oldman River, he had recorded, there was lignite, resting on dark brown, sandy clays. He examined the geology of the hills where they finally stopped to camp; their chalky surfaces and white muddy flats reminded him of the Hand Hills.

CHAPTER NINETEEN

Barriers beyond the Rockies

ow, at last, Hector's party was getting near the mountains again. The pasture was much better than it had been on the plains. When they struck the Bow River once more there were trees at last, a good growth of pines and large poplars. Along the banks they found a profusion both of wild fruit and of game.

There was another welcome difference: they were back among friendly tribes. They saw two Indians on the opposite side of the river; hidden, they watched them through a field-glass. Suddenly Nimrod, who had been looking attentively for some time, gave a great shout, and in a high state of excitement announced that they were Stoneys of his own tribe. Making signals to them, Hector and Nimrod climbed down through a dense thicket of berry bushes to the river and had a long talk with them.

Hector now camped in a most beautiful spot by the river, among large trees—a pleasant relief from the treeless, waterless plains. Exploring the woods, they came to a wigwam, carefully closed and with logs laid up against it for security. Hector slashed a hole in it with his knife and found that it contained a corpse, supported in a sitting position just as if alive. The inside of the tent was in good order; it was filled with offerings of buffalo robes and other furs, tobacco, paint, dresses, and other Indian valuables. It was probably the remains of some great Blackfoot chief, as the Indian bags, moccasins, and other worked articles were those of that tribe.

A few miles on, they came to the Stoneys' camp at the mouth of the Ispasquehow or Highwood River, in one of the prettiest spots Hector had seen in the country. There were thirty-five tents, a much larger band than was usually seen of the Rocky Mountain Stoneys. They had been south along the mountains to meet the Kootenay and had come farther east than usual in the hope of seeing buffalo. As they were close to the Blackfoot country, they had formed a large party for their protection. Even so, they were nervous about their enemies. A party of nineteen hunters out after deer and grizzlies failed to come back one evening. Had the Blackfoot surprised them? Tracks of strange Indians had been seen. There was general alarm but, at last, about two in the morning, most of the hunters returned, loaded with wapiti and bear meat. Bears, not Blackfoot, had caused the delay. They had killed three grizzlies, but one of the hunters had been wounded, though not badly.

Hector stayed with these Stoneys for two nights. They were all Christians. Some of them could read and even write in their own language, using the syllabic characters that the Wesleyan missionaries had invented. They were uneasy about their future. Every year they were finding it more difficult to keep from starving—even the buffalo could not be depended on any more. They very badly wanted tools and a few simple agricultural implements. Hector thought that if they were supplied with these they would use them and soon settle down, giving up their vagrant mode of life. The chiefs at least seemed quite in earnest about the matter. Some of them already cultivated little plots of ground, growing turnips and potatoes, though more as curiosities than as a practical supply of food.

Through trade with the Kootenay, they had acquired some good horses. As these were accustomed to mountain travel, Hector thought they would be well suited for his westward journey; he had no difficulty in effecting six good exchanges, as he had met most of these Indians before and they all looked on him as an old friend.

Nimrod refused to leave his wife at this camp, as he said he would need her company coming back; he could not travel so far in the mountains all alone. Hector agreed and, as well, engaged another capital Indian named William, who was also to take his wife but only on condition that they would not under any circumstances expect him to broach the stock of pemmican as long as they were with him.

Hector's party of nine, now including two Indian women, set off at the same time as the whole Indian camp. The long, straggling train of men, women, and children with their loaded horses and dogs, winding up the zigzag trail from the pretty little valley to the level plain above, made a picturesque sight.

The evening, when they camped, was dull and overcast, and the river looked favourable, so they tried their luck at fishing. They had only crude twine for lines and a few large unmounted cod-hooks. In spite of the lack of gut, hair, line, rod, or any other civilized appliances, in an hour and a half they caught thirty-six trout, of two kinds, none of which weighed less than three-quarters of a pound and most of which ranged from a pound to a pound and a half.

Rain kept them from going on next day, but they killed an antelope within a mile of the camp. The country made Hector think of a deer park, it was so beautiful with its rich pasture, clumps of wood, and bands of small deer. The mountains were completely covered with snow, though it was only the middle of August. The small lake they camped beside was frozen over in the morning, and the ground was covered with hoar-frost.

At last they reached Old Bow Fort, where they found the ground strewn with a litter of broken carts, which a party of Americans had left when they started the day before to cross the mountains by the Kananaskis Pass. Hector, the provident Scot, used these fragments for repairing their pack-saddles.

William proudly took him to see a garden that he and another Stoney had made that summer, in which some very fair turnips were growing. It was very small and surrounded by a rude fence. William pulled up a few turnips to take to the camp. Hector was amused that he blazed a tree and wrote on it with charcoal the number of turnips he had pulled and whose rows he had taken them from.

Now they were ready to start across the mountains. Hector made observations on the boiling-point and rearranged the packs so they would be easier to carry in the mountains. They followed the route Hector had travelled the year before, camping again on the Bow Lakes (Lac des Arcs) at the same place as before. As they went along, Nimrod killed a fat buck. They had been making a sort of tea from the twigs of what Hector called the *missasktomina*—saskatoons, as service-berries are called to this day in Western Canada. These now failed them, so they tried using the tops of spruce trees instead. Again hunting was good; William bagged a black-tailed deer and Hector a Virginia deer.

Hector wanted to climb the mountains to the north-east. He started alone at six in the morning. He climbed slowly, examining the strata as he went along, and got to the top at one o'clock, after climbing up 3,000 feet from the camp.

> *The scene from the summit was very remarkable, the great distinctness with which the eye was able to follow the gigantic and complex plications giving it more the look of a magnified geological model than a natural view. There would not be the slightest difficulty, with time and provisions, in working out completely the structure of this portion of the Rocky Mountains, and, perhaps, from the clear manner in which the enormous faults and foldings of the strata are displayed, obtaining most valuable inductions for application to the general principles of geological science.*

Usually the practical geologist has to piece together and picture in his mind the nature of complicated disturbances, from detached and superficial observations, but here the whole formation of the mountains could be clearly seen, not obscured by the outbursts and intrusions of igneous rocks that in other mountain chains render the study of their structure so hopelessly difficult.

Besides geologizing, Hector was hunting. He wounded a mountain (Hector always said 'white') goat with two kids, but she escaped to an inaccessible place. The Indians said these goats were the hardest of all animals to kill. Once one was wounded and got up onto a ledge beside a waterfall. It stood there for seven days before it fell down over the precipice. It had been shot in five places.

Hector did not get back to camp till nearly seven o'clock. The mountain was so steep and smooth that, like many other mountaineers, he found the descent more fatiguing than the climb.

When, by a different route from the one he had followed the previous year, they again reached the wonderful mass of rock that forms the Cascade Mountain, he was surprised to find that his recollection of the heights and distances had, in the year since he had seen it, grown less than the reality. Now the mountain seemed even more striking than it had on the first visit. Hector was revelling in the beauty of the mountains, as well as in their beautifully clear geological formations. Crossing a high hill, he had a splendid view. Mount Ball, visible to the south-west, had a cone of snow on it, and all the mountains to the westward were snow-clad. He could see right through the Vermilion Pass gap.

Hector checked last year's observations as the party went along. They were glad to find what he called muskeg tea (more usually called labrador tea, the *ledum palustre*), which made a capital beverage in the absence of a better.

At the crossing for the Vermilion Pass, which Hector had used the year before, he halted to hold a council with the Indians. He wanted to keep to the east of the Rockies as long as possible while he made his way north-west. He remembered vividly the devastating want of game on the western side of the mountains that he had experienced the previous summer. Could he reach the North Saskatchewan and find a pass from its head-waters to the north of his last year's crossing-places? William said he could go by Pipestone Pass from Bow River to the North Saskatchewan. There, at the Kootenay Plain, they would get plenty of sheep—and they would find a better trail. As they had not been able to increase their stock of food, this seemed a wise plan. Hector's calculations, based on the plants he had seen last year, both as to when there would probably be heavy snow on the western side of the mountains and where it was likely to be deep, made him think that he had nearly two months still for travelling. Shrewdly, he realized that though there was likely to be heavy snow on the west of the high mountains themselves, there would probably be relatively little on their lower slopes and in the dry valleys and plateaux between them. As it turned out, it was not deep snow that kept them from crossing to the Fraser Valley and the coast, but piles of fallen timber.

They worked their way up the valley of Pipestone Creek, passing a very wide valley leading to the west, on the side of which they saw a singularly shaped mountain so much resembling a large tooth that they called it Mount Molar. There William added a young moose to their dwindling stock of provisions and he and Hector managed to kill all of a flock of five sheep they had seen grazing surprisingly low down on the mountain.

Near the divide they camped opposite a waterfall that leapt and rushed down a gutter-like channel, from a height of 450 feet, to form Pipestone Creek. There the Indians found some soft, fine-grained, grey-blue stone, which they used for making pipes. The Stoneys called the creek 'pa-hooh-to-hi-agoo-pi-wap-ta', and the Cree 'moni-spaw-gun-na-nis-si-pki', both meaning 'blue pipestone river'.

Hector climbed a mountain above the camp to the level to which several small glaciers came down, 9,400 feet above sea level, as he reckoned. He collected a number of fossils and fifty species of alpine plant, besides killing three large marmots, one the biggest he had seen anywhere. William said that two years earlier he had killed a buffalo cow there out of a band of seven. She was one of the Thickwood species, larger and blacker and with wider-spread horns than the prairie variety. Next day, while the horses followed the rocky path over the bare, bleak height of land, Hector chased some big-horns up another mountainside. Looking to the west over a shallow valley, he could see another, higher range, with its valleys filled with snow and with several fine glaciers. Even where he was there was snow left over from the previous winter. He saw again the tall peak that, when he had seen it from the west the summer before, he had named after Sir Roderick Murchison. This new view of it from the south-east convinced him that he had overestimated its height, as indeed he had. He was now beginning to think that none of the Rocky Mountains rose above 13,000 or 13,500 feet—though the aneroid barometer no longer gave them any help. It refused to indicate any further rise after it reached its old limit of 21.20 inches at an altitude of some 7,400 feet, considerably lower than the summit of the pass.

They found their way down a gentle descent over a bleak moorland on the other side of the height of land, into the valley of a river that Hector named Siffleur—the French name for the whistling marmots. An abrupt descent through thick woods brought them to this tributary of the North Saskatchewan; William had been right about the second lateral pass from Bow River to the North Saskatchewan.

The Indians were both off hunting; without their help Hector found he could not follow, over the rocky ground, some buffalo tracks he discovered. The Indians came back with the skin of a very large he-goat which the women cured for him and which he later presented to Edinburgh University Museum.

They followed the Siffleur Valley down along a path cut through dense and very tangled woods, to the wide valley of the North Saskatchewan. They still had to cross five miles of shingle terraces, which ranged step above step to a height of 500 feet. The steep descents and the loose surfaces of the slopes, on which the pack-horses had difficulty in keeping a footing, gave them trouble. After they camped that night,

Nimrod came in to say he had wounded a moose and had killed three sheep out of a band of several hundred he had encountered a little way up the river. They had good luck again next day, finally killing the wounded moose and getting a wapiti as well, and four more sheep, while Hector took observations for latitude and reckoned the longitude, confirming his results of the year before.

They set to work drying and making pemmican of all this meat, as Hector now intended to send the Indians back and go on alone. He gave them a supply of ammunition, and, in part payment for their services, some of the horses. He gave them orders on the Hudson's Bay Company for the rest of the wages due to them and sent letters by them to Edmonton. Nimrod was persuaded to leave his wife with William for two days while he showed Hector the entrance to the pass, which he said he knew, leading from the bend of the North Saskatchewan across the mountains.

There was no trail. Going up-stream, the diminished party followed along the margin of the river without much difficulty, except at one place where there was a good deal of fallen timber; one of the pack-horses in trying to get round a bog fell into the river, which was deep and swift, and was nearly drowned.

For the moment there was abundant game. There were plenty of spruce grouse, and Hector shot nine; they started a black bear and saw fresh tracks of six moose, besides those of wapiti and smaller deer. The district seemed to deserve its reputation among the Indians as a good hunting-ground.

Nimrod had been very dull and sulky at the idea of going back alone. Next day he said he was going to hunt. Hector somehow felt that they had seen the last of him, and so it proved. He took only his gun and went on foot, but he did not meet them at the appointed camping-place. He never rejoined them. Hector heard afterwards that he reached Bow River safely on his way back; that Lord Southesk found him and William there, ten days later, and took them on as guides. Lord Southesk was on a hunting-trip. It was strange that the only two travellers, apart from Indians and a few employees of the Hudson's Bay Company, that had ever been in that region, should have travelled through the Pipestone Pass and so nearly met, one going north and one south. Neither knew that the other was there; but Southesk noticed a date and latitude mark left by Hector on a tree ten days earlier.

Hector's problem now that he had no hunters was to go as far and as fast as he could with the 320 pounds of pemmican the party carried, eked out with anything they might be able to shoot for themselves as they went along. Hector went ahead of the party of four men, each of whom had one horse to ride and two to drive. He noted that, now, without any guide, he was the actual explorer of the country. He added: '. . . it needed all the little experience I had picked up of the Indian's tact in threading through forest country in a given direction: and I daresay that, without knowing it, we often followed a roundabout and bad line of route, when a better existed.'

Soon enough they struck a baffling problem. They came to a point where the North Saskatchewan is formed by three large branches joining. The question now was: which of these led to the pass to the Columbia that they were looking for? Leaving the horses to graze on a good patch of goose-grass, Hector explored the valley to the west and Beads the one to the south. They came back in a couple of hours, both having found blazed trees, showing that someone had passed, but no regular trail. They decided to try Hector's valley first. Hector reported: '. . . after a good deal of hewing and climbing through dense woods, we made four miles by sunset, when we encamped about 700 feet above a roaring torrent, upon a narrow strip from which the forest had been cleared by a land-slip, and where our horses could manage to pick a little; but among the angular blocks of rocks we found it by no means easy to find a place to stretch ourselves.'

At daylight he started with Beads to see where the valley led. After five miles of very thick woods they suddenly emerged at the foot of a great glacier—the Freshfield Icefield—

which completely filled the valley. There was no hope of getting through with the horses by this route. They explored the glacier, after a slippery climb to reach the surface of the ice. It was about seven miles long, lying in a valley bounded to the west by a row of high conical peaks that were completely snow-clad.

In the afternoon they tried Beads's valley. They found that the stream in this rose from a glacier in a high valley to the right, but the main valley ahead seemed to stretch on, wide and spacious, with a flat, level bottom, densely forested. They went on up it, passing little swampy streams which showed that the water was still flowing to the Saskatchewan. After three miles they observed a small creek, issuing from a number of springs, which flowed in the direction in which they were travelling. They could hardly believe it was a branch of the Columbia as they had made no appreciable ascent since leaving the main Saskatchewan and had encountered nothing like a height of land, but they were indeed now on the western slope of the mountain. This was the pass David Thompson had crossed in 1807 and Howse in 1810. It is still called Howse Pass. They camped beside a small lake among beautiful open woods, where the timber was of very fine quality.

Hector and Beads set off again at daylight to search for a trail; their attention was much divided between their work and the blueberries and raspberries, which grew in the greatest abundance. The blueberries, Hector noted, exactly resembled in appearance and flavour those in Scotland, except that they were about the size of small musket-balls. He called the river whose head-waters he had rediscovered Blaeberry River.

They notched a line for the track, went back for the horses, and started again at ten a.m. The valley sloped steeply down, filled with dense timber, so Hector kept along the side without seeing very well where they were going. At noon they emerged on an open strip, luckily enough, to find that they were just on the brink of a deep, rocky chasm, through which boiled and leapt a large stream, 700 feet below, issuing from a glacier above them. They had to go down into the valley again, forcing their way through dense alder thickets ten or twelve feet high. At last, with much sliding and tumbling, they reached the river in the afternoon; the horses had been a good deal bruised and cut in the descent. Three streams converged to make a good-sized river, flowing with a violent current through a rocky channel. Not a vestige of grass or anything that horses could eat was to be seen, although the trees and bushes were very luxuriant. They pressed on, but at last had to camp, willy-nilly, on a small gravel bank of the river on which grew a few shoots of goose-grass, which their horses cropped in a few minutes; that was all they had to eat that night. It was an uncomfortable night for the men as well as the horses; it rained all night and the river rose, so that the small camping-ground grew smaller still. By morning some of the horses had crossed to the other side of the river and the rest were so cramped for space that during the night they were stepping over the campers as they lay on the ground.

After the cold weather they had been accustomed to on the eastern slope of the mountains, the morning felt stifling— until they crawled out of their blankets; then the continued rain and the raw, damp air made them feel actually colder than they had felt the previous morning, when the thermometer was thirty degrees lower and they were 1,000 feet higher up. A thunderstorm came on and the higher mountains were quite covered with a fresh fall of snow down to within 600 or 800 feet of their camp.

Next night they found a camp-site on a fine, level flat in the valley of the river where, at last, the horses got something to eat. In the morning Hector sent two of the men to cut out a trail, while he and Burnham climbed the side of the valley. It was very steep and they had to scramble up a cleft in the slate rocks. Though they went up 1,500 feet they got no view because there was a dense fog which even prevented them from seeing how much farther on the woods stretched.

The men had cut their way to the best place where there was pasture for the horses. Even so, they only managed to travel five miles next day. Again Hector climbed the mountain side in the evening. It was wooded almost to the top, with very fine trees, especially the tall cedars and pines, and a dense undergrowth of cedar, white maple, and alder. The forest had clearly been undisturbed for untold ages, and Hector was able to study the way in which new, young trees grew up to replace fallen giants.

Things went better next day; they came out through a narrow chasm into a wide valley running to the south-east. Again, the north-western end was closed by a large glacier on the slopes of Mount Mummery. They made sixteen miles, getting along faster on the shingle flats of the river. This brought them to the place at which the Blaeberry River breaks through the west wall of the valley; here the going got bad again. They camped for the night where there was a profusion of ripe blueberries and a plant with a very thin, prickly stalk, called *panax horridum,* or devil's club. It was slow going next day, but they fought their way over a high ridge and then through heavy woods along the edge of the river, reaching an open space at last in the evening. The only cheering event was the discovery of a horse track, not older than last summer. It was the first track of any kind they had seen since crossing the height of land. There was no sign of game and already one bag of pemmican was gone. They were using nine pounds a day among the five of them.

Hector went ahead, carrying nothing but his gun. The fallen timber was very bad; some of it measured four or five feet across. Being on foot he found the tangle only a slight impediment, though in the sixteen miles he walked he must have done a lot of clambering and dodging, to say nothing of wading the river several times. He got on pretty fast and found that the narrow valley of the Blaeberry River widened out, leading to the north-west just before joining the Columbia. He pressed on, seeing a great number of panther tracks and a few tracks of small deer. After six more miles, he reached a low range of hills in the centre of the valley. He could now see the western side of the valley, six miles away; there the wall of hills seemed quite unbroken. He concluded that he was at last in the valley of the Columbia and started back to meet his men. Night came on when he had only retraced his steps four miles—a fairish walk, in all, of twenty-six miles under gruelling conditions! He made a fire, roasted a couple of grouse he had shot, and waited till morning.

The morning brought a very thick fog and he awoke wet through, stiff, and sore, and started off when it was still grey dawn. He met the men after a four-hour walk. They had managed only six miles in a day and a half. It was not till the next day that they once more reached the low hills from which Hector had turned back two days before. Then they all set off in various directions to find a track through the canyon, where the river broke through the confining range.

Their goat pemmican had got so rotten that they had had to fling it away some days before and now they opened their last bag of buffalo pemmican. They were horrified to find that, although it had been well prepared to keep in the dry prairie country, the damp weather on the western slope had already ruined the greater part of it; instead of ninety solid pounds, there was only a mere shell, amounting to about forty pounds, that it was at all possible to eat, the central part of the mass being completely rotten. On half rations this would last them nine days.

The men spent the morning cutting a track, and Hector found to his dismay, when he checked the latitude at noon, that in their tortuous course down the valley they had taken nine days to make sixteen miles of latitude, and without altering their longitude much. They managed to shoot several dark-plumaged grouse; these sat so close that Hector killed one on the ground by hitting it with a stick. Even so their nine days' supply of half rations was not likely to bring them to a possible pass to the Fraser Valley, let alone to the coast, especially as, incredibly enough, they had only one axe for cutting through fallen timber. They searched for a trail but there was no sign of one, as the Shuswap Indians of the region always travelled by canoe.

Matters were worse that afternoon. They only made three

miles before they were again at fault. There was a good feeding-place for the horses, at least, so they made camp to let them get something to eat.

Burnham said the rocks in the hills they had passed were just like the California gold rock, so some of them set out to hunt gold and found a few specks of what was thought to be the precious metal, though Hector had his doubts on the subject. If the prospectors did not find gold, the scouts did find that the Columbia was only two miles away. They returned in great glee at being at last out of their difficulties, as they supposed.

The party reached the Columbia early next day and followed it down towards the north to a good feeding-place. There were plenty of horse tracks but no sign of a trail. Immediately beyond this pasture the river wound close under wooded hills where the forest was on fire; there was so much fallen wood that it was clear that they would not be able to travel more than two miles a day. The mountains on the other side of the valley did not seem to be very high, but were very steep, so they could not cut through due west to the coast. They were astonished to find along the banks of the river a good many dead salmon which had, no doubt, been worn out by their long ascent from the sea. Afterwards they saw them all the way to the source of the Columbia, a distance, Hector noted, of 1,100 or 1,200 miles from tide-water, at an altitude of 2,600 feet above the sea.

They now had almost constant rain, with only short glimpses of sunshine, yet it was very cold, with frost every night. The thermometer had become deranged, and a few days later, trying to mend it, Hector broke it completely, so he could keep no more temperature records.

The men had half rations for themselves for only six more days; the woods ahead were dense. Hector could plainly see that with their single axe it would be useless to attempt to push their way on to the Boat Encampment at the northernmost point of the Big Bend of the Columbia, where the main work of exploration would only begin, with an attempt to find a route for horses between the Columbia and Fraser rivers. Many of the horses were much enfeebled by the long fast they had undergone in descending the Blaeberry River. If, as seemed certain, they failed to penetrate to the coast, the party would have to come back and would probably lose all the horses. Hector was tempted to send them south, with three of the men, to find Palliser, while he looked for some kind of canoe in which to follow the Columbia down to the north, and then make the traverse to the Fraser River on foot, but he decided against this. He knew it would settle nothing; the Shuswap Indians, he was aware, could leave the Thompson River and reach Jasper House in fourteen days, carrying heavy loads, presumably by the Yellowhead Pass. He was satisfied that there were but few places in the Rocky Mountains where an active and determined man could not pass on foot; the great object he sought to effect was to pass *with horses* from the Columbia to the Fraser.

With great reluctance, they started on what they all felt was very much like a retreat, up the Columbia to the south. They had been defeated, not so much by soaring mountain precipices and great glaciers and snow-fields as by fallen timber, dense woods, lack of food for themselves and pasture for the horses, and by the sheer size of the country.

Recrossing the Blaeberry River, they headed south, only to find that the woods were bad in this direction, too, but they knew they were moving towards the open country of the Kootenay, who were horsemen and were therefore sure to have good trails. Meanwhile they had to choose between scrambling and log-hopping along the rocky hill-side; cutting, hewing, and squeezing through the willows along the river-bank; or plunging and splashing through the swamps in the bed of the river itself. They tried them all in turn during the following ten days and could hardly tell which was worst. At least they eked out their scanty provisions with several grouse and a skunk, which latter Beads prepared for supper in a most skilful manner, so that it was really very good eating.

Then, suddenly, after they had camped, they heard someone calling out down by the river. It was Capôt Blanc (White Coat) with his son. He was the Chief of the Shuswaps, who had for a long time been the Jasper House guide for crossing the mountains; they had heard firing and had come up the river in a rough wooden dug-out in search of them. Hector thought they looked the most miserable, dirty pair of Indians he had seen, but they exchanged some bear meat for ammunition and tobacco. They had killed the bear while he was feeding on dead salmon. Hector's party also tried dried siffleur and goat meat, but found it was of no use to them as it was rather highly flavoured for any stomach but a Shuswap Indian's. In a mixture of French, Cree, and English, Capôt Blanc explained that it would take three days to go downstream in a canoe to the Boat Encampment; from there he knew a road by which he thought horses could be taken to the head of Thompson's River, which he called Kamloops. The route was so obstructed with fallen trees that the journey could not be made this season before the snow. Going south, he told them, they would sleep six times before they reached the Columbia Lakes. The road was bad and it might take them longer, as no one ever travelled it with loaded horses. The Shuswaps had a few horses; they sometimes brought them as far down the river as Hector had gone, but they used to drive them through the woods like deer, transporting all their belongings in canoes by water.

Constant rain and dense fog added to the party's troubles. When, two days later, they came to the Kicking Horse River (particularly memorable to Hector) where it joins the Columbia, they found it deep and difficult to ford; the current was so strong that it swept one of the horses a long distance down before he managed to get ashore in safety.

Hector was still taking careful geological notes and notes of plants and trees and wild life. Now every evening large flocks of geese passed on their way south through the valley and they saw swans and other wildfowl, but did not succeed in getting a shot at them.

At last, on September 29, they reached what Capôt Blanc

had described as a 'rub-a-dub' track, which meant one so good that the horses could trot. They had been travelling all day, every day, but had made very slow progress, though Hector thought that they might perhaps have gone a little faster, except that the rotten pemmican and the constant wading in the swamps made some of them ill for a few days; as they were afflicted with boils, walking was hard and riding impossible.

As they went farther south the woods thinned out. Dry, level terraces replaced the swampy bottoms of the river valley, and at last they could get along at a good pace. A group of old lodge poles and a well-beaten track showed them that they had reached the country of the Kootenay.

Yet it was again Shuswaps, not Kootenay, that they first fell in with. Two, who had seen them from the river the day before, joined them, and made them understand that their camp was some days' travel farther south, up the river. They were riding good fast horses, and Hector made a bargain with them, exchanging three of his worn-out horses for their two fresh ones. The open country cheered them all; it even seemed to put new life into the horses. They had come into dry country again and were enjoying splendid weather, with clear hot sunshine all day. Sage-brush was common, the first they had seen almost since leaving the Cypress Hills. If they had only had enough food, they would have enjoyed riding through what, apart from the dusty ground and sparse bunch-grass, seemed almost like the open glades of a deer park—except that there were few enough deer, even small ones, though piles of antlers showed that there had once been plenty of wapiti. Hector was fascinated by the great fishing eagles—as he called the ospreys—perched on the tops of dead trees that overhung the river, watching for salmon. He stalked two, very carefully, and shot both. Their wing-spread was five and a half feet.

The mountains to the west were not high, but they presented an almost unbroken wall—a wall that was to give the railway engineers trouble later on.

They noticed the trail from Vermilion Pass but found

when they camped in the evening that they had passed the Shuswaps' camp on the Lower Columbia Lake (Lake Windermere) without seeing it, the woods were so thick. The trail now resembled a well-beaten cart-road, the parallel horse-tracks forming deep ruts like those produced by wheels. To pass the Upper Columbia Lake (Columbia Lake), the source of the tremendous river, they had to climb about 400 feet and wind along the face of a precipice by a rocky and difficult path. The other side of the lake was low, and they could see a wide valley branching off to the south-south-west and cutting, as it seemed, through the mountains; it does not, in fact, provide a through route.

When they got to the upper end of the long, narrow lake, Hector found that the valley still went on. Only a level tract two miles broad, covered with open timber, separated the source of the Columbia from the Kootenay River, which flows along the same valley, but to the south, in the opposite direction to the Columbia. The swift-flowing Kootenay breaks into this wide valley from the north-east through a rocky gorge.

Here two families of Kootenay Indians were drying salmon which they had caught in the Columbia Lakes; there were no salmon in the Kootenay River, as they could not pass the great falls close to where it joins the Columbia.

Hector was tremendously impressed with the ponderosa pine and a gigantic larch (western larch), which formed a forest of noble trees where they camped. The bark of the pine made a splendid fuel, as it was full of resin. This was lucky, as there was almost no small wood and, had it not been for the great sheets of bark lying about, the travellers would often have had to go without a fire, even though they were in the midst of a forest.

They were now on the well-beaten track that Palliser had followed the year before. They came up with a family of Kootenay Indians, one of whom spoke Cree fluently. He was Alick, who had guided Blakiston through the South Kootenay Pass the year before. He had just been up at the Vermilion Plain, and told Hector that he had seen his horse-tracks and encampment of the previous summer. Alick knew the country well to the south and the west of the Columbia; he had made the traverse from the Boat Encampment to the Thompson and thought there would be no difficulty in taking horses over it if it were not for fallen timber. He said that there had once been a good trail from the Columbia Lakes to the west, but it had not been used for years and was probably blocked up with fallen timber. To the west he knew of no snowy mountains, except in the north, near the Boat Encampment—only wooded hills, but they were steep and high.

Eight miles farther south they came on a Kootenay camp of twenty tents. Here they met the old chief who had traded the young ox to Palliser's party the previous summer. They went on with these Kootenay another six miles and camped where the Indians did. The Kootenay's band of 500 horses, as wild as deer, contained many very beautiful animals. They had ten or twelve cows, too, and in the evening Hector got them to lasso one for them to milk.

The Kootenay had just come back over the Rocky Mountains from hunting buffalo. They had plenty of dried buffalo and moose meat, as well as dried berries. Hector soon got a good stock of provisions, by trading with them. As soon as the tents were pitched, the women crowded round them to give them meat and berries in exchange for needles, thread, awls, and small trinkets. They got rather too many of the cherries and saskatoons, which the Indians beat up into a paste and then dried in cakes. It was one of their principal foods, but Hector did not think it very appetizing.

Hector was as much impressed by the Kootenay as Blakiston had been:

> *These Kootanies are very fine Indians, being remarkably free from all the usual bad qualities of the race. The women are rather comely, and the men, though small, are well built. However, they were in good condition, having plenty of food at present; for Captain Palliser described them as being last summer the most miserable tribe he had seen. They are all very*

religious, having been converted by the Roman Catholic priests. Frequently, and at stated times, a bell is rung in the camp, and all who are within hearing at once go down on their knees and pray. This well-meant custom had rather a ludicrous effect on us once, for, in the evening, when a couple of Indians were holding a cow they had lassoed for us, and Beads was busy milking it in spite of its kicks and struggles, the little bell was heard, and down popped the Indians on their knees, letting go their hold of the cow without any warning to poor Beads, who was, of course, doubled up in a twinkling, but without any damage beyond the loss of the milk.

At first Alick agreed to guide them to Fort Colvile by a short but difficult route. This pleased Hector, as to try to find it on his own meant a risk of again getting entangled in woods—which neither the condition of their horses nor of their larder would warrant. Later Alick went back on his promise and advised them to follow the trail by the Kootenay trading-post. They took his advice, but were sorry afterwards. If they had gone by the short route, they would (if they had been lucky) have met Sullivan, coming from the west, on the height of land where he camped on October 6, when Hector was only twenty miles farther east, in the Kootenay Valley. This would have filled in the short distance that Sullivan left untravelled when he had to turn back.

Instead, they went on with the Indians, trading their tired and footsore beasts for two more fresh horses and revelling in the good pasture and good weather. Alick left them just before they crossed the Elk River, close to where it joins the Kootenay. A little farther on, Hector estimated, they crossed the boundary. Here the valley narrowed, but it widened out again into a second broad expanse of prairie, where they found the Kootenay Post. This was, as Blakiston had remarked so scornfully, 'merely a little log cabin'. Mr. Linklater, the company's clerk, was now there, alone, living in a canvas tent. He had arrived ten days before, after a nineteen-day journey from Colvile. Linklater was glad to see them and supplied them with a few luxuries which Hector was afraid he could ill spare from his own slender supplies. Among these was tea, which they now tasted for the first time in over two months, during which time they had tried a variety of what Hector now called 'abominable' substitutes for that best of luxuries to the traveller. So much for the 'capital beverage' he had mentioned earlier!

Hector found that the post was five miles south of the boundary line and about the same height above sea level as Edmonton. Here they had news of the party of American miners who had

> ... *so unwisely started in the beginning of last October from Edmonton, to cross the mountains by the Kootanie Pass. They arrived in a sad plight at this place in December, one of their number having slid over a precipice on a snow bank and been killed, and several of the others having lost parts of their feet, and been otherwise injured by frostbite. Those of the party in this state remained with Linklater till spring, and the rest tried to push on to Colvile on snow shoes, but only two of them got there, and not till long afterwards. The rest, four or five in number, straggled about the different Indian camps they met with in a dreadful state of privation, living even on the bark of trees. At least one more of the party died, but it is thought that the rest got down to the settlements.*

Hector commented severely:

> *The disastrous consequences of this fool-hardy journey, which they attempted in opposition to the advice we gave them at Edmonton, did not arise from any great difficulty which they encountered more than is incident to all winter travelling, which no one used to the country is mad enough to attempt without a suitable equipment, but with which they were totally unprovided. From what I have heard and seen of the country, I believe it would be no great feat to travel from Fort Edmonton to Fort Colvile by the Kootanie Pass in 30 days,*

using dogs and snow shoes, but any possible display of pluck and energy would not take through a party of travellers inexperienced in the ways of the country and encumbered with horses. However, I do not think that the party of Americans got any of their horses as far as the Kootanie Post.

An Indian arrived with a foaming horse, bringing news of another party of eight Americans that was crossing by the south Kootenay Pass, having come by way of Fort Benton on the Missouri. He said that their horses were tired out and their provisions had failed, so he had come to get food and fresh horses for them. The gold-rush was clearly in full swing.

The great Columbia-Kootenay Valley seemed to go on to the south-east, but the Kootenay River, which they were following, broke away from it. The trail was well marked, but rocky and bad, and they got on very slowly. They met a party of Indians paddling up-stream. They used canoes of a most singular shape.

They are made of a large sheet of the bark from a particular kind of spruce-fir, which is sewn up at both ends, but sloping outwards at each end, so as to form a conical point. The length of the bottom is, therefore, about 10 feet, while the space within the gunwales is only seven feet. They are sewn and gummed together, and have light gunwales and ribs of split willow. They carry a fair load for their size, and are most easily paddled by only one person, who, sitting at the extreme end, sinks one conical point that acts as a tail, while the other is canted out of the water. The round smooth surface then presents the smallest possible resistance to the water. The point, being strongly bound with wattles, will stand a severe blow, and therefore acts like a beak to ward off the rocks in running rapids. From their shape they are, of course, more easily upset than any other kind of canoe; but in skilful hands are well adapted to the work.

Hector knew they would have to cross the river next day

and tried to get the Indians to go back to take them over. They got sullen and refused because Hector would not agree to some ruinous horse-trading that they proposed. That night an old chief and his wife overtook them; they said that they would put them across at the right place next day and made it clear that they were ashamed of the young men's behaviour in refusing to help them.

They crossed, with the elderly Indians' assistance, where the river abruptly changes its course to the west-north-west. The plants in the narrow valley made them think of the Blaeberry River. Hector realized it was the climate rather than the altitude that caused the marked differences in the flora of the different parts of the mountains. The narrow valley broke through a succession of low mountain ranges. The track through each canyon was very bad; between the canyons there were wide valleys.

They were hurrying on, as it was getting very cold and snowy. Hector lamented that he did not have time for proper observations. Once again they had to cross the river, which was here 160 yards wide, deep, and with a current of three miles an hour. By good luck they found a party of Indians who for a little tobacco soon ferried them over.

They cut across to Pend'Oreille Lake, which Hector called 'Kalispilin' and 'Kallespeline' Lake. They followed down Clark's Fork and once again were lucky in finding Indians to ferry them over when they needed to cross the river. Some travellers from Fort Colvile advised them to go round by the Spokane Plain, as there was snow on the short route through the 'Kalispilin' Mountains. A hard ride and a night spent without water for the horses or supper for themselves brought them to Plant's farm. Here they got some flour; a little farther on they met some Indians, from whom they got a fine dried salmon. With these supplies they pushed on and struck the American Military Road, sixty-six miles from Colvile. Hector left his men to follow slowly and rode on alone. He reached Colvile the same evening, October 23, and found Palliser and Sullivan both there, just dispatching letters for England.

CHAPTER TWENTY

A Twelve-Mile Gap

While Hector was making his gallant but vain attempt from Howse Pass to pierce the mountains west of the Columbia through to the Fraser Valley, Palliser and Sullivan were much farther south, looking for a route through to the Pacific Coast from the Columbia within British territory, but as near as possible to the international boundary.

Between the Cypress Hills and the entrance to the Kootenay Pass they crossed an arid stretch of prairie. They toiled over sandy plains with only scattered and insignificant swamps and pools, most of which were salt. Heavy rain at night saved the situation more than once; without this welcome supply of good water they would have been in serious difficulties.

As they travelled over the level plains they could see to the south, across the boundary line, the Trois Buttes, which Hector had noticed. Palliser thought they seemed like the tops of three distinct rocks seen over a sea horizon—a vivid description of these remarkable hills in northern Montana. As they travelled on to the west they, like Hector, could still see them until they came within view of the Rocky Mountains.

Their well-worn carts, so often previously patched up, now began to give out altogether. The first total smash occurred one day out from the Cypress Hills; the wrecked cart was crushed beyond hope of any effort to repair it. Soon another cart broke down, and they had to distribute its load among the five that remained. Palliser cut off the shafts and brought away portions that might prove useful for future repairs.

They came on a large, perfectly dry river-bed about 500 or 600 yards across. The Blackfoot half-breed assured them that there had been no water in it since the time of the flood. Palliser agreed with him that the waters of this singular river had probably once flowed into the Missouri. They had great difficulty in getting down the steep, 200-foot banks into the ravine, but, after travelling several miles along the crest of the left bank, they managed to do so, and followed it to the south, at last finding a cluster of small springs of excellent water. They needed their compasses next day, going over a dry plain so level that there were no landmarks by which they could steer to keep their direction unvaryingly; the sun was overcast. They had to camp without water, but again rain brought them a supply.

They were now in sight of the Rockies, and, as danger from horse-thieves was daily growing less, they no longer had to guard their horses. Two more days of travel brought them to the Oldman River in the evening. Palliser encouraged the men to cross the river that same evening by promising a treat of tea and sugar, now rare luxuries, if they could get over successfully. After a day's hot sunshine the water would be warmer than in early morning, and they would save time. Everyone worked hard. They rolled up the tents into the form of bowls, using them as boats to transport the baggage, and swam the horses across. Beyond the Oldman they were still troubled by a shortage of good water and grass, but managed to kill some deer along a tributary.

Now they had to strike off, across burned-over ground, to find the entrance to the Kootenay Pass; by August 12 they were in the mountains. They could take the carts no farther. They made a present of two, the best of them, to the men, in which to take their things back to Edmonton, along with everything that Palliser and Sullivan no longer needed. They broke up the other carts, using the wood and the raw hides of the animals they had killed to make pack-saddles. They paid off their men in horses and orders on the Hudson's Bay Company store at Edmonton. Then they started off for the height of land with twenty horses.

They soon fell on the Kootenay track, which led between steep, thickly wooded mountains. The undergrowth was very dense. Here they lost one of their horses, abandoning him after laborious search and much delay. They met a band of Kootenay going off to hunt on the plains. One of them found the missing horse and brought it back. Palliser was impressed: it was a valuable horse and the Indian could easily have kept it; instead he had travelled all night to overtake Palliser to restore his lost property. Palliser rewarded him handsomely with a blanket and fifty rounds of ammunition.

When they reached the height of land, they found themselves at an altitude of more than 6,000 feet above the level of the sea, contemplating, on the north-western horizon, snowclad mountain masses of more than double that altitude—a magnificent view. They camped there, and next day, after very severe work for the horses, came out of the mountains, on the bank of the Wigwam River, which flows into the Kootenay system.

Here they came on two tents of Kootenay. These Indians had cows and oxen as well as horses. Palliser exchanged some tired horses for fresh ones and bargained as well for a lean young bullock, the party's provisions being almost exhausted.

Palliser had intended to go north to the entrance of the Kananaskis Pass and try to find a route westward from this to the Columbia, but he discovered that there would be no chance of getting food supplies; the Indians had gone off to the Arrow Lakes (which Palliser called the Great Columbia Lakes, not to be confused with Hector's Columbia Lakes at the source of the Columbia River). There was no one fishing up the Kootenay; there was, therefore, no one from whom food supplies might be obtained. Palliser decided to strike south for Fort Colvile, exchange his tired horses there, lay in a new stock of provisions, and, using it as a base, renew his explorations.

They travelled fast, starting early, breakfasting at eleven, and pressing on till late evening. Their way lay between chains of mountains which formed the tremendous banks of the river. When they had to cross this, they once again made a boat of the tent and a raft with logs and the horse lines. The river was very deep and the water icy cold, but they got over safely. The track, though good in places, was mostly very bad indeed. One night the horses strayed far away and they lost a great deal of time hunting them up. Two of them came to a bad end. Palliser wrote: 'Our horse which carried the ammunition fell over the cliff into the river and was drowned; we fished him up however, and recovered the ammunition.' Next day he had the misfortune to lose another horse; this was once the finest of the whole band, his own horse Carlo, brought by him from Red River in his spring trip of 1858. Poor Carlo was unable any longer to make his way across the rocky, precipitous track. They tried hard to force him onwards to a grassy spot where he could stay, but they did not succeed. Palliser had to leave him behind, and sent back two of the men to shoot him, considering this a more merciful way of terminating the faithful old animal's existence than leaving him to endure the protracted agonies of starvation.

Like Hector, Palliser was impressed with the magnificent falls on the Kootenay; but the rough, rocky track gave them increasing trouble. At last they reached what Palliser called the 'Paddlers' Lakes'—probably by the Kootenay River where it widens out near today's Bonner's Ferry. The Indians who were camped there were quite amphibious, spending the greater part of their lives in their small canoes, the kind that Hector had described. They were usually manned by two Indians who both paddled on the same side, first giving a few strokes on the right, then changing, at the same time, to the left side. Palliser thought that their canoes, though skilfully put together, were far inferior to the birch-bark canoes of the Canadian *voyageurs*. These Paddler Indians lived principally on fish, which seemed to agree with them, particularly the women, who were remarkable for their comeliness, clear complexion, and the symmetry of their limbs.

Here Palliser and Sullivan parted to take different routes to Colvile. Sullivan, in charge of the men and horses, was to go round by land, while Palliser went down the river by canoe. He got the canoe on credit, promising to send back, by the two Indians who accompanied him, sufficient calico to dress the owner's wife and two children, and a little ammunition for the owner. By noon next day Palliser was north of the border again and he came, after sunset, to a wide, rushy lake (today's Duck Lake) with quantities of wildfowl and very beautiful orange water-lilies. Across the lake they found an ingeniously constructed fish weir at which a large number of Flat Bow (Kootenay) Indians were encamped. Next day he could not persuade his two Indians, with whom he could only communicate by signs, to budge.

When, after a day's delay, they set off again, on September 1, they had nothing left to eat but a few berries. They started north through a dense fog. When it cleared after a couple of hours they turned west. The sun was visible at noon so that Palliser could take the latitude, which proved to be 49° 36′—still north of the border. He had saved some pemmican, which they now ate. In the afternoon they reached the western extremity of Kootenay Lake (Palliser's 'Flat Bow'), finding another camp of Indians there. His men gorged on the plentiful fresh fish so voraciously that they were unable to stir for the rest of the day.

Another day of canoe travel and portages ended with a supper of duck and a goose that Palliser had shot. The following day again they travelled steadily, and they met some Indians coming back from the Columbia. Palliser exchanged a shirt for two salmon; one fish was four feet and the other four feet, four inches, long. They had a fine feast.

Starting again before sunrise, they soon reached the Columbia River and Fort Shepherd, opposite the mouth of the Pend'Oreille River. Miners had been working for gold on both the Columbia and the Pend'Oreille. No one knew for certain whether the gold-diggings—or, for that matter, Fort Shepherd itself—were in British or U.S. territory. This well-built Hudson's Bay Company post had been established, in what was believed to be British territory, to replace Fort Colvile after the Oregon Treaty moved the border north to the forty-ninth parallel. When Sir George Simpson had sent instructions that the new post should be set up north of the border, the Hudson's Bay Company officer in charge had written that he was not sure where the boundary ran, though he believed that the mouth of the Pend'Oreille was in British territory. Palliser set to work to make observations to settle the question by determining the latitude. A circle of Scotsmen, Americans, and Indians surrounded him, anxiously awaiting his decision. The latitude proved to be 49° 1′: they were three-quarters of a mile within British territory. Palliser commented: ' . . . strange to say the Americans were quite as much pleased at my pronouncing in favor of Her Majesty, as the Scotchmen; and the Indians began cheering for King George.'

Going on again in the afternoon, Palliser reached Fort Colvile next day. Sullivan had arrived the day before. He and the men had suffered a good deal from want of provisions and had been for several days compelled to live on nothing but berries. These had disagreed with them very much, causing an attack of stomach cramps, which gave them great uneasiness, but at the settlement in Colvile Valley they had been most hospitably received by a Scottish settler. With his kind treatment, a little laudanum and brandy, and good wholesome food, they soon recovered from the pernicious effects of the berries.

Palliser was anxious to get to work again as quickly as possible, to find out whether there was any practicable route from the main chain of the Rocky Mountains through British territory to the Pacific; he wanted to press on as far to the west as the season would permit. Having secured the supplies they needed at Fort Colvile, they went north across the forty-ninth parallel again, to Fort Shepherd. To the east, between Fort

Shepherd and the Kootenay-Columbia Valley, there was still a stretch of country they had not as yet examined. Through this Sullivan was to try to force his way as best he could, to see if any route north of the border would be feasible. Meanwhile Palliser was to push the exploration westward from Fort Shepherd towards the Pacific.

Sullivan came back from his branch expedition to the east to report that he was 'rejoiced to say' that a route through British territory was entirely possible, but it had not been an easy trip. He had had to contend with the Selkirk and Purcell Ranges; though these mountains are not as formidable in the neighbourhood of the forty-ninth parallel as they are farther north, they are sufficiently rugged to make travel extremely difficult, and, as usual, dense timber obstructed progress.

At the start of the trip Sullivan engaged three Indians, whom he called 'Sanihk' Indians. They were perhaps Snakes. Two of them were an elderly couple, whom Sullivan described in his diary as 'two slow old coaches'. He sent two other Indians in search of still another Indian, the only one, it was said, who knew the country to be explored. Meanwhile the Hudson's Bay Company clerk from Fort Shepherd, Herbert Margary, joined the party. He proved an invaluable companion.

Before they started, Sullivan took observations for latitude, confirming Palliser's conclusion that Fort Shepherd was three-quarters of a mile within British territory. Then they crossed the Columbia, started up the Pend'Oreille, and camped to wait for their Indian guide. The road was already proving very difficult. Sullivan asked Mr. Margary to go back to find the guide and bring him on at any price.

While he waited, Sullivan reported on the gold-diggings:

> *The gold mines on this river are at present confined to this small portion of the valley, and the miners are engaged in mining the flats and bars of the river only. They realize from 15s. to 20s. per day with the rocker, and from 35s. to 40s. with sluices. They are prevented from reaping rich harvests, owing to the quantity of water in the stream, as well as the absence*

*of capital for the purposes of ditching and carrying water to
advantageous places in the neighbouring mountains.*

He thought that there was every prospect of gold being
found and prospected himself on a little tributary, the Salmo
River (Sullivan called it Salmon), and washed out two and a
half dollars' worth of gold in one pan of dirt, and two dollars'
worth in another. One of his Indians was luckier; he picked
up in the crevice of the rock a nugget worth 15s. 6d.

Mr. Margary finally came back with the guide, but, in spite
of his help, they began to have the familiar trouble with
masses of fallen timber and dense undergrowth—the latter so
tightly interlaced as almost to defy the power of the axe
altogether. The Indians wanted to go back; Sullivan was
determined to go on. He packed onto the horses everything
they did not absolutely need for the journey, including about
half their provisions, and for six dollars sent this surplus back
to Fort Shepherd by a half-breed who had been mining on the
Salmo River. Sullivan then divided what baggage was left into
as many parcels as there were people in the party. Margary
explained Sullivan's determination to the Indians and shoul-
dered his pack as cheerfully as he would have started on a
more pleasant occupation. Sullivan told the Indians that the
sooner they started the sooner the journey would be done,
but it was with reluctance, at very best, that the Indians
followed their example. Sullivan was not enthusiastic himself,
despite his brave show of determination. He wrote in his
diary: 'We then packed ourselves and plodded on a most
miserable road, fallen timber, dense green woods and bad
mountains.' They forced their way through the woods, eventually, and enjoyed a good supper and a most comfortable
night's rest at the forks of the Salmo River.

By following the more easterly branch of this river, despite being delayed by torrents of rain, in five days they
attained the summit of the dividing ridge between the Lower
Columbia and the Kootenay—the Nelson Range of the Selkirk
Mountains, at an elevation of 1,500 feet above Fort Shepherd.

An observation for latitude here assured them that they were still in British territory, as Sullivan judged they had been throughout the journey. The ascent had been gentle, and Sullivan felt there was not the slightest obstacle—except fallen timber—to prevent the accomplishment of an excellent road. Today a secondary road leads to this summit and a trail leads on down the other side to the Kootenay Valley. Then, decaying masses of vegetation, the young scrub pines, and the stunted undergrowth were almost impervious barriers, but they would disappear entirely before the woodsman's axe; lacking axemen, Sullivan's party were driven to climbing about, almost like squirrels. On the other side of the height of land the descent to Summit Creek, a tributary of the Kootenay, was abrupt but short; the valley was only 300 yards away. Sullivan began to hope that they had struck an Indian trail, but the guide suddenly informed him that they had been travelling for half an hour, not upon an Indian path, but on what Sullivan called a 'carriboeuf road', and that they must now leave it. The woods were traversed by the beaten tracks of the so-called caribou, which frequented the country in large numbers.

The journey on down Summit Creek towards Kootenay Lake was long and tedious. They had to cross and recross the stream to avoid fallen timber, but this did not make them any wetter than they were already, from all the rain that had fallen in the past few days. That night, though it rained still harder, they were very comfortable; they had constructed an excellent shelter with cedar branches, and had as much wood as they were disposed to burn.

At last they came to Kootenay Lake and found that they were still fifteen miles north of the border. They were all more or less fatigued and needed new moccasins. The numerous sloughs and swamps south of the lakes were teeming with wild ducks, geese, and other aquatic birds that made a special rendezvous of these marshy lands in the fall of the year, when they deserted the less genial climate of the north. From these swamps, also, the Kootenay Indians obtained the *klusquis,* or thick reed, with which they built their lodges, and which they used for barter with other tribes that did not have this necessary product.

At the lake the Kootenay met them and treated them very hospitably, giving Sullivan a great deal of information about the country to the east. They told him of a trail to the lakes at the source of the Columbia, now for many years out of use but altogether in British territory. The Kootenay said that two very precipitous mountains had to be crossed before arriving at the source of the Columbia River. They were not exaggerating the difficulties presented by the Purcell Mountains. Sullivan said he wanted to travel this road. The chief replied: 'If you take all the young men of my tribe and furnish them with axes, they will cut through but a very small piece in a day, your camp fire of one night will be in sight of your camp fire the night following; the fallen timber is too bad; the trail that once was clear is now blocked up by reason of the fires.' There was a second trail, which the Indians described as 'very practicable'; this they decided to take.

The Indians were sent off to hunt sheep, but, since they did not return, Sullivan faced a journey with nothing but some flour for food. He made a few presents to the chiefs and principal men, obtaining from them the loan of four horses and the services of two young men as guides, as well as a few provisions. They left the 'Sanihk' Indians at the lake, with a supply of ammunition with which to support themselves while they were away. They were delayed by the fact that there was no canoe at the crossing-place, nor any wood suitable for making a raft. Once again Mr. Margary went back, this time to find canoes. They were delayed a second day at their first camp, by losing one of the horses, but pushed on at last over another hill, to camp in a small prairie where there was excellent water and grass for the horses. None the less, the homesick beasts strayed twenty miles back on the trail towards the Kootenay camp during the night. Sullivan complained in his diary that the Kootenay were the laziest Indians he had ever met; he had to go back after the horses himself!

Clouds prevented Sullivan from taking observations, but, from his dead reckoning, he considered that this camp was one or two miles north of the border. He had probably made a short detour south of the border (along the route of today's highway 35) but he was confident that a practicable trail might be made through British territory farther north. It seemed clear that the mountains thereabouts might be penetrated in many directions and that the wide valleys between offered facilities for more than one road. This was just as well, for, as Sullivan wrote in his diary: 'Unfortunately the road commences in American Territory.' Today a road and railway run from Creston in the Kootenay Valley, up the Goat, down a tributary to the Moyie, up the Moyie and over the divide, via Cranbrook, to the Upper Kootenay Valley, thus justifying Sullivan's belief that a practicable way could be found through the valleys north of the border, even though his own route seems to have carried him south of it.

When the party reached the Moyie, they followed its beautiful valley north-eastward, with fine grass and water everywhere and splendid camping-places. They saw signs that a large party of Kootenay, in search of beaver and 'carriboeufs', had preceded them by four or five days. When at last they reached the lakes at the source of the Moyie, their guides gave them the welcome intelligence that they were only one day's journey from the place on the Kootenay River where the Indians used to cross the stream on their way to trade at the small Kootenay Post. There, on that very day, Hector was debating which route to follow. Sullivan climbed a mountain and studied the heights bordering the right bank of the Kootenay. These were about twelve miles away and a broad open valley extended all the way without any obstruction, apart from the usual tangle of burnt and fallen timber. Sullivan was reluctant to abandon this twelve-mile stretch of country without travelling over it, but provisions were running out. His Indians were possessed of most extraordinary appetites; they had used up their own provisions and were making demands on Margary's and Sullivan's little store.

Going back they would have to depend on the few small pheasants chance might throw in their way. Sullivan decided they would have to give up the last twelve miles. He thought he could depend on what the Kootenay told him: the Kootenay never stole, rarely lied, and were decidedly the best converts to Christianity of all the Indian tribes he had encountered in his travels. So Sullivan turned back. The party rode from sunrise to sunset, fasting for two days on the return journey to Kootenay Lake, where the 'Sanihk' Indians were anxiously waiting for them. Sullivan hired two canoes, which carried them down to Colvile in five days. It had been a trip that Sullivan would always remember with great pleasure, despite the difficulties, largely on account of Margary's most friendly society and cheerful assistance.

Palliser's explorations north of the boundary, westward from Fort Shepherd, had also shown that a route entirely within the British territories was possible, though very difficult.

With an Indian and an old Blackfoot half-breed hunter, who brought two of his own horses, which were in better condition for the severe journey ahead than Palliser's exhausted animals, Palliser set off, a few days after Sullivan, in the opposite direction. The party travelled through wooded hills, crossing the first three ranges without much difficulty. They had to camp just south of the border to get good water from a small lake, but struck north next day before starting again to the west. After this they had to cut their way with axes through country which, although not impassable to horses, presented great difficulties for road-building. They worked till six p.m. but covered only three miles. Another day of very severe hacking and climbing took them four miles farther. They had spent it in alternately chopping through twenty or thirty yards, then jumping the horses and driving them up. Before they arrived where there was grass, the Indian's horse failed and could go no farther. Soon they came to a small swamp. By a great exertion they brought the horse to it and left him there. In the afternoon one of the mares rolled down a precipice, pack and all; they climbed down and carried up her load and, by taking a circuitous route, brought her up again. Here the Indian declared he could stand the work no longer, took off his coat and shirt (advance payment for the trip), threw them back to Palliser, and departed. He came back next evening. Palliser received him kindly and restored his property; after that he continued faithful throughout.

Again, they let the horses feed for a short time when they found some grass and, again, when they had descended a deep ravine, they failed to find any more grass for them. Another day of chopping and clambering brought them up a mountain about 1,200 feet high, which was steep, rocky, and densely piled with fallen timber. (A drive over the road on the Canadian side of the border from Grand Forks to Lake Christina even now gives a clear impression of what Palliser's difficulties must have been.) It was easier coming down the other side. They found both grass and water for the horses when they camped, so Palliser stayed there for a day to recruit them. The entry in the journal for the following day reads:

> *Our labours not so severe; the mountains not so steep, and the fallen timber not so heavy as heretofore. Passed the horses over one very bad place, across a face of rock. This place at first appeared impassable for horses, but by availing ourselves of the slate shingle, which we levelled with our hands, building it up in some parts, and rolling it over the precipice in others, we made a causeway, and passed triumphantly. Camped on a little tributary to the Columbia, called Sheep River. Made seven miles.*

Difficulty in crossing this river (now called Big Sheep Creek) and heavy timber held them up again; they only travelled one mile next day, but did some chopping for the following day's journey. By then the worst was over. They had to do a good deal more chopping and climbing, but the forest thinned out and there was pasture for the horses. They rode along the crest of a grassy hill, and, at last, when they sighted Lake Christina (which Palliser called by the Indian name,

Lake Nichilaam), they were back in country the Indians knew. The horses were worn out. They had to abandon the two mares, which broke down for want of food, want of water, and the constant jumping over fallen timber. With the half-breed Pichena's two horses, they set off down the mountain, but did not manage to reach the lake by nightfall. To add to their troubles it rained hard; they were wet, cold, and miserable. The mountains above them were covered with snow. Again they had to camp in the cliffs without anything to eat; their only food was a little flour, and without water they could not cook it. As soon as they reached the beautiful Christina Lake next morning they cooked and ate the last ounce they had.

Now they struck an Indian trail, leading to the south down the valley of the Kettle River. Palliser decided to go back to Colvile for more supplies. They were now walking, driving the two remaining horses ahead, with light packs containing only a couple of blankets and buffalo robes, axe, kettle, and sextant. By good luck they discovered a fine cache of dried salmon that an Indian had made for the subsistence of himself and his family during the winter. Palliser records: 'I broke into it, and took out enough for supper for us three, and also for breakfast to-morrow morning, and leaving my black silk handkerchief, and a dozen charges of gun-powder, with a handful of duckshot, I carefully reclosed the Indian's caché.'

Next day he met the Indian himself; he was on his way to take up his cache. Palliser invited him to breakfast; he evidently suspected where it came from. Palliser told him the salmon was his own, and what he had left to replace it. The Indian replied, 'I wish I always had you for to steal from me.' Palliser persuaded him to try to recover the mares. This he undertook very unwillingly, on account of the desperate nature of the country, but he did find one of them a month later.

After a few days at Colvile they set off again. This time Vital and another half-breed went along. They swam the horses back across the Columbia and had gone five miles when they met Lieutenant Palmer of the Royal Engineers. He had been exploring routes from the coast inland and had now come down the Hudson's Bay Company trail from Fort Hope, on the Fraser, over the Cascade Mountains to the Okanagan Lakes, and so eastward to Fort Colvile, with the company clerk who was on his way to relieve Mr. Blenkinsop there. The Lieutenant confirmed Palliser's belief that the Hudson's Bay Company trail lay entirely within British territory, at least as far as the American camp on Lake Osoyoos, which Palliser called Little Okanagan Lake. Palliser walked back with the Lieutenant to Fort Colvile and spent the evening with him discussing routes north of the border; the Lieutenant gave him a sketch of the route by which he had travelled from the Okanagan Valley eastward; this lay partly in British and partly in American territory.

Equipped with Lieutenant Palmer's information, Palliser went back to rejoin his men and start off again westward from Lake Christina, to find, if possible, an all-British route. His men had gone on ahead, but he found them easily by the camp-fire they had lighted some eight miles up the Columbia on the Kettle River. He had not been able to make observations for latitude at the southern end of Lake Christina when he was there before, but now a clear night, between cloudy days, gave him a chance to make an observation by the pole-star. This gave them a latitude of 49° 4' 30". Palliser sent the horses by the trail, which followed the main valley of the Kettle and which, it was thought, here swung south of the boundary. He did not think that the country north of the border was impracticable for horses, but the fallen timber was very dense and he did not have time enough to chop through it. He started off on foot, with two days' provisions, over the hills to the west of the lake. He had to do a great deal of scrambling until they reached a height of land commanding a fine view of prairie country, affording a choice for continuing a road in several directions. They slept in a ravine and went on again next morning almost before there was sufficient light to allow them to pick their steps through the broken and fallen timber. By nine o'clock they had again climbed down into the valley of the Kettle River, just below the junction of its two forks near today's Grand Forks. About two hours later the horses arrived, with the sextant in their packs, so Palliser made a noon observation; they were still north of the forty-ninth parallel at 49° 4' 30", presumably in the Kettle Valley, through which both a highway and a railway run today.

They made another early start, following the Kettle River along the route that No. 3 Highway follows now. Suddenly they caught sight of a soldier in American uniform in pursuit of some wild ducks on the river. He told Palliser that the boundary survey party was not more than two miles off, to the south-west. A little farther on they saw the observatory used by the commission for laying down the boundary line. They rode into camp and were most hospitably received by the scientific gentlemen employed on the survey.

Palliser's work was done. He had travelled overland in British territory from the last outpost of settlement, on the Red River, to join forces with the Boundary Commission, which was working eastward from the Pacific Coast.

He spent a happy day with the scientific gentlemen employed on the boundary survey. He visited the observatory, in which was the zenith telescope used by the commission for laying down the boundary line. This greatly impressed him: 'The zenith telescope is an American invention, used in observing pairs of stars, one north, one south of zenith, but of nearly the same declination. A far greater number of results can be obtained in a given period than by means of the transit instrument formerly in use for obtaining very accurate latitudes.' Even so, there were three parties engaged in the survey, each with an observer, a computer, and a topographer, protected by an officer and a company of regular soldiers. Palliser must have thought a little ruefully of his small party and the enormous territory it had covered! Next day the Chief Commissioner for the United States, Mr. Campbell, arrived, but Colonel Hawkins, the British Chief Commissioner, whom Palliser had hoped to meet, had gone back to London to unravel another problem, about the island of San Juan.

From this point, as Lieutenant Palmer had assured Palliser, the Hudson's Bay trail ran altogether through British territory, over the Cascade Range to the coast. Between them, Palliser and Sullivan had satisfied themselves that there was— or could be—a practicable route connecting this old established Hudson's Bay Company trail with the Kananaskis Pass through the Rocky Mountains. Palliser did not deem it necessary—or, indeed, justifiable, so late in the season—to try to cross the Cascade Range himself; such a course would most probably have resulted in the loss of all the horses and no further increase in knowledge. Summing up, later on, he wrote that one of the results of the expedition had been that they had found a way across the prairies and the Rocky Mountains to the mouth of the Fraser River, but he added:

> *Although I consider this fact established, viz., that a line for a route has been discovered from Red River Settlement to the west coast of the continent, and that line moreover entirely within British territory, yet, I wish [it] distinctly to be understood that I think it far from being the best that could be discovered. Time did not admit of a series of attempts in a more northerly direction.*

Neither Palliser nor Hector had been able to find a really good route from the Columbia-Kootenay Valley to the Fraser Valley and the coast. That would have to wait for another twenty years, until the railway surveyors got to work on the problem. Their leader, Sandford Fleming, remarked that he always took Palliser's report with him on his survey trips; he found it of great use. At his special request he met Palliser in 1876 and again several times afterwards. No doubt, when they dined together in London, before Sandford Fleming went back to the wilderness of western mountains to make his final successful surveys with Palliser's findings to help him, he and Palliser discussed over the port the whole question of routes through the Rockies.

CHAPTER TWENTY-ONE

Return, Report, and Reckoning

O n October 22, 1859, Palliser wrote to the Secretary of State for the Colonies: 'Snow has commenced to fall, the season of 1859 is terminated, and in conformity with the directions of Her Majesty's Government, I am drawing the affairs of the expedition to a close.'

The expedition had linked its westward explorations with the eastward survey of Colonel Hawkins's Boundary Commission. It had carried its work as far as it could. Palliser would dearly have liked to ascend the Columbia by canoe from the point at which the Kootenay joined it, to find out at first hand whether it was in fact navigable, as it was said to be, for steamers all the way to the head of the Arrow Lakes, and whether horses could travel overland from the Arrow Lakes to the Forks of the Fraser and Thompson rivers. An intelligent Hudson's Bay Company officer who knew the country had assured him that this was so, as had several half-breeds. Palliser thought this was dependable information, indicating a possible connection between the Saskatchewan plains and British Columbia. He had to leave without checking for himself this potential route to a known pass through the Rockies. There was no more time and no more money—but there were more adventures still to come and a lot more hard work to be done.

The first problem was to get back to London. Hector had joined them at Fort Colvile late in October, and now, on November 2, they started on their homeward journey, accompanying Mr. Margary and Mr. Blenkinsop's family who were travelling under his care. They followed the wagon-road that had been constructed at great expense for the use of the American army, first through a magnificent forest of pines and then over the Great Columbian Desert, where they had to carry corn for their horses. There was very little water and almost no wood, a special hardship as here there was no *bois de vaches* (buffalo dung) to take its place.

On the journey across the Snake River and on to the army camp at Walla Walla, they experienced bitter cold and heavy falls of snow. These, and lack of food, had so reduced their horses that it was clear that it would be folly to attempt to proceed any farther with them, especially as there was likely to be deep snow ahead. They left them with an agent to be sold, dismissed their only remaining man (but not the faithful Beads, who stayed with them until they reached San Francisco) and went on to old Walla Walla, on the Columbia, thirty miles away. They had hoped to travel down the Columbia to Des Chutes by the American steamer, but on their arrival the agent informed them that she had unfortunately blown up. They were now very much perplexed to know how to proceed with all their luggage—instruments, books, and specimens. There were no boats and no Indians. At last some Indians arrived with the news that a schooner was making its way up the river, but the American agent calculated that the schooner would not arrive for some time, owing to the prevalence of a contrary wind and the disadvantage of a course up-stream. It was now the middle of November; Palliser was afraid of being caught in the ice. He bought two canoes from the Indians; though these were very small and of the most wretched description, they were the best to be had. The whole district was devoid of timber, so for canoe-building material the Indians had to depend solely on the logs of drift-wood that from time to time floated down from the Columbia's upper waters. The best of these they burned and hollowed out, but even the best were always small, misshapen, rotten, and dangerous. The explorers were prepared to trust themselves to these hazardous craft, but not their books, papers, maps, or instruments. These they left with the agent, to be sent on by schooner whenever she should return. As it transpired, she stuck fast in the ice when the river froze over, and their baggage did not reach them until March 14, in a wretched state, damaged by water.

They set off in the canoes and reached Des Chutes, 140 miles down-river, in two and a half days, running the rapids by moonlight, the solitary Indian they had engaged steering the foremost canoe. The ice was actually forming around them as they arrived. They went on overland by an excellent wagon-road past the succession of rapids between Des Chutes and the Dalles, which are now the basis of tremendous hydro-electric developments. An American steamer took them on to the Cascades, where James Sinclair had met his death three years before. At the Cascades, a boarded platform and tramway, not two miles long, connected with another steamer at the lower end of the portage, from which point navigation was open to the Pacific at Astoria, 135 miles away. Always fascinated by the 'capability' of rivers for steam navigation, Palliser kept careful notes about all he saw and heard of the Columbia in this respect and used the information about its upper reaches, north of the forty-ninth parallel, in his report, in assessing transport possibilities in British territory.

On the last day of November they arrived at Fort Vancouver (in United States territory). From Portland, just down-river, there was regular steam communication with San Francisco and Victoria, on Vancouver Island. After two and a half years, they were back in territory served by a system of public transport. Dr. Hector waited at Portland for the baggage; Palliser and Sullivan went on to Victoria, where they were most kindly and hospitably entertained by Governor Douglas, Admiral Baynes, and Captain Haig, who was acting for Colonel Hawkins of the Boundary Commission. They noted great commercial industry and much promise of progress.

Hector arrived on January 16, 1860, with the news that their luggage was frozen in on the Columbia, as they would have been, too, had they waited. Sullivan had already left, on January 5, for England. Sir Roderick Murchison had asked Hector to examine the coal structures at Nanaimo, Vancouver Island. Accordingly, he went off with Beads in a canoe with bedding and provisions for a week's trip. Short as the time was, he turned in a most comprehensive report on the subject. As the baggage still had not arrived, Hector made one further trip from Victoria some way up the Fraser River. Palliser, meanwhile, visited the new mainland colony of British Columbia. There he was heartily welcomed by Captain Parsons, Colonel Moody, and other officers of the Royal Engineers at New Westminster.

The baggage came at last, on March 14, almost simultaneously with the steamer for San Francisco. By some exertion Palliser and Hector managed to get both their baggage and themselves on board in time. The connecting steamer for Panama was full, so they had to wait a fortnight for the next one, and they took the opportunity to visit the interior of California, seeing the gold-mines and the giant trees in the Sierra Nevada Range. They went on together to Panama, crossing the isthmus overland (as, of course, there was then no canal). Hector waited for the British steamer direct to Southampton; Palliser set off, via Havana and New York, to Montreal, where he had to see Sir George Simpson about the complicated accounts of the expedition. He reached London at last, in mid-June, just over three years after the expedition had set off.

The long, eventful journey was over: now the accounts had to be settled up with the government and the Hudson's Bay Company; the notes and observations and specimens had to be studied and worked over; a careful map had to be made; the detailed report had to be written. All this involved a lot of gruelling, tedious work—without the excitement of hunting grizzlies and buffalo to make up for the drudgery.

There was a long wrangle over the accounts. The Hudson's Bay Company bills were, for many reasons, far bigger than Palliser had expected. For one thing, the gold-rush had pushed up all prices west of the Rockies; buffalo had been unexpectedly scarce; John Ball had insisted on adding to the expedition's work the canoe trip from Lake Superior to Red River. It took the best part of a year to get the whole thing straightened out and to convince the Colonial Office that the bills should be met out of public money. Bulwer Lytton and Carnarvon, with their enthusiasm for an all-British route from the Atlantic to the Pacific, were no longer in office; their places had been taken by the Duke of Newcastle and Chichester Fortescue, who were not greatly interested in the Hudson's Bay Company territories west of Lake Superior and were determined not to get involved in establishing new British colonies in remote regions, which chiefly impressed them as all too likely a source of heavy expense to the British taxpayer. Merivale, too, had gone: he was now at the India Office. His successors at the Colonial Office rather agreed with old 'Bear' Ellice, the veteran Whig politician and Hudson's Bay Company stalwart, that Palliser had simply been on a buffalo-hunting jaunt.

It was some time before people realized how wrong this opinion was and how useful '*Palliser* J.'s Plan' had turned out to be. The report took a long time to write and print. It was presented to the Colonial Secretary in 1862 and was published in 1863; the map was not published for another two years. Arrowsmith, the great map-maker, had started to draw the map, using the expedition's reports and checking their findings against all his earlier sources of information. He took so long to do this that the Colonial Office lost patience and handed over the job to another map-maker, Edward Stanford. He took even longer, and the map did not appear till 1865.

Meanwhile, Palliser, Hector, and Sullivan were all being asked to give lectures about their explorations, first of all, of course, to the Royal Geographical Society. The lectures there roused up the old controversy as to whether the expedition had really made any discoveries. The Hudson's Bay Company people, especially 'Bear' Ellice, insisted that David Thompson, Peter Fidler, and other fur-trader explorers had long before covered all the ground that Palliser's expedition had traversed. So they had—or at least a large part of it; but their work had been forgotten and neglected, and, in any case, new problems had come up as settlement pushed westward across North America, especially since steamboats and steam engines had come into use.

Palliser's final report discussed many of these problems. It was a bulky document, half of it a day-by-day diary and half a collection of detailed notes on plants and animals; on the changing seasons, on rainfall, snowfall, temperatures, and wind; on the latitude and longitude of the places where they had made observations; on the comet; on the Indian tribes and their customs and languages, with short vocabularies for four tribes; and, above all, on the geology of the enormous territory they had covered. Hector's geological observations, sketches, and records of sections became the basis of the first complete description and explanation of the geological make-up of the whole country west of the Great Lakes. This work laid the basis for future detailed geological surveys in what became the Canadian West. It also threw a great deal of new light on how the earth had developed, on the nature of the arrangement of rocks and soil and their comparative ages. There had been, as well, Blakiston's important magnetical observations.

Besides accumulating this wealth of new scientific and geographical knowledge, the expedition had made a careful study of the 'capabilities' of the country it had traversed—as well as making it clear to the United States authorities that Great Britain had an interest in these Indian territories, which, Palliser wrote, are 'far more extensive than seems to be imagined'.

With the expert help of Hector and Bourgeau, he had satisfied himself that much of this vast country, especially the valleys of the Red River and the North Saskatchewan, was well suited for settlement. He realized that in other parts of the country, particularly in the south-western part of the true prairie lands, there were large areas where limited and uncertain rainfall and lack of water and timber would make settlement difficult, if not impossible. This was the area that is, to this day, called 'Palliser's Triangle'—an area where magnificent wheat crops have been grown in the century since Palliser reported, but where many farmers have ruined themselves and broken their hearts trying to cultivate land that was not suited for cultivation. Now, a hundred years later, a great dam is being built across the South Saskatchewan just below the Elbow, which Palliser's party explored. It will hold back the spring floods on the river to make a tremendous lake, so that water can be brought to the thirsty lands of Palliser's Triangle. A second dam is being built across the connecting valley, which Hector explored, to keep the water in this new lake from running off down the Qu'Appelle River.

In their travels from Lake Superior to Red River, over the passes in the Rockies, and, beyond the Rockies, in the tangle of mountains west of the Columbia, the members of the expedition had received a vivid impression of the difficulties that would be involved in trying to link the prairies of British North America by transport routes entirely through British territory either with the old colonies on the St. Lawrence or with the new colony on the Pacific Coast. In his trip from Toronto to Red River, through United States territory south of Lake Superior, Palliser had seen how much more easily settlers and merchandise could be transported to the British prairies by American routes than by any entirely British route. This problem of easier connections with the United States than from coast to coast across British North America has proved to be a crucial one—perhaps even the most crucial problem that has had to be faced in building the Canadian nation. A way was 'forced through' all obstacles in the end, when the Canadian Pacific Railway was built, but the difficulty and cost were as imposing as Palliser had forecast that they would be.

Palliser foresaw, too, that when settlers moved in to begin farming there would be difficulties with the Indians and half-breeds who already lived in the country, hunting and roaming freely over its splendid spaces. The furtraders, willy-nilly, had always had to keep the friendship of the Indians who brought in the furs they wanted for sale overseas and the pemmican they needed to feed the men stationed at their posts and travelling in their boat brigades. Settlers and farmers, with their new way of life, would, on the contrary, clash with the Indians and half-breeds. Even the coming of explorers and surveyors made both the half-breeds and the Indians anxious and uneasy.

Perhaps the most important thing Palliser's expedition did was to travel through the heart of the Plains Indians' territory without getting into a fight, even with the proud, independent, and warlike Blackfoot, Bloods, Piegans, and Sarcees. The explorers had managed to carry out their work and had still kept the peace—even though it was a precarious peace—with the Red Men. This was no mean achievement.

In his reports, and particularly in a confidential letter to the Secretary of State for the Colonies, Palliser discussed the whole problem of the future of the Indians and half-breeds and of setting up a government in the huge, wild country he and his colleagues had come to know as no one else knew it (except the furtraders and missionaries, who naturally looked at the matter from their own special point of view). Palliser's approach was impartial, as John Ball had long ago emphasized. Later, the problems about which he had warned the British government (and on which his advice was not taken) came to a head in the Riel rising of 1869-70 in Red River and the North-West Rebellion of 1885 on the North Saskatchewan.

When Palliser's report was completed and had been duly laid before the House of Commons, there seems to have been little stir about it. Perhaps it was too detailed, too difficult to follow, and too full of scientific observations; it looked too much like a stodgy blue-book. Even friends who bought it—or some of them at least, like Lord Dunraven—seem to have put it away unread.

In any case, by the time the report was published, the

United States was embroiled in the Civil War, which raised new problems and distracted attention from the development of the North American West. Besides, the great Sioux uprising of 1862 had checked the expansion of American settlement west of Red River.

By the time the report came out, Palliser himself was off in the West Indies, running the Yankee blockade into the Confederacy, in a schooner called *Rosalind.* He wrote with mischievous glee that he had been able to attend the great ball at Charleston, while his neighbour, the Marquis of Hartington, heir of the Duke of Devonshire, could not do so, since he had no dress clothes, having penetrated the Yankee lines on horseback, without baggage. Before that, Blakiston had gone off to explore the Yangtze Kiang and Bourgeau to botanize in the Caucasus. Hector went to New Zealand in 1861: there he explored the Southern Alps and he eventually became Sir James Hector, the first head of the Geological Survey. Palliser went with Hector to Marseilles to see him off to New Zealand. There, by an astonishing chance, they met Blakiston, on his way home from China. They all had dinner together. Though rather awkward at first, they nevertheless spent a pleasant evening. Sullivan had a bad time looking for a job, but he, too, eventually went to New Zealand, where as reporter for the *Otago Times* he accompanied Hector on his mountain journeys. We owe a record of these journeys to him: he wrote a fine series of articles about them.

It was not till twenty years after the expedition had originally set out that there was tangible, official recognition of Palliser's work. The Royal Geographical Society had awarded him its gold Patron's Medal in 1859, while he was still in British North America, and, at last, in 1877 he was given a C.M.G. for what the second prime minister of Canada, Alexander Mackenzie, described as 'very great services in that then new country'.

John Palliser's niece, Caroline Fairholme, who inherited the family estate when her uncle died in 1887, wrote many years later still that 'his days spent among the Rocky

Mountains and hunting and travelling in Canada were amongst the very happiest, if not *the* happiest of his life'. He himself wrote in 1877 to Sandford Fleming, the Canadian Pacific Railway survey engineer: 'How I should enjoy going out again and seeing a few of those old wilds which you have metamorphosed and utilized and I dare say it is not impossible that I may do so.' Hector, when a very old man, visited British Columbia, but we do not know that Palliser ever did revisit the prairies and mountains of Canada, though he did a lot of other travelling, which included a walrus-hunting trip with his brother Frederick to Novaya Zemlya in 1869. This trip had important implications for the exploration of the Siberian Arctic.

In his last years, John Palliser spent much of his time striding over the wild Comeragh Mountains behind his home in Ireland. On the day he died, August 18, 1887, he had been for one of his long, solitary walks. Perhaps, as he walked, he was seeing again in his mind the wide Canadian prairies and wild mountain passes that he had explored and loved. He came home, sat down in the drawing-room at Comeragh House to read Creasy's *Fifteen Decisive Battles of the World*—and died. There is no monument to him in the little church at Kilrossanty, County Waterford, where he is buried, but his memory lives on in Western Canada. There, in the names that they gave to the scores of mountains, rivers, and lakes, the voices of Palliser, Hector, Blakiston, Bourgeau, and Sullivan still echo, a living memorial of Palliser's British North American Exploring Expedition.

out bloodshed, 248, 296. *See also specific tribes*
Indians, 40, 46, 59, 61, 78, 99, 108, 109, 172, 182, 187, 191, 209, 212, 213–14, 270–71, 281, 282, 283, 284–85, 290; warlike, 59; only war parties come to Elbow of S. Saskatchewan, 69, 70; wars, 65–66, 70, 104; Sinclair killed by, 137; passes known to, 8, 136–37; offerings, 57, 106, 122–23, 249; customs: mourning, 65, 66, and discharge of vows, 124; careless about starting disastrous fires, 75, 126; American settlers attacked by, 85; trade with Hudson's Bay Company, 102, 104; trade transferred to free-traders for American goods and whisky, 97; buffalo pound, 102, 105–6; *travails (travois)*, 116; beliefs: Roche Percée, 57, Manitou's Rest, 96, buffalo drive, 105–6, fire-flies, 122, glaciers unlucky, 162; sign language, 143; will not eat beef, 144; anxious for post at Forks of Little Red Deer, Medicine River, and Red Deer, 188; remote Indians uncorrupted by proximity of white population, 193; future discussed by Palliser, 295–96; still use traditional weapons, 188–89, 221; women and children, 26, 30, 32, 33, 63, 64, 80, 98, 102, 112, 122, 124, 131, 158, 159, 173, 178, 181, 219, 222–23, 227, 230, 231, 236, 237–38, 251, 255, 267, 271, 276, 278; lodges

and tents, 19, 56, 63, 64, 65, 114, 230. *See also* Plains Indians, Cree, Stoneys, Blackfoot, Sarcees, Bloods, Piegans, Sioux, Minitarees, Kootenay, Ojibwa, Sanihk, Shuswaps, Iroquois
International Boundary Commission, *see* Boundary Commissions, International
International Peace Garden, 53
Ireland, 1, 2, 5, 9, 15, 298
Iroquois Indians and half-breeds, 17, 197–98, 200, 203–4
Isle Royale, 18
Ispasquehow River, *see* Highwood River

Jack Fish (Pike) Lake, 90, 92, 102, 116
James, hunter and guide, 170, 178, 181
Jasper House, Hudson's Bay Company post on Upper Athabasca, 133, 164, 195, 198, 199, 200, 202, 203, 204, 206, 208, 213, 217, 263, 264
Joffre, Mt., 180
Johnson, Recorder of Assiniboia, 43

Kakabeka Falls, 21, 24, 25
Kalispilin Lake, *see* Pend' Oreille Lake
Kalispilin Mountains, 271
Kaministikwia River, 19, 21, 22, 24; ascent of, 19–26
Kamloops River, Shuswap name for Thompson River, 264
Kananaskis, legendary Indian, 138
Kananaskis Lakes, 140